Contents at a Glance

Pro Android Web Apps

Damo

and

Sébastien Blanc

Apress®

Pro Android Web Apps: Develop for Android Using HTML5, CSS3 & JavaScript

ISBN-13 (pbk): 978-1-4302-3276-6

ISBN-13 (electronic): 978-1-4302-3277-3

Printed and bound in the United States of America 9 8 7 6 5 4 3 2 1

President and Publisher: Paul Manning
Lead Editors: Steve Anglin and Douglas Pundick
Technical Reviewer: Kunal Mittal
Editorial Board: Steve Anglin, Mark Beckner, Ewan Buckingham, Gary Cornell, Jonathan Gennick, Jonathan Hassell, Michelle Lowman, Matthew Moodie, Jeffrey Pepper, Frank Pohlmann, Douglas Pundick, Ben Renow-Clarke, Dominic Shakeshaft, Matt Wade, Tom Welsh
Coordinating Editor: Mary Tobin
Copy Editor: Damon Larson
Compositor: MacPS, LLC
Indexer: BIM Indexing & Proofreading Services
Artist: April Milne
Cover Designer: Anna Ishchenko

Distributed to the book trade worldwide by Springer Science+Business Media, LLC., 233 Spring Street, 6th Floor, New York, NY 10013. Phone 1-800-SPRINGER, fax (201) 348-4505, e-mail orders-ny@springer-sbm.com, or visit www.springeronline.com.

For information on translations, please e-mail rights@apress.com, or visit www.apress.com.

Apress and friends of ED books may be purchased in bulk for academic, corporate, or promotional use. eBook versions and licenses are also available for most titles. For more information, reference our Special Bulk Sales–eBook Licensing web page at www.apress.com/info/bulksales.

The source code for this book is available to readers at www.apress.com.

Contents

About the Authors

Damon Oehlman is an experienced software developer and technical manager who currently lives in Brisbane, Australia. Having developed for a variety of platforms, from Windows to web development and now mobile, Damon has a unique perspective which fuels his passion for the "write once, run anywhere" promise of mobile web app development.

Seeing the growing trend toward mobile development, Damon left the stable environment of the corporate world and co-founded mobile development company Sidelab (`www.sidelab.com`). Sidelab offers professional development services for mobile web apps with particular expertise in mapping, location-based services and data visualization. Damon also maintains a technical blog, Distractable (`www.distractable.net`) and created the HTML5 mobile mapping JavaScript library Tile5 (`www.tile5.org`).

When not coding or writing, Damon enjoys spending time with his wife and kids, who help him to remember that there is more to life than writing software.

Sébastien Blanc is a senior JEE software engineer. He works for E-id (`www.e-id.nl`), a Dutch IT company. Additionally, Sébastien spends a lot of time providing expertise for mobile web apps. He is a regular conference speaker and really believes in the success of web-based mobile applications. Like Damon, when not coding, Seb enjoys spending time with his family.

About the Technical Reviewer

Kunal Mittal serves as an Executive Director of Technology at Sony Pictures Entertainment, where he is responsible for the SOA, Identity Management, and Content Management programs. He provides a centralized engineering service to different lines of business, and he leads efforts to introduce new platforms and technologies into the Sony Pictures Enterprise IT environment.

Kunal is an entrepreneur who helps startups defining their technology strategy, product roadmap, and development plans. With his strong relations with several development partners worldwide, he is able to help startups and even large companies build appropriate development partnerships. He generally works in an Advisor or Consulting CTO capacity, and he serves actively in the Project Management and Technical Architect functions. He has authored and edited several books and articles on J2EE, cloud computing, and mobile technologies. He holds a Master's degree in Software Engineering and is an instrument-rated private pilot.

Acknowledgments

Firstly, my thanks go to my awesome wife and kids. 2010 was a massive year, filled with so many opportunities, and you not only supported me with all the work I had to do, but also reminded me that taking time to spend with family was just as important. I love you all so much.

Secondly, I want to thank the team at Apress for both the opportunity to write this book and for the support and advice along the journey of writing it. I've certainly learned a great deal through the process, and have appreciated your patience and professionalism from start to finish.

Damon

To Mathilde, my kids, Damon, Douglas, Mary, Kunal, and Steve.

Sébastien

Introduction

As we move into a world where mobile devices are becoming the primary mechanism for people to connect with the Internet, it should come as no surprise that the ability to develop applications for mobile devices is becoming a sought after skill. We also have very strong vendor competition in the space, resulting in a marketplace filled with a variety of devices.

We see vendors promoting development tools and marketplaces for their own devices, attempting to create software ecosystems around their products. For the most part, the strategy is working too (for some vendors more than others). Developers are using those tools and creating "native" applications for a particular device, and then having to rebuild large portions of their applications to target each different device.

For some companies building mobile applications, this is an acceptable approach. It is, however, one that is entirely unsustainable for the longer term. Consider that each company with a web product will be expected to provide both a desktop web application and suitable mobile clients for multiple devices in the next few years (if not months). Then consider the number of software developers - people like you and me, that there are in the world. Do we have the required resources to meet this demand? I would venture not. There must be a better way. And there is.

Building mobile web apps is this better way. It is an approach to mobile app development that when done right, will have you rewriting a lot less code to target the variety of devices that exist in the marketplace. This book focuses on writing mobile web apps for Android, but in reality many of the concepts can be easily ported across to other mobile devices (which is the whole point).

What's a Mobile Web App?

A mobile web app is an application that is built with the core client web technologies of HTML, CSS, and JavaScript, and is specifically designed for mobile devices. Helping mobile web apps get a bit of attention are the trends toward HTML5 and CSS3—the latest "versions" of two of the technologies. We explore both HTML5 and CSS3 in detail in the book, along with **a lot** of JavaScript.

JavaScript is the language that many developers love to hate. Some don't even regard it as a programming language at all. However, JavaScript is here for the long haul, and is likely to be one of the most in demand skillsets for the next five years.

Which Technologies Are Used in This Book?

In the book, we work through lots (and lots) of JavaScript code. There's obviously quite a bit of HTML and CSS there too, but JavaScript really **is** the language of mobile web app development.

If you haven't worked with JavaScript in the past, we don't completely drop you in at the deep end, but we would recommend getting hold of some learning materials, as this isn't a

JavaScript fundamentals book. We also make extensive use of the excellent jQuery JavaScript library to make life generally easier during development. If that is something that is new to you, we recommend having a jQuery tutorial or two handy as well. If you have experience with Prototype, MooTools, or another of jQuery's "competitors," then you should be able to adapt the sample code in the book with relative ease.

In terms of mobile web apps (and other JavaScript-rich web apps), learning how to structure your applications for readability and maintainability is important. This is one of the reasons that we have chosen to work through a couple of small application-sized projects in the book rather than small code-snippets showing particular functionality. This will allow you to become familiar with the different technical aspects of mobile web app development, and also gain an understanding of how you might effectively put a real-world mobile web application together.

If you are already familiar with web application development, this book should make the transition to mobile web app development simple. If, however, you are coming from a mobile application development perspective, and are looking to explore the web app approach, having those extra learning materials will make a big difference.

What's in This Book

This book is structured around two application samples that will teach you the various aspects of mobile web app development. Chapters 2–6 deal with the first mini application of a simple "To Do List", and Chapters 8–12 guide you through the beginnings of building a simple location-aware game.

In and around these two "main meals" we have three "snack" chapters. Chapter 1 is focused on getting you up and running with the basic concepts for writing Android web apps. Chapter 7 is a short look at working with interactivity and the HTML5 canvas. And finally, Chapter 13 takes a look at some of the things that might be coming our way in the world of mobile apps.

Getting Started

Welcome to the wonderful world of web app development for Android. Over the course of the book we will walk through the process of building mobile web apps. While targeted primarily at Android, most (if not all) of the code will work just as well on Chrome OS. Actually, the reusability of the application code will go beyond Chrome OS—the code from this book should be able to run on any device that provides a WebKit-based browser. If you aren't familiar with WebKit or Chrome OS at this stage, don't worry—you will be by the end of the book.

In this chapter, we will go through a few topics at a high level so you can start building applications as quickly as possible:

- An overview of the platform capabilities of Android

- Which of those capabilities we can access through the web browser (either by default or by using bridging frameworks such as PhoneGap)

- Configuring a development environment for coding the samples in this book and your own applications

- An overview of the tools that come with the Android development kit, and some supporting tools to assist you in building web apps

Understanding Android Platform Capabilities

The Android operating system (OS) was designed as a generic OS for mobile devices (including smartphones and tablet PCs). The plan was that Android would serve multiple device manufacturers as their device OS, which the manufacturers could then customize and build upon. For the most part this vision has been realized, and a number of manufacturers have built devices that ship with Android installed and have also become part of the Open Handset Alliance (http://openhandsetalliance.com).

Android, however, is not the only mobile OS available, and this means that a native Android application would have to be rewritten to support another (non-Android) mobile device. This leads to having to manage the ongoing development of mobile applications for each of the platforms that you wish to support. While the large companies of the world can afford to do this, it can be difficult for a smaller organization or startup. Here in lies the attraction of developing mobile web apps—write the application code once and have it work on multiple devices.

This section of the book will outline the current features of the Android OS, and if relevant whether you can access that functionality when building web applications.

For those who would prefer a summary of the system capabilities and what you can actually access via the browser or a bridging framework, then head straight to Table 1–2, toward the end of this section.

BRIDGING FRAMEWORKS

A bridging framework provides developers a technique for building *web applications* that can be deployed to mobile devices. The framework also provides access to portions of the native device capabilities (such as the accelerometer and camera) through a wrapper (usually JavaScript) to the native API.

During the course of the book, we will work through some examples that use PhoneGap (http://phonegap.com) to bridge to some of this native functionality. While PhoneGap was one of the first, there are many more bridging frameworks available. In this book, though, we focus on PhoneGap, as it provides a simple and lightweight approach for wrapping a mobile web application for native deployment.

For more information on the various mobile web app frameworks, I have written a couple of different blog posts on the topic. In particular, the following post has some great comments from contributors on the projects that help to show their areas of strength: http://distractable.net/coding/iphone-android-web-application-frameworks.

While I would have loved to talk more about each in this book, the focus here is on building mobile *web applications*. From my perspective, these are applications that can be deployed to the Web and accessed via a device's browser. The addition of a bridging framework should be an optional extra rather than a requirement. Given this particular use case, PhoneGap is a clear winner.

Device Connectivity

While as consumers we are all probably starting to take the connectivity options of our own mobile devices for granted, it's important not to do this as a mobile developer (web app or native). If mobile applications are built assuming that a connection to the Web is always available, then this limits the usefulness of an application when connectivity is limited—which is more often than you might think.

Understanding that your application will have varying levels of connectivity at different times is very important for creating an application that gives a satisfying user experience at all times.

In very simple terms, a mobile device can have three levels of connectivity from a web perspective:

- A high-bandwidth connection (e.g., WiFi)

- A lower-bandwidth connection (e.g., 3G)

- Limited or no connectivity (offline)

At present, when building a pure web app, you can really only detect whether you have connectivity or not (without actually attempting downloads or the like to test connection speed). This is different from building native Android applications, as these applications can access native APIs that provide information regarding the device's current connection type and quality.

In Chapter 5, we will investigate features in the HTML5 API for enabling your applications to work well offline, and in Chapter 9 we'll explore examples using bridging frameworks to access some of the native connectivity detection.

Touch

One of the features that helped the current breed of mobile devices break away from the old is the touch interface. Depending on the version of Android, at a native level you will either have access to multitouch events or just single-touch events. Web apps, on the other hand, only allow access to single-touch events at this stage.

> **NOTE:** Not having multitouch event support for web apps certainly gives native applications an edge when it comes to application UI implementation. This will almost certainly change in the future, but for some time we will likely have a situation where some Android devices support multitouch for web apps and others don't.
>
> It will be important at least for the next couple of years to always code primarily for single-touch, and offer improved functionality (time permitting) for those devices that support multitouch events in the web browser.

We will start exploring touch events in some depth in Chapter 7.

Geolocation

The Android OS supports geographical location detection through various different implementations, including GPS (Global Positioning System) and cell-tower triangulation, and additionally Internet services that use techniques such as IP sniffing to determine location. At a native API level, geolocation is implemented in the `android.location` package (see `http://developer.android.com/reference/android/location/package-summary.html`), and most bridging frameworks expose this functionality from the native API.

Since HTML5 is gaining acceptance and has been partially implemented (full implementation will come once the specification is finalized in the next couple of years), we can also access location information directly in the browser, without the need for a bridging framework. This is done by using the HTML5 Geolocation API (www.w3.org/TR/geolocation-API). For more information on the HTML5 Geolocation API, see Chapter 6.

Hardware Sensors

One of the coolest things about modern smartphones is that they come equipped with a range of hardware sensors, and as technology becomes more pervasive this is only going to increase. One of the most widespread sensors currently is the *three-axis accelerometer*, which allows developers to write software that tracks user interaction in innovative ways. The list of hardware sensors that the Android OS can currently interact with goes beyond the accelerometer, however, and a quick visit to the current hardware sensor API reference for native development reveals an impressive list of sensors that are already supported in the native API (see http://developer.android.com/reference/android/hardware/Sensor.html). Table 1–1 lists the various sensors and provides information on whether access to the sensor is currently supported with the bridging framework PhoneGap. If you are not familiar with one of the sensors listed, then Wikipedia has some excellent information – simply search on the sensor name. Note that while the Android SDK (software development kit) supports a number of hardware sensors, most are not accessible via mobile web apps (yet).

Table 1–1. *Sensors Supported by the Android SDK*

Sensor	PhoneGap Support
Accelerometer	Yes
Gyroscope	No
Light	No
Magnetic field	No
Orientation	Yes
Pressure	No
Proximity	No
Temperature	Yes

One of the most compelling arguments to go with native development over web development is to gain access to the vast array of sensors that will continue to be added to mobile devices as technology progresses. While definitely a valid argument, building a web app in conjunction with a bridging framework can allow you to access some of the more commonly used and available sensors.

Additionally, PhoneGap is an open source framework, and the ability to write plug-ins is provided (although hard to find good information on), so it's definitely possible to access additional sensors.

Local Databases and Storage

Mobile devices have for a long time supported local storage in one form or another, but in more recent times we have started to see standardized techniques (and technology selection) for implementing storage. Certainly at a native API level, Android implements support for SQLite (http://sqlite.org) through the android.database.sqlite package (see http://developer.android.com/reference/android/database/sqlite/package-summary.html).

SQLite is quickly becoming the de facto standard for embedded databases, and this is true when it comes to implementing local storage and databases for web technologies. Having access to a lightweight database such as SQLite on the client makes it possible to create applications that can both store and cache location copies of information that might normally be stored on a remote server.

Two new, in-progress HTML5 standards provide mechanisms for persisting data without needing to interact with any external services apart from JavaScript. These new APIs, HTML5 Web Storage (http://dev.w3.org/html5/webstorage) and Web SQL Database (http://dev.w3.org/html5/webdatabase), provide some excellent tools to help make your applications work in offline situations. We explore these APIs in some depth in Chapter 3.

Camera Support

Before touch became one of the primary sought-after features for mobile devices, having a reasonable camera was certainly something that influenced a purchase decision. This is reflected in the variety of native applications that actually make use of the camera. At a native level, access to the camera is implemented through the android.hardware.Camera class (see http://developer.android.com/reference/android/hardware/Camera.html); however, it is not yet accessible in the browser—but the HTML Media Capture specification is in progress (see www.w3.org/TR/capture-api).

Until such time that the specification is finalized, however, bridging frameworks can provide web applications access to the camera and picture library on the device.

Messaging and Push Notifications

In Android 2.2, a service called *Cloud to Device Messaging (C2DM)* (http://code.google.com/android/c2dm/index.html) has been implemented at the native level. This service allows native developers to register their applications for what are commonly known as *push notifications*, whereby a mobile user will be notified when something is new or has changed.

It will be some time before push notifications are implemented in browsers, as a working group has only recently been announced to discuss and provide a recommendation on this particular area (see www.w3.org/2010/06/notification-charter).

Unfortunately, with C2DM being reasonably new, it will probably be some time before the bridging frameworks implement this for Android.

WebKit Web Browser

The Android OS implements a WebKit-based browser. WebKit (http://webkit.org) is an open source browser engine that has reached a notable level of adoption for desktop and mobile browsers alike. The WebKit engine powers many popular browsers like Chrome and Safari on the desktop, and mobile Safari and the native Android browser in mobile (to name a few). This alone is a great reason to build web applications for mobile rather than native applications. As both Android and the iPhone implement a native WebKit browser (Mobile Safari is WebKit at its core), you can target both devices very simply if you consider WebKit as your common denominator.

Why is having WebKit in common so important? Given HTML5 and CSS3 are both still emerging specifications, it will probably be a couple of years before web standards are concrete and mobile browsers all behave in a consistent way. For now, having WebKit as a common element between the two dominant consumer smartphone platforms is a huge advantage. As developers, we can build applications that make use of the components of HTML5 that are starting to stabilize (and are thus being implemented in more progressive browser engines, such as WebKit), and actually have a good chance of making those applications work on both an Android handset and an iPhone. Try doing that with either native Android Java code or iPhone Objective-C code.

> **NOTE:** Adoption of WebKit as the "mobile browser of choice" appears to be gaining momentum. Research In Motion (RIM), the company responsible for BlackBerry, has adopted WebKit and HTML5 in its new BlackBerry Torch. This is good news for mobile web application developers, and I believe shows the future is in cross-platform web development rather than the current trend of native development.

Process Management

Process management is handled similarly on Android and iOS devices since Apple's release of iOS 4; however, prior to that there was a fairly significant difference between the way Android and iPhone applications behaved when a user "exited" them. On the iPhone, once you left an application, it essentially stopped running—which meant there really wasn't any ability to do anything in the background. On Android, however, if a user left an application (including a web application) without quitting, it would continue to execute in the background.

To validate this, we ran the following code on an Android handset to ensure that requests were still coming through while the application (in this case the browser) was not the active application.

```html
<html>
<body>
<script type="text/javascript">
setInterval(function() {
    var image = new Image();
    image.src = "images/" + new Date().getTime() + ".png";
}, 1000);
</script>
</body>
</html>
```

Using the JavaScript `setInterval` call in this context means that an image request (for an image that doesn't exist) is issued every second. When the code runs, that image request is made to the web server every second (or thereabouts) regardless of whether the web browser is the active application or not. Additionally, as the browser on Android supports multiple windows being open at once, the request will continue to execute even if the browser is active but a different window is selected as the current window.

Having this kind of background processing ability provides developers some excellent opportunities. It is, however, important to make sure our applications are built in such a way that when in the background, applications aren't downloading unnecessary information or consuming excessive battery power.

Android OS Feature Summary

Table 1–2 shows a matrix of device features, the Android version from which they are supported, and whether they can be accessed in the browser. In some cases the browser support column uses the term *bridge*. This refers to the use of bridging frameworks (such as PhoneGap, Rhodes, etc.) to expose native device functionality to the browser.

Table 1–2. *Android OS Features and Browser Accessibility Matrix*

Device Feature	OS Version Support	Browser Access
Connectivity detection	≥ 1.5	Bridge
Geolocation (GPS)	≥ 1.5	Yes
Hardware sensors	≥ 1.5	Bridge
Touch screen and touch events	≥ 1.5	Partial
Local storage and databases	≥ 1.5	Yes
Messaging/notifications	≥ 2.2	No
Camera	≥ 1.5	Bridge

Preparing the Development Environment

Now that you have a high-level understanding of what you can do on the Android platform with regard to web apps, let's move on to getting our development environment set up so we can start developing applications in the next chapter.

There are multiple approaches that can be taken when putting together an effective development environment for mobile web apps on Android. The basic components of the setup outlined in this section are a text editor, a web server, and an Android emulator (or handset). You could, however, choose to use an IDE like Eclipse instead (see http://eclipse.org).

Eclipse is an IDE that is tailored for Java development, and the Android team offers native Android development tools for Eclipse. If you are working with both web and native Android development, you may prefer to continue with the Eclipse environment—and if this is the case, there is nothing in this book that will preclude you from doing so.

> **NOTE:** While there are many merits to using a full-featured IDE for web development, I personally prefer using lightweight and separate tools. Using a standalone web server and accessing the content from your device's browser will allow you to more easily test multiple devices simultaneously without the overhead that might be imposed by using tools provided within the IDE.
>
> Additionally, if I decide to focus on another mobile device as a primary development target, I can continue to use the same tool set to develop for that platform. I anticipate that we will see two or three dominant players and a long trail of perhaps ten-plus platforms in the mobile space, so having an approach that works across devices is definitely appealing.

Text Editors and Working Directories

Any text editor that you are comfortable using will serve you more than adequately when writing web apps for Android. If you really aren't sure which text editor you want to use, then Wikipedia (as usual) has an excellent comparison list (see http://en.wikipedia.org/wiki/Comparison_of_text_editors).

With your trusty text editor now beside you, it's time to set up the directory that you are going to work from as you progress through this book. The actual location of the directory is completely up to you, but I would recommend building a folder structure similar to the following, as this will assist you in working through the examples:

- PROJECT_WORKING_DIR
    - css
    - img
    - js
    - snippets

Reusable CSS, image, and JavaScript resources will be stored in the css, img, and js folders, respectively. As we progress through the book, we will build folders for each chapter under the snippets directory for that chapter.

Web Server

Having a web server serving your application code as you develop it really helps streamline your development process. Throughout the book we will be working primarily with client-side technologies, so our requirements for a web server are quite lightweight. This means pretty much any web server will do the job, so if you already have a web server that you wish to work with, that is absolutely fine.

For those who don't, however, we will quickly walk through getting a lightweight web server called Mongoose running on Windows, Mac OS, and Linux. Mongoose is extremely simple to get running; just follow the installation guide for your platform as described following (there may be some differences depending on your individual configuration).

Mongoose on Windows

Firstly, download the Mongoose standalone executable (mongoose-2.8.exe at the time of writing) from the project downloads page: http://code.google.com/p/mongoose/downloads/list.

There is an installer package available, but installing Mongoose as a service won't be as simple as using the standalone executable. Once the file has been downloaded, put the executable file somewhere on your path (recommended but not required), and then skip to the "Running Mongoose" section of this chapter.

Mongoose on Mac OS

The simplest way to install Mongoose on Mac OS is by using MacPorts (www.macports.org). If you don't already have MacPorts installed, install it now by following the simple instructions provided on the MacPorts web site.

With MacPorts installed, to install Mongoose run the following command:

```
sudo port install mongoose
```

If MacPorts is installed correctly, this should download, build, and install Mongoose, after which it should be ready for your immediate use. Proceed to the "Running Mongoose" section of this chapter.

Mongoose on Linux

With Mongoose being so lightweight, it is actually very simple to build Mongoose from source on most Linux systems. The following instructions are for systems running

Ubuntu, but only minor modifications will be required to adapt this to another Linux system.

Firstly, download the Mongoose source from `wget` http://mongoose.googlecode.com/files/mongoose-2.8.tgz.

Next uncompress the downloaded archive file:

```
tar xvzf mongoose-2.8.tgz
```

Change directory to the Mongoose source directory:

```
cd mongoose
```

And then run `make` targeting Linux:

```
make linux
```

You will now be able to run Mongoose using the full path of the Mongoose executable. If you would prefer to be able to run Mongoose without specifying the full path, then copy the Mongoose executable into a path such as /usr/local/bin:

```
sudo cp mongoose /usr/local/bin/
```

That's it—you can now run Mongoose.

Running Mongoose

Running Mongoose is refreshingly simple. Configuration defaults are sensible, so running `mongoose` from the command line produces a web server that runs and serves that folder as the web root.

Additionally, Mongoose will bind to all of the IP addresses assigned to your computer, which means that you will be able to browse from other devices on your network using the IP address (or one of the IP addresses) of the machine you are running Mongoose from.

Let's try running Mongoose now. Open up a command prompt/terminal window and then change directory to `PROJECT_WORKING_DIR`, which you set up in the previous step. If Mongoose is located on your path, you will be able to run `mongoose` from the command line; and if not, then you will need to run it using its absolute path. Either way, once you have run the command (no command-line options required), you should then be able to browse to http://localhost:8080/ and see the directory file list of the folders you set up earlier (as shown in Figure 1–1).

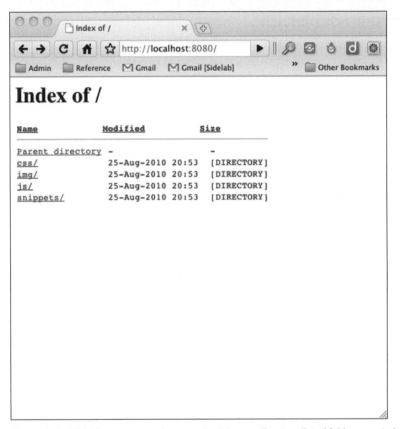

Figure 1–1. *With Mongoose running, you should see a directory list of folders created earlier.*

Alternative Approaches

You can also copy files across to an emulated SD card image and load them from the image by using the `file://sdcard/<filelocation>` syntax. If you are interested in more information on how to create SD card images and copy files to and from them, I recommend checking out the information at the following URL: `http://developer.android.com/guide/developing/tools/emulator.html#sdcard`.

Emulator

To test the samples, you will either need an Android handset or the Android emulator that comes bundled with the SDK. If you don't already have the SDK, you can download it from `http://developer.android.com/sdk`. Follow the instructions on the Android site, with the exception of installing Eclipse and the ADT plug-in (unless you already have it installed and are comfortable using it). Once you have the Android SDK installed, the emulator and associated tools can be found in the `tools` directory of the SDK installation directory.

Creating an Android Virtual Device

Creating an Android Virtual Device (AVD) is straightforward when using the GUI tools that are provided as part of the Android SDK. First, locate the android executable and run it. The location of the executable will depend on the SDK installation path, but essentially you are looking for the file android (android.exe on Windows) within the tools folder of the SDK installation directory. This will launch the Android SDK and AVD Manager application, which is shown in Figure 1–2.

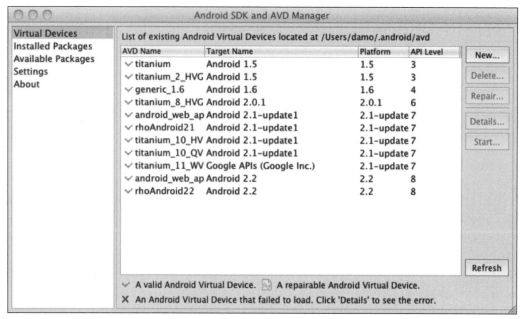

Figure 1–2. *The Android SDK and AVD Manager*

Here we will create a device for running our samples. Nothing too fancy is required, just the standard emulator running with version 2.1 of the SDK or greater. Press the Add button to start creating the image. Once you have done this, you should see a screen similar to the one shown in Figure 1–3.

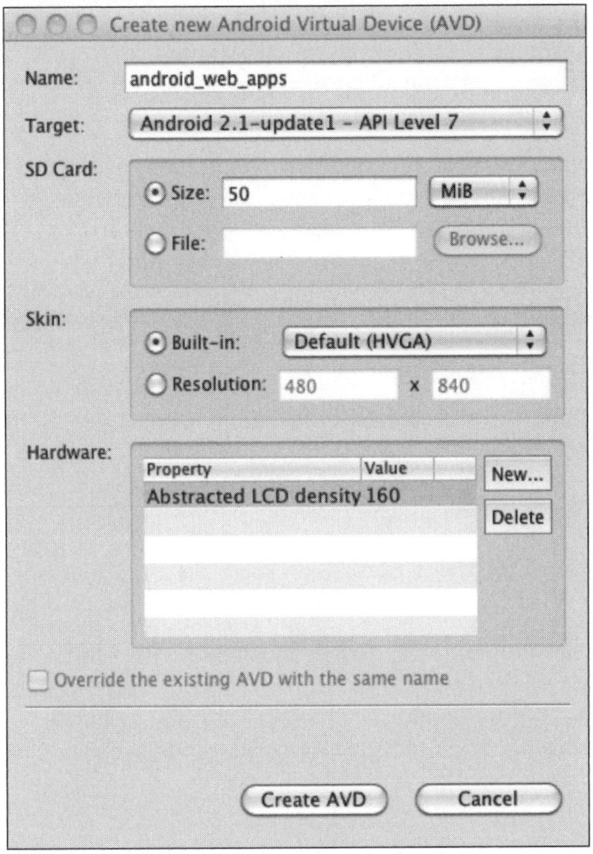

Figure 1–3. *Creating a new AVD for the emulator*

You need to provide at least three pieces of information when creating a new AVD file:

- The name of the device (no spaces are allowed). Here we are creating a device called "android_web_apps." This is the name that is used when launching the emulator from the command line.

- The target Android API we are developing for. At the time of writing, both Android OS versions 2.1 and 2.2 have the highest levels of market penetration, with 1.5 and 1.6 now in the minority (see http://developer.android.com/resources/dashboard/platform-versions.html). For the examples in the book, we will primarily work with a version 2.1 emulator. By using a version 2.1 emulator rather than a version 2.2 emulator, we can make sure our code will work on both versions of the OS—but it is still important to test on as many versions of the OS as possible.

- The size of the SD card. You can also specify an existing SD card image if you want to, but that's not required for running through the samples in the book. I'd recommend just specifying a size of 50MB or thereabouts.

Other information, such as the skin value (somewhat synonymous with screen resolution), will be automatically populated based on the API version selection, but you can tweak these options if desired. All of the samples in the book have been designed with a standard mobile device screen size of 320×480, so I'd recommend working with that.

> **NOTE:** Some of the examples in the book illustrate the difference between standard dpi (dots per inch) and high dpi, and how that will impact your applications. For these samples, you will need an AVD that is configured with a higher screen resolution than standard. When configuring this device, select a resolution such as WVGA800 (or similar) to emulate a device with a high device dpi.

Starting the Emulator

Once the AVD has been created, you can then start the device by pressing the start button, which is displayed to the right of the device images. You will be prompted with a couple of options (as shown in Figure 1–4), but in general selecting the defaults is fine (although wiping user data can sometimes be very useful for getting back to a clean slate).

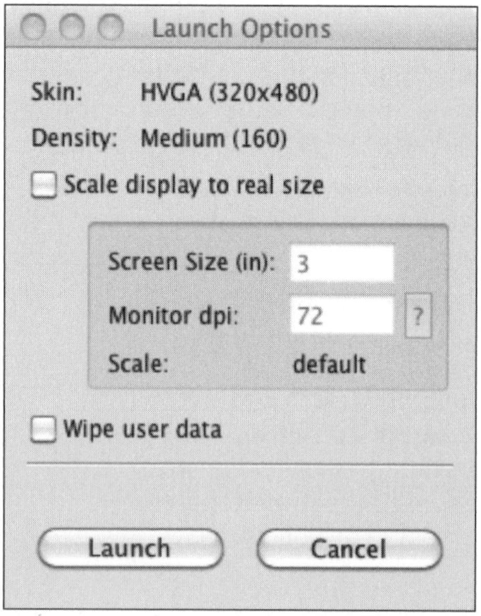

Figure 1–4. *Launching a new virtual device for our emulator using the AVD Manager*

Once the emulator has started, a screen similar to Figure 1–5 will be displayed, indicating that the Android emulator is starting.

Figure 1–5. *The Android emulator starting—a good time to get some coffee*

Be aware that the emulator does take quite a long time to load, so once you've got it loaded, try to avoid closing it. When it's finally loaded, you will see an Android home screen like the one shown in Figure 1–6.

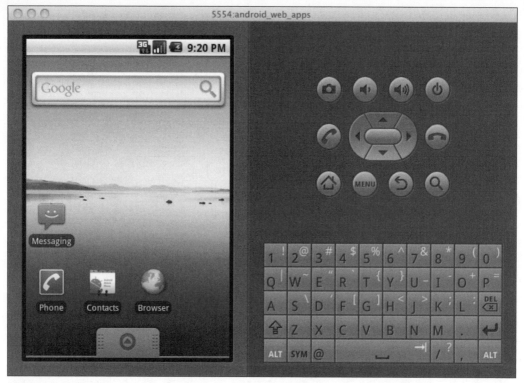

Figure 1–6. *The Android emulator has loaded successfully; open the browser to get started.*

From the home screen, run the browser and you will be able to access the local web server that you configured previously.

Hello World

Before we get into the working through the specifics of mobile web applications and sites in the next chapter, let's make sure our development environment is set up correctly with a very simple Hello World example.

First we will create a very simple HTML file that we will use to validate that we can view our development files in the mobile browser on our Android device:

```
<html>
<style type="text/css">
body {
  font: 4em Arial;
}
</style>
<body>
Hello World
</body>
</html>
```

Save the preceding code sample to a file named `helloworld.html`, and then access the directory in which that file is stored from your terminal or command prompt. Run Mongoose (either using the absolute installation path or just `mongoose`, depending on how you installed it and your path configuration) from that location.

Figure 1–7 shows a screenshot of some example command-line output you will see if Mongoose has been run correctly.

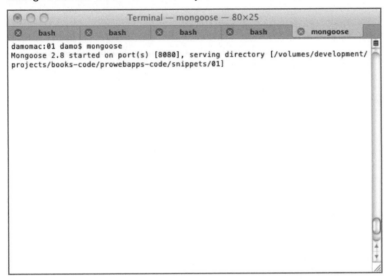

Figure 1–7. *Mongoose web server example output showing the port and directory that content is being served from.*

While Mongoose will inform you of the port it is running on, you will also need to find the IP address of your machine so that you're able to browse the server from both the emulator and an actual Android device connected to your local network via WiFi. One of the simplest ways to determine your IP address is through the use of the `ifconfig` or `ipconfig` commands on Mac OS/Linux and Windows, respectively. If you are unfamiliar with the technique then the following links may be of assistance:

- *PC:* `www.wikihow.com/Find-the-IP-Address-of-Your-PC`

- *Mac:* `www.wikihow.com/Find-Your-IP-Address-on-a-Mac`

- *Linux:* `linux-ip.net/html/tools-ifconfig.html`

Armed with the knowledge of your IP address, you will now be able to view your test page in the emulator (or your Android device). Figure 1–8 shows example screen captures from the Android browser, showing both browsing to the `helloworld.html` file that we created and what is displayed in the browser as a result.

NOTE: While you may be accustomed to using *localhost (or 127.0.0.1)* when browsing a development webserver when operating on your own machine, when you are working with an Android emulator (or device) you will need to access the webserver via the IP of your machine on your local network. Mongoose is very helpful in this regard and will happily serve web pages from any IP (including 127.0.0.1) that is associated with your machine.

Figure 1–8. *Browsing to our Hello World example demonstrates that our development setup is working.*

Now that you have successfully created a Hello World example, it is time to move on to actually learning what makes a web application or site mobile. This is the topic for the next chapter.

> **NOTE:** To keep things simple, in this example we ran Mongoose from the same directory that the `helloworld.html` file was stored in. For the remainder of the examples, we will be working in a slightly more complicated directory structure to ensure that we can reuse certain files between chapters. For instance, in the example source code repository on GitHub (`http://github.com/sidelab/prowebapps-code`), this file is stored in the following location: `/snippets/01/helloworld.html`.
>
> This is the kind of directory structure that will be used for the rest of the book, with each chapter's code samples being stored within a directory under the `snippets` directory. Some larger examples, such as the geospatial game covered in Chapters 9 through 11, will use a variation on this structure, but this is the general rule.
>
> In future examples, Mongoose will be run from the directory above `snippets`. This in turn means that the path you will use to browse the majority of future examples will match the following pattern: `http://YOURIP:8080/snippets/CHAPTER/SAMPLE.html`.

Summary

This chapter covered the basic capabilities of an Android device and what can be achieved in web apps as opposed to native apps. This included looking at what is available via standard browser support, as well as through using bridging frameworks to extend native functionality to a web browser embedded in a native application.

We also walked through the very simple requirements for running a development environment for building Android web apps. Additionally, we took a preliminary look at some of the tools that will help you debug your code as you work through the samples in this book and later you create your own applications.

In the next chapter, we will look at some of the simple techniques that are used to create mobile-friendly web pages and the foundation pieces of a mobile web app. We'll begin with some simple standalone examples, but quickly move on to working through a practical example: building a simple to-do list application. We will continue to explore and build this in Chapters 3 and 4 also.

Chapter **2**

Building a Mobile HTML Entry Form

Creating a simple, mobile-friendly web page is very easy. By the end of this chapter, you will know not only how to build a mobile web page and form, but understand how to apply some simple CSS (including some CSS3) to give a web form a very similar feel and experience to what you would find in a native application.

The samples in this chapter and subsequent chapters work towards creating a simple to-do list web application optimized for Android. Building mobile web applications has a heavy focus on JavaScript in addition to HTML and CSS. So, in addition to understanding mobile web app development techniques, understanding how to structure JavaScript-heavy applications will be explored.

HTML for the Mobile Web

HTML for the mobile web is much the same as it is for the desktop—just with smaller screen sizes (in most cases at this stage). Additionally, there is an increased focus on optimizing for performance given the reduced bandwidth that a mobile device has access to when browsing via a mobile broadband connection.

The focus in this chapter is on the techniques and tools required to make the jump into mobile web app development, primarily from an application presentation perspective.

Mobile-Ready Web Pages

Building mobile-ready web pages is quite simple, and only requires the addition of some extra information to tell the mobile browser to recognize the page as "mobile ready." Let's start this chapter by having a look at a simple web page.

We will first have a look at a mobile browser *without* the appropriate tweaks applied. This will give you an understanding of *why* you need to optimize your web pages for mobile if you want people to be able to use them effectively. This is especially important if you are building applications that people may compare side by side with an Android application that has been constructed using a native user interface (UI).

Our test web page is a simple page that consists of nothing more than a heading and a paragraph of text (*lorem ipsum* paragraph condensed):

```
<html>
<head>
  <title>Simple Mobile Web Page</title>
</head>
<body>
  <h1>Welcome</h1>
  <p>Lorem ipsum dolor sit amet ... </p>
</body>
</html>
```

Figure 2–1 shows how the preceding HTML appears in the Android browser.

Figure 2–1. *Our simple web page with no mobile readiness applied*

While the browser has successfully rendered the page, there are a few things that it hasn't done well:

- The text on the page is quite small; this is because the browser has assumed that it has been built for a desktop screen resolution and has thus applied some scaling to ensure the page will fit properly.

- Because the browser believes the page is designed for desktop display, it is permitting zoom and xy-axis scroll operations on the page.

- The URL bar for the browser is displayed, and while this isn't a problem now, when we get into more complicated applications, it would be nice to know how we can get the Android browser to hide the URL bar.

Now that you know a few things that you want your mobile browser to do (or not to do) when displaying the page, let's have a look at what is required to get there.

Introducing the viewport Meta Tag

The HTML `viewport` meta tag was introduced by Apple for use in Mobile Safari on the iPhone, and is used to tell the mobile browser exactly what it is seeing. Without a `viewport` meta tag, the browser will assume it is looking at a web page that is built for desktop browsing and thus scale the display down to fit. An example `viewport` meta tag definition is as follows:

```
<meta name="viewport" content="width=device-width; user-scalable=0;" />
```

In this particular instance, we are telling the browser that we wish to have the page displayed at the screen width of the device, and that the user should not be permitted to zoom in and out on the viewport. Zooming in and out on the display is generally pretty handy when looking at a site that hasn't been optimized for mobile; however, when viewing a mobile-ready page, it's not generally required, and can sometimes be a hindrance to other functionality that you want to offer in your app.

> **NOTE:** While the `viewport` meta tag is something you would expect to be part of the HTML5 specification, this is not the case at this stage However, both WebKit and Mozilla browsers are actively using the tag, and will be working with the W3C to have it incorporated as part of the specification.

While this `viewport` meta tag is sufficient for telling the WebKit browser on Android how you would like the page sized, other mobile devices may require some extra information to configure the display properly. To help with constructing a `viewport` meta tag that will work on the majority of mobile devices, I've included a quick reference table. Table 2–1 outlines the various parameters you can include in the content section of the meta tag and a brief explanation of each.

Table 2–1. *viewport Meta Tag Parameters and Their Effects*

Parameter	Overview	Valid Values
Standard viewport Meta Tag Parameters		
width	Specifies the width of the viewport. This can be a specific value in pixels (not recommended) or keywords that describe the required display width.	device-width: The screen width of the device. A numerical value for the absolute width of the viewport.
height	Specifies the height of the viewport.	device-height: The screen height of the device. A numerical value for the absolute height of the viewport.
user-scalable	Specifies whether the user is permitted to adjust the scaling of the screen.	1, yes, or true: User scaling is permitted. 0, no, or false: User scaling is not allowed.
initial-scale	Specifies the initial scaling value for the display.	A value that indicates the scaling that will be applied when the page is initially loaded. A value of 1.0 indicates that 1 viewport pixel equates to 1 screen pixel.
minimum-scale	Specifies the minimum scaling that can be applied to the display.	A value in the range of 0 to 10.0.
maximum-scale	Specifies the maximum scaling that can be applied to the display.	A value in the range of 0 to 10.0.
Android-Specific Meta Tag Parameters		
target-densitydpi	Informs the device exactly what screen density the current web page/application was designed for.	device-dpi: Sets the viewport dpi density to match the dpi density of the device. high-dpi, medium-dpi, or low-dpi. A value in the range of 70 to 400 specifying the specific pixel density of the device.

* dpi (dots per inch) is a measure of screen pixels per inch (DPI stands for Dots Per Inch). The Android platform caters for devices of varying pixel densities and broadly categorizes those into high, medium, and low.

NOTE: It's worth reading the article "A pixel is not a pixel is not a pixel," by John Gruber, which explores the issue of increasing screen densities on mobile devices and the impact this will have for web developers as we move forward (see www.quirksmode.org/blog/archives/2010/04/a_pixel_is_not.html).

Considering these extra configuration parameters, the following `viewport` meta tag declaration offers the some extra robustness for cross-platform device compatibility:

```
<meta name="viewport" content="width=device-width; initial-scale=1.0; maximum-scale=1.0;
user-scalable=0;" />
```

For the moment, we will not specify a `target-densitydpi`, but I'll introduce this setting later when discussing the HTML5 canvas so you can understand its effect on a display.

With the preceding `viewport` meta tag applied, our page will now be displayed in a more readable fashion; additionally, the zoom controls have been removed, as shown in Figure 2–2.

Figure 2–2. *A simple page with the viewport meta tag applied*

Autohiding the URL Bar

Given that the goal of this book is to provide you with the techniques required to successfully build a web app that will compete with a native app, having a URL bar visible in your app isn't going to help with convincing people. Depending on the direction you take for deploying your application (remember it is possible to deploy mobile web apps as native applications using tools like PhoneGap[1]) you will be able to hide the URL bar automatically, or you may have to implement some workarounds to get it to hide effectively.

In the case where you are building an application that will be deployed online and primarily accessed through the mobile browser, a workaround is going to be required. Currently, the most effective workaround is to tell the browser to scroll to the top of the screen once it has finished loading the page. This works because the vertical scrolling behavior for the browser when viewing web pages is to first scroll off the URL bar, and then through the rest of the content. So, executing window.scrollTo(0, 1) when the window has finished loading will do the trick. For now, we will just add it to the body onload tag like so:

```
<body onload="window.scrollTo(0, 1);">
```

> **NOTE:** Successfully implementing this technique requires the page height value to be at least as large as the display size of the screen. This is generally best achieved by telling the body tag that it has a min-height in the stylesheets for your web app. For an example, have a look at the CSS implemented in the "Adding Some Style" section later in the chapter.

Adding Form Elements

In terms of the actual HTML code, HTML form elements are the same for mobile devices as they are for desktop browsers. It's just the interaction with those controls that changes for a mobile device, and thankfully Android takes care of all that for you. This is not that surprising given that a HTML form element is simply an instruction to the browser saying, "Put native control here."

For the sake of simplicity, we will initially set a "task" in our to-do list application to have three properties:

- Name
- Description
- Due date (and time)

We now need to create a very simple form that will allow a user to supply those details. The following HTML code (which is again very simple) creates such a form:

```
<h1>Create Task</h1>
<form>
  <div>
  <label for="taskname">Task Name:</label><br />
  <input type="text" name="task[name]" id="taskname" />
```

---

[1] http://phonegap.com/

```
    </div>

    <div>
    <label for="taskdesc">Task Description</label><br />
    <textarea name="task[description]" rows="5"></textarea>
    </div>

    <div>
    <label for="taskdue">Task Due:</label><br />
    <input type="text" name="task[due]" id="taskdue" />
    </div>
    <input type="submit" name="Save" />
</form>
```

Figure 2–3 shows the preceding HTML rendered in the browser of the Android simulator.

Figure 2–3. *Rendered output from simple HTML for a Create Task form*

As you can see in the figure, using vanilla HTML to generate a form isn't really going to have the appeal required to convince people to use Android web apps over a natively built app. We are definitely going to have to do something about this.

Adding Some Style

The easiest way to apply a native feel to form controls for most mobile platforms is not to apply any style to the control at all (very Zen sounding, isn't it?). Rather, we will tell the control just to leave the styling to us, and we will apply some CSS styles to some surrounding HTML elements.

In this next example, we are going to need some surrounding HTML elements that will have CSS styles applied to improve the look and feel of the form. While we probably could work with the div elements we created previously, let's move to using an unordered list (ul), as this will provide us more options for further styling later on. Replace the form code from before with something that looks like this:

```
<form id="taskentry" onsubmit="return false;">
<ul>
  <li><input type="text" name="task[name]" id="taskname" placeholder="Task Name"/></li>
  <li><textarea name="task[description]" id="taskdesc" placeholder="Description"
rows="5"></textarea></li>
  <li><input type="text" name="task[due]" id="taskdue" placeholder="Task Due" /></li>
  <li class="naked"><input type="submit" name="Save" /></li>
</ul>
</form>
```

This HTML generates output that is displayed in Figure 2–4.

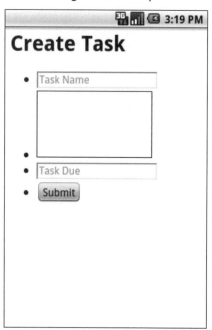

Figure 2–4. *Updated layout using HTML5 placeholders*

In addition to restructuring the form to use a list, we have also removed the label elements and replaced them by using the HTML5 placeholder attribute for the input fields and text area. This provides a simple (and limited-screen-real-estate-friendly) mechanism for giving the user cues for what is required in each form field.

HTML5 ALERT: You may be wondering why HTML5 is sneaking in so soon. What happened to writing some JavaScript and applying some CSS to achieve that placeholder trick the way we used to do for desktop web applications? The reason is that the `placeholder` attribute, while simple, demonstrates some of the useful features that have been added to HTML5 to make a web developer's life easier.

With the `placeholder` attribute and the new layout, we are halfway to having a pretty nice-looking form. Let's have a look at some CSS that will get us the rest of the way there. Now we just need to add some CSS to style the HTML elements. This is probably a good time to start building our `todolist.css` file, which will be used by a number of the pages in our app.

```css
body {
    margin: 0px;
    min-height: 480px;
    font-family: Arial;
}

form ul {
    margin: 0px;
    padding: 6px;
    list-style-type: none;
}

form ul li {
    margin: 0 0 4px 0;
    -webkit-border-radius: 4px;
    border: 1px solid #666666;
    padding: 4px;
}

form ul li.naked {
    -webkit-border-radius: 0px;
    border: 0;
    padding: 0;
}

input, textarea {
    -webkit-appearance: none;
    border: 0;
    width: 99%;
}

input[type=submit] {
    border: 1px solid white;
    background: -webkit-gradient(linear, left top, left bottom, color-stop(0.0,
#F8F8F8), color-stop(1.0, #AAAAAA));
    -webkit-border-radius: 6px;
    -webkit-box-shadow: 0 0 4px #333333;
    width: 100%;
    padding: 6px;
}
```

This stylesheet can now be included in your form code, with the following HTML tag placed in the head section of the page:

```
<link rel="stylesheet" media="screen" href="todolist.css" />
```

Notice that some nonstandard CSS definitions that have been included in the code (shown in bold in the preceding code snippet). I will discuss these in more detail in the following section.

> **NOTE:** These kinds of CSS definitions will be used throughout the book. They represent early WebKit implementations of CSS3 (the next generation of CSS) that are often used in conjunction with HTML5 to achieve some nice visual effects. HTML5 and CSS3 are very complementary technologies, and their combined use is really the enabler for mobile web apps to compete with native mobile apps.

Figure 2–5 shows the browser output displayed after the preceding CSS is applied to our adjusted HTML.

Figure 2–5. *The updated form layout with CSS applied*

Form Styles with a Splash of CSS3

About 75 percent of the preceding CSS is a mix of CSS1 and CSS2, which has been around now for some time. However, there is also a smattering of CSS3, and most of this is quite new. This stylesheet includes some WebKit-specific CSS3 definitions that enable us to make our form look very nice without requiring the use of external image resources.

> **NOTE:** The CSS3 specification (like the HTML5 specification) is not yet finalized. For this reason, the CSS3 definitions here are implemented using the proprietary `-webkit` prefix (for the WebKit browser family, other browsers will implement their own proprietary prefix). This indicates that the folks at WebKit are confident that these sections of the CSS3 spec will make the final cut. Once the CSS3 specification is locked down, then the `-webkit` prefix will be dropped and replaced by the standard name.
>
> As an example, `-webkit-box-shadow` will simply become `box-shadow`. This is definitely worth keeping in mind when building your mobile application—especially given that there is nothing stopping someone from installing a different mobile browser on their Android device. If you want your web app to display in browsers other than WebKit, try to use proprietary CSS3 extensions for eye candy only. Either that or include definitions for the other browser-rendering engines that you want to support in the style definitions also.

Let's have a brief look through the CSS3 extensions used in this example (more detail is provided in the Appendix of the book).

appearance (-webkit-appearance)

This CSS3 property is used to tell the browser what type of native of control we would like to be displayed. There are many different control types that can be specified. For this example and many other instances, it is simplest just to set the appearance to none and to apply the look and feel through surrounding elements.

border-radius (-webkit-border-radius)

The `border-radius` property provides a very simple and nice way of applying a border to your HTML elements. In addition to being able to specify the corner radius for all corners of your element with this property, you can specify specific and different radii for each individual corner using the following properties:

- `border-bottom-left-radius`
- `border-bottom-right-radius`
- `border-top-left-radius`
- `border-top-right-radius`

A `radius` property will take either one parameter that specifies the overall corner radius, or two parameters, specifying the horizontal radius and vertical radius for the corner(s), respectively.

box-shadow (-webkit-box-shadow)

The box-shadow property is used to apply a shadow to HTML elements without requiring external image resources—very nice. The property takes four parameters that allow you to specify how the shadow should appear:

- *Horizontal offset*: This defines where the shadow should be positioned relative to the control in the horizontal direction. Positive values position the shadow to the right of the control, and negative values position it to the left.

- *Vertical offset*: This works like the horizontal offset, but on the vertical axis. Positive values position the shadow below, and negative values position it above.

- *Blur radius*: This specifies the radius for the blur effect. Basically, bigger numbers mean a larger shadow that fades out gradually; smaller numbers mean a smaller, crisper shadow.

- *Shadow color*: This specifies the color of the shadow—pretty self explanatory, really. Most commonly, you'll be using shades of gray here, but colors can be used to create glow effects.

gradient fill style (-webkit-gradient)

So far, we've used shadows and rounded corners in our form; now we'll take a look at using gradients, which can help capture the visual appeal of many current mobile apps. Gradients in CSS3 are not implemented as a CSS3 property, but rather as a fill style—and they are very powerful and quite configurable. I'm sure there are whole chapters dedicated to gradients in a CSS3 book, so I won't attempt to cover all the detail here. Essentially, there are two types of gradients: *linear* and *radial*. This chapter's example uses a linear gradient, so I'll cover that here. Specifying a linear gradient requires a minimum of five parameters (to actually make a gradient effect occur), but more can be used to specify additional color stops.

- *Gradient type*: This is the type of gradient you are going to display—linear or radial.

- *Point 1*: This is the starting point of the gradient. It's a pair of space-separated values that specifies the position. We used names in our example (**left top** and **left bottom**), but additionally numeric values (in the range of 0.0 to 1.0) or percentages can be used.

- *Point 2*: This is the ending point of the gradient.

- *Stop 1*: This is the starting color stop. Defining a color stop is done using the `color-stop` function. The function takes two arguments. The first specifies the relative position between point 1 and point 2 at which the color is used. You can use numbers or percentages to define the position. If using numbers, `0.0` equates to "at point 1" and `1.0` equates to "at point 2." Using percentages, `0.0` is equivalent to 0 percent and `1.0` is equivalent to 100 percent. The second argument is used to define the color that will be used at the specified position.

- *Stop 2*: This is the next color stop. To create a gradient effect, only two stops are required, but more can be specified.

This should start to make more sense when you look at the example in the preceding code sample. If it doesn't, however, then I'd suggest that you just flip to the reference section and have a look at some gradient samples.

Improving the Page Title Appearance

Now that the form is looking a little more presentable, that run-of-the-mill h1 tag for a title is looking a little out of place. Let's see what we can do to improve the presentation. We'll have a look at a couple of options. First, we'll apply a vanilla styling that looks similar to what you might see as a subsection title in a native Android app. Second, we'll use some of the CSS3 styles that we played with previously to dress it up a bit.

The two different CSS classes we are going to experiment with follow—just add them to the end of the `todolist.css` stylesheet, and depending on the look you would like for the application, apply one and delete the other.

```
h1.simple {
    font-size: 0.9em;
    padding: 4px;
    background: #333333;
    color: #AAAAAA;
    border-bottom: 2px solid #AAAAAA;
    margin: 0 0 4px 0;
}

h1.fancy {
    background: -webkit-gradient(linear, left top, left bottom, color-stop(0.0,
#666666), color-stop(0.5, #3A3A3A), color-stop(0.5, #222222), color-stop(1.0, #000000));
    -webkit-box-shadow: 0 2px 1px #AAAAAA;
    -webkit-border-bottom-left-radius: 6px;
    -webkit-border-bottom-right-radius: 6px;
    font-size: 1.1em;
    color: white;
    padding: 10px 8px;
    margin: 0 6px 6px 6px;
    text-align: center;
}
```

Once these styles are applied to the h1 tag (by setting the `class` attribute of the tag), you'll get the results displayed in Figure 2–6.

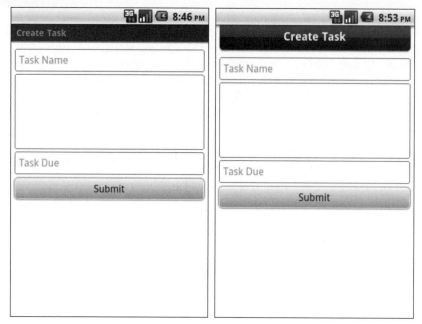

Figure 2–6. *Two header styles compared*

Coding for Different Screen Sizes

Devices powered by the Android OS can come with in a variety of screen sizes, which means that we really want to build our forms and apps to be able to adjust their appearance to make the best use of the available screen real estate. In most cases, this is done best by using relative dimension specifications (i.e., percentages) rather than specific, absolute values (i.e., pixels).

While this might be enough to ensure that a form looks presentable for all screen sizes, it certainly won't guarantee that it's going to look good. For these situations, we need to provide customized stylesheets for the varying device sizes. This is surprisingly simple, and can be done by specifying the appropriate device widths in the media attribute of the link tag. For instance, the following code would include the stylesheet smallscreen.css for devices with a width of 480 pixels and the stylesheet largescreen.css for larger screen sizes.

```
<link media="only screen and (max-device-width: 480px)" href="smallscreen.css" type=
"text/css" rel="stylesheet" />
<link media="only screen and (min-device-width: 481px)" href="largescreen.css" type=
"text/css" rel="stylesheet" />
```

TIP: I would recommend using three stylesheets (instead of two, as just shown) when it comes to writing anything more than a simple app. If you can effectively separate your CSS styles into those that apply regardless of screen size and those that are dependent on screen size, you will have an easier time managing your code in the long run.

Using this approach, the preceding example would have a core stylesheet (say, `allscreens.css`) that is brought into the HTML document without the device width rules in the `link` tag. All CSS that is not dependent on screen size would be moved to this file, and the `smallscreen.css` and `largescreen.css` files would only contain the size-specific rules.

Handling Device Orientation Changes

In addition to handling differing screen sizes, our apps will likely have to respond to the user changing the orientation of the device. Up until now, we have been designing for our applications being used in portrait mode. While the form we have built will play nicely in landscape mode (as demonstrated in Figure 2–7), it is important to know when the orientation changes, as particular applications you write might need some special treatment.

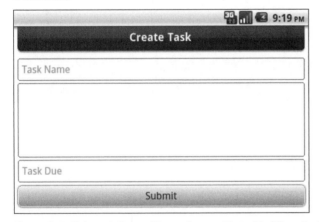

Figure 2–7. *Using relative position makes working with different orientations simple.*

To demonstrate the techniques for dealing with screen orientation changes, let's create a simple page that will provide some feedback as to when orientation changes are occurring.

We will now look at some example code that implements an orientation detection routine that works on both current and previous versions of Android. Additionally, we'll bring in jQuery here so we can do things a little more concisely. If you aren't already familiar with jQuery, it is probably worth quickly running through a jQuery tutorial (an extensive list of tutorials can be found at `http://docs.jquery.com/Tutorials`), or else the JavaScript that is used in this exercise will appear a little confusing.

First is the page HTML:

```html
<html>
<head>
    <title>Orientation Checker</title>
    <meta name="viewport" content="width=device-width; initial-scale=1.0; maximum-
scale=1.0; user-scalable=0;" />
    <link rel="stylesheet" media="screen" href="orientation-monitor.css" />
    <script type="text/javascript" src="../../js/jquery-1.4.2.min.js"></script>
    <script type="text/javascript" src="orientation-monitor.js"></script>
</head>
<body>
    <h1 class="simple">Orientation Monitor</h1>
    <ul class="details">
        <li class="header">Event Details</li>
        <li><label>Type:</label><span id="event-type" /></li>
        <li class="header">Window Details</li>
        <li><label>Width:</label><span id="window-width" /></li>
        <li><label>Height:</label><span id="window-height" /></li>
        <li><label>Orientation:</label><span id="window-orientation" /></li>
        <li class="header">Detection Results</li>
        <li><label>Orientation:</label><span id="orientation" /></li>
        <li><label>Rotation Class:</label><span id="rotation-class" /></li>
    </ul>
</body>
</html>
```

NOTE: I haven't included the CSS here for this example, as it isn't the point of the exercise. You can, however, review the full source at the following URL:

http://sidelab.com/code/pawa/snippets/02/orientation-monitor.css

Next is the content of the orientation-monitor.js file:

```javascript
$(document).ready(function() {
    var canDetect = "onorientationchange" in window;
    var orientationTimer = 0;

    var ROTATION_CLASSES = {
        "0": "none",
        "90": "right",
        "-90": "left",
        "180": "flipped"
    };

    $(window).bind(canDetect ? "orientationchange" : "resize", function(evt) {
        clearTimeout(orientationTimer);
        orientationTimer = setTimeout(function() {
            // display the event type and window details
            $("#event-type").html(evt.type);
            $("#window-orientation").html(window.orientation);
            $("#window-width").html(window.innerWidth);
            $("#window-height").html(window.innerHeight);

            // given we can only really rely on width and height at this stage,
```

```
        // calculate the orientation based on aspect ratio
        var aspectRatio = 1;
        if (window.innerHeight !== 0) {
            aspectRatio = window.innerWidth / window.innerHeight;
        } // if

        // determine the orientation based on aspect ratio
        var orientation = aspectRatio <= 1 ? "portrait" : "landscape";

        // if the event type is an orientation change event, we can rely on
        // the orientation angle
        var rotationText = null;
        if (evt.type == "orientationchange") {
            rotationText = ROTATION_CLASSES[window.orientation.toString()];
        } // if

        // display the details we have determined from the display
        $("#orientation").html(orientation);
        $("#rotation-class").html(rotationText);
    }, 500);
  });
});
```

Once you have implemented the code, a simulator or device will display a screen similar to what is shown in Figure 2–8.

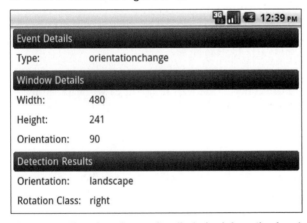

Figure 2–8. *The orientation monitor displaying information for a landscape orientation.*

Let's take a walkthrough of the meaningful parts of the preceding code. Firstly, we make a determination as to whether the version of WebKit that the Android device we are using supports the orientationchange event:

```
var canDetect = "onorientationchange" in window;
```

Then we use the jQuery bind method to attach ourselves to the relevant event—based on the previous detection. Here I use the ternary (or elvis) operator to save some keystrokes. (I apologize if you aren't a fan of Elvis, but I am, so expect to see more of him.)

```
$(window).bind(canDetect ? "orientationchange" : "resize", function(evt) {
  ...
});
```

Next, we'll do something pretty subtle, but very important. As `orientationchange` and `resize` events can occur quite rapidly, we need to wait until things have settled down before actually attempting to handle the event. In this case, I am using the JavaScript `setTimeout` and `clearTimeout` functions to clear and reset a timer that will run once the event queue has stabilized.

```
var orientationTimer = 0;
clearTimeout(orientationTimer);
orientationTimer = setTimeout(function() {
  ...
});
```

This wraps up the preparatory work that is required to properly capture appropriate events for detecting orientation changes. Let's now have a look at what is required to interpret the information we are receiving.

First, let's work out the screen aspect ratio, and from there determine whether the screen is being displayed in portrait or landscape mode:

```
var aspectRatio = 1;
if (window.innerHeight !== 0) {
    aspectRatio = window.innerWidth / window.innerHeight;
} // if

// determine the orientation based on aspect ratio
var orientation = aspectRatio <= 1 ? "portrait" : "landscape";
```

As I mention in the comments in the full code sample, the preceding code is really the only reliable way *at the moment* to write detection code that is going to work for most devices. In my testing, an Android device that did not support the `orientationchange` event still reported results for the `window.orientation` value, but always returned 0, regardless of the device's actual orientation.

Based on the aspect ratio of the display, we can infer the orientation of the screen. We can go a little further with the next section of code to get a value-add for those devices that do actually provide us accurate orientation information:

```
var ROTATION_CLASSES = {
    "0": "none",
    "90": "right",
    "-90": "left",
    "180": "flipped"
};

var rotationText = null;
if (evt.type == "orientationchange") {
    rotationText = ROTATION_CLASSES[window.orientation.toString()];
} // if
```

In this code, we first look to see if the event was an `orientationchange` event. If so, then we take the `window.orientation` integer value, convert it to a string, and then map it to an array value that we will use in conjunction with CSS classes at a later stage.

> **NOTE:** As a platform, Android is continuing to evolve and the particular code may have differing effects on different versions of the Android OS. One of the common criticisms of the Android platform relates to the fragmented OS versions available across devices.
>
> To that end, the preceding code worked for Android 1.6, 2.1, and 2.2 in the emulator, but failed to behave correctly on an Android 2.1 device. This is something that is going to prove challenging for Android developers (including web app developers) until Google works with the device manufacturers to ensure Android OS releases are distributed to consumers.
>
> Until that time, it is very important to perform thorough device testing with your apps and be aware of any limitations that particular OS versions may have.

What this code produces for us is essentially two string values that we can utilize for effectively applying stylesheets (or individual styles) for our mobile web apps.

Once we have done this, it's a very simple matter to tweak the code so that we can use it in future exercises. Essentially, we need to remove the feedback elements from the code (where jQuery is being used to update spans for our example app), and use the jQuery `trigger` function to fire a new event:

```
$(window).trigger("reorient", [orientation, rotationText]);
```

Once this is done, you should be able to tweak your code to update the detected orientation display elements by using jQuery `bind` to handle "reorient" events. If you run into trouble, just have a look at the final exercise JavaScript code on GitHub:

```
http://sidelab.com/code/pawa/snippets/02/orientation-monitor.js
```

> **BUILDING A TOOL SET:** We are starting to build up our tool set of reusable code that will be used in later examples. While I won't cover the detail of how this is being done, you can have a look at the library at any time. Like the exercise code, the library is available for review at the URL :
>
> ```
> http://sidelab.com/code/pawa/js/prowebapps.js
> ```

Adding Form Validation

Now that we have the form looking presentable, we need to add some form validation to make sure we are getting accurate data so that we can actually start saving new tasks in the next chapter.

We will continue using jQuery from this point forward, which will give us access to some excellent validation plug-ins that will save us from having to write validation routines from the ground up. Before we get to integrating that validation plug-in, however, let's consider how we are going to provide validation feedback in our application, as that is something we are not going to be able to just use as is.

I know it's been mentioned before, but we need to again consider limited screen real estate. Additionally, if you have come from a desktop web application background, you will also have to come to terms with not having hover tips and associated mouseover-type functionality in your mobile web apps.

So we need an effective way of communicating validation errors that doesn't take up excessive screen space, but provides the user enough detail to fix the problems with the data they have entered.

We will explore one option for providing that feedback by looking at an example.

Providing Feedback with Limited Screen Space

The approach we are going to take in this application is to first indicate any field that has a problem with the data that has been provided with a visual cue that something is awry—nothing new here. While a common practice for web applications would also be to provide an overall summary of the validation errors that have been encountered for the entire form, we will not be able to incorporate this given the limited screen real-estate. As an alternative, let's look at ways that we can leverage the power of jQuery to alter the page at runtime and display those errors when a user enters a particular field.

Given that we haven't actually hooked up the jQuery validation plug-in yet, we'll just use mock JavaScript to simulate some failed tests to check that our display behaves in the desired fashion.

First, let's add some basic style information to the todolist.css file for invalid fields:

```
input.invalid, textarea.invalid {
    background: url(exclamation.png) no-repeat 2px 2px;
    padding-left: 22px;
}

#errors {
    margin: 8px 6px 2px 6px;
    padding: 6px 14px;
    background: -webkit-gradient(linear, left top, left bottom, color-stop(0.0,
#cc0000), color-stop(0.7, #770022));
    -webkit-border-radius: 4px;
    color: white;
    display: none;
}
```

NOTE: I've included an external image resource to draw attention to the invalid field. This is definitely one way to do things, and is great for what we are doing currently. Later in the book I will discuss how you can actually embed image data directly into your stylesheets to reduce the number of HTTP requests required by your app.

Oh, and you may notice that I've used another gradient. It might be time to start admitting I have a problem with gradient addiction.

With a way to see that a field is invalid, let's implement some code to trigger the display of validation errors:

```javascript
var errors = {};

function displayErrors() {
    // initialize variables
    var haveErrors = false;

    // remove the invalid class for all inputs
    $(":input.invalid").removeClass("invalid");

    // iterate through the fields specified in the errors array
    for (var fieldName in errors) {
        haveErrors = true;
        $("input[name='" + fieldName + "']").addClass("invalid");
    } // for

    // if we have errors, then add a message to the errors div
    $("#errors")
        .html(haveErrors ? "Errors were found." : "")
        .css("display", haveErrors ? "block" : "none");
} // displayErrors

$(document).ready(function() {
  $("#taskentry").bind("submit", function() {
        errors = {
            "task[name]": ["Task name is required"],
            "task[due]": ["Due date is invalid"]
        }; //

        displayErrors();
        return false;
    });
});
```

This code is the start of our todolist.js file, which we will build up to contain the application logic for our web app. Right now, there isn't much to it, but by the end of Chapter 4, this will be quite a substantial amount of code. For now, the code simply binds to the submit event of the task entry form and provides the skeleton of a displayErrors function. If you click the Submit button on the web form, you should now see something similar to Figure 2–9.

Figure 2–9. *The Create Task form simulating an error condition*

Let's move on to providing the user additional information when they focus back on a field in the form. If you play around in the emulator or on an actual Android device, you may notice that the screen positioning of elements when the onscreen keyboard is displayed is going to make it difficult to choose a suitable location to provide the additional validation feedback. If you haven't yet experienced this firsthand, then just take a moment to throw a few extra dummy input fields in the Create Task form and experiment with the interface.

Figure 2–10 highlights the dramatic reduction of available screen real estate when the keyboard is displayed.

Figure 2–10. *When the onscreen keyboard is displayed, the available display height is roughly halved.*

From my own investigations and experience, I have found that using the screen real estate above a control is a little more reliable than below (given that scrolling is limited by the height of the current HTML document). To provide the detailed feedback, let's add some additional JavaScript to our `todolist.js` file. We'll start with adding an additional function that will be used to display any errors for a form element that is passed to it:

```
function displayFieldErrors(field) {
    var messages = errors[field.name];
    if (messages && (messages.length > 0)) {
        // find an existing error detail section for the field
        var errorDetail = $("#errordetail_" + field.id).get(0);

        // if it doesn't exist, then create it
        if (! errorDetail) {
            $(field).before("<ul class='errors-inline' id='errordetail_" + field.id +
"'></ul>");
            errorDetail = $("#errordetail_" + field.id).get(0);
        } // if

        // add the various error messages to the div
        for (var ii = 0; ii < messages.length; ii++) {
            $(errorDetail).html('').append("<li>" + messages[ii] + "</li>");
        } // for
    } // if
} // displayFieldErrors
```

This code is then triggered by attaching to the focus handler of the control—the following code demonstrates how to do that when the document is loaded:

```
$(document).ready(function() {
    $(":input").focus(function(evt) {
        displayFieldErrors(this);
    }).blur(function(evt) {
        $("#errordetail_" + this.id).remove();
    });
    ...
});
```

Now we just need add an additional style definition so the inline errors are displayed differently from other ul elements:

```
ul.errors-inline li {
    border: 0px;
    color: red;
    padding: 0px;
}
```

Once that has been implemented, errors should display above an input field when it receives focus, as per Figure 2–11.

Figure 2–11. *Detailed error messages are now displayed above an entry field when it receives focus.*

That's pretty much it in terms of providing error feedback; from here all that is required is to include the jQuery validation plug-in and let it do the hard work of validating data.

Setting up the jQuery validation plug-in requires the following steps:

1.   Importing the jquery.validate.js library into our HTML code

2.   Adding some validation information to the class declarations of input fields that we want to validate

3. Calling a customized version of the `validate` method for our form to override the default jQuery validation plug-in behavior to what we created previously

Let's start with the tweaks to the HTML:

```html
<html>
<head>
    <title>Simple Mobile Web Page</title>
    <meta name="viewport" content="width=device-width; initial-scale=1.0; maximum-scale=1.0; user-scalable=0;" />
    <link rel="stylesheet" media="screen" href="todolist.css" />
    <script type="text/javascript" src="../../js/jquery-1.4.2.min.js"></script>
    <script type="text/javascript" src="../../js/jquery.validate.js"></script>
    <script type="text/javascript" src="../../js/prowebapps.js"></script>
    <script type="text/javascript" src="todolist.js"></script>
</head>
<body>
    <h1 class="fancy">Create Task</h1>
    <div id="errors"></div>
    <form id="taskentry">
    <ul>
        <li><input type="text" class="required" name="task[name]" id="taskname" placeholder="Task Name"/></li>
        <li>
            <textarea name="task[description]" id="taskdesc" placeholder="Description" rows="5"></textarea>
        </li>
        <li><input type="text" class="required date" name="task[due]" id="taskdue" placeholder="Task Due" /></li>
        <li class="naked"><input type="submit" name="Save" /></li>
    </ul>
    </form>
</body>
</html>
```

That takes care of steps 1 and 2; now we just need to replace the mock validation code (the jQuery bind for the submit and the associated callback) with the following code:

```javascript
$("#taskentry").validate({
    submitHandler: function(form) {
        // TO BE COMPLETED IN THE NEXT CHAPTER
    },
    showErrors: function(errorMap, errorList) {
        // initialize an empty errors map
        errors = {};

        // iterate through the jQuery validation error map, and convert to something we can use
        for (var elementName in errorMap) {
            if (! errors[elementName]) {
                errors[elementName] = [];
            } // if

            errors[elementName].push(errorMap[elementName]);
        } // for

        // now display the errors
```

```
        displayErrors();
    }
});
```

Once this is done, the application should behave exactly as before, but rather than displaying our mock errors it will display error messages that have been produced from the jQuery.validate plug-in.

Summary

This chapter should have familiarized you with the basic requirements of building a mobile web app. It included a look at the viewport meta tag, and explored some of the CSS3 styles that can be used in Android's WebKit browser to create a clean user interface. It also covered some of the extra things to be considered when creating web apps for mobile devices, including device orientation changes and the extra constraints applied when designing an app given limited screen real estate. Finally, we made use the jQuery validate plug-in to bring robust forms validation into our application without having to write it from the ground up.

In the next chapter, we will look at saving our data using the various client-side storage mechanisms that are provided as part of HTML5. This will involve starting to get a bit more serious with our code, and as a result, I'll be moving to using the JavaScript module pattern in the code samples. Employing the module pattern will provide us the solid foundation required to build more complicated applications in JavaScript, so while it takes a bit of getting used to, it's well with the effort.

Chapter **3**

HTML5 Storage APIs

In the last chapter, we looked at creating a simple mobile web page and a simple Create Task form for our to-do list application. In this chapter, we will look at options for being able to store data locally on the device. HTML5 introduces a couple of APIs that permit this kind of client-side storage.

Previously when writing a web app, if you needed to save data to a database, you would need to use a server-side script (PHP, Python, Ruby, etc.) to do this for you. Some emerging elements of the HTML5 API offer a client-side alternative for this, and investigating these and how to effectively use them will be the primary focus of this chapter.

Essentially, three different types of client-side storage mechanisms are being implemented as part of the HTML5 specification:

- *Web storage*: Often referred to as HTML5 local storage, this is a client-side mechanism for storing key/value pairs. It's simple, but very powerful (see http://w3.org/TR/webstorage/).

- *Web SQL database*: This provides access to a SQLite-like database, which is a client-side alternative to a traditional RDBMS that you might find on a server (see http://w3.org/TR/webdatabase/).

- *Indexed database*: A draft specification that has been proposed by the W3C to replace the currently implemented Web SQL database specification, geared towards providing a "database of records holding simple values and hierarchical objects" (see http://w3.org/TR/IndexedDB/).

In this chapter, we will be focusing on the first two storage APIs listed above, providing both an overview and sample code for both.

Although the Indexed DB API has been put forward by the W3C to replace the Web SQL database, currently no versions of Android have shipped with support for the specification. For this reason, we have focused on the two that you can implement and use right now—Web Storage and Web SQL database.

It is our firm belief that WebKit browsers (as used natively on Android) will continue to support the Web SQL database for some time to come so you should feel comfortable using that specification even though the W3C have indicated that they will not be creating any further revisions to the standard.

The Web Storage API

Both the localStorage and sessionStorage objects implement the Storage interface, and this provides the following methods:

- getItem
- setItem
- removeItem
- clear

These four methods capture pretty much the entire functionality of the Storage API, and while they appear simple, they open up some great opportunities. The magic lies in the fact that you can save any object into Storage. You just provide a key to access the value later, and away you go.

In a simple case, you might simply save a string or other simple type values into storage. Consider the following code:

```
localStorage.setItem("preferences-bgcolor", "#333333");
localStorage.setItem("preferences- textcolor", "#FFFFFF");
```

This creates two values in localStorage for tracking application preferences for a background and text color. You could, however, achieve the same result by just storing a single object in localStorage with the following code:

```
localStorage.setItem("preferences", {
    bgcolor: "#333333",
    textcolor: "#FFFFFF"
});
```

You can retrieve your preferences object by using a simple call to getItem:

```
var preferences = localStorage.getItem("preferences");
```

You should then be able to access the background color and text color preferences from the preferences object. Let's try that now. Just show an alert to display the background color:

```
alert(preferences.bgcolor);
```

Um, well, that's embarrassing. Depending on the implementation of the Web Storage API browsers are using at the time you are reading this book, you may well find that the preceding call just shows you a message as per the JavaScript alert displayed in Figure 3–1.

Figure 3–1. *Accessing objects in localStorage may not yield the expected/documented results.*

What does that mean for you right now? Can you only store simple values in localStorage and sessionStorage? Yes . . . but you can always use JSON (JavaScript Object Notation) to serialize your objects first and then save them as strings. This is definitely worth investigating, so the first exercise of this chapter relates to that.

NOTE: If you haven't encountered a situation like this previously, then welcome to the world of the early technology adopter—things change. We discussed this earlier, but here is a firsthand example in which the browser builders believed part of the HTML5 spec had stabilized enough for implementation, when in actual fact there were still some tweaks on the way. This is all part of the fun, and we are likely to come across more examples of this through the course of the book.

If you do come across something that doesn't work as expected, or something in the book isn't in line with the current HTML5 spec, then please provide some feedback online: www.apress.com.

Saving Objects to Web Storage Using JSON

We will now investigate saving JavaScript objects to Web Storage using JSON. JSON provides an elegant and efficient method of storing JavaScript object data as a plain text string. Once in string format, the data can then be sent to external services or saved as per the samples here. Before you begin saving objects in JSON format, however, you are going to need Douglas Crockford's `json2.js` library for serializing/deserializing objects to JSON strings. This library is available at the following location: `http://json.org/json2.js`.

You can download that file into your top-level js directory so you can use it for other exercises later on.

> **NOTE:** Doug Crockford has included an alert in the first line of the `json2.js` file to discourage people from using the library via a direct link to his site. You will need to remove this line before running code samples from the exercise. If you forget, though, everything will work; you'll just have to click through an annoying alert each time you run an exercise using JSON. We're fairly confident that by the end of the book that first line will be removed.

Let's create a simple page that will set up the environment for us to run our tests:

```html
<html>
<head>
    <title>Web Storage Tester</title>
    <meta name="viewport" content="width=device-width; initial-scale=1.0; maximum-scale=1.0; user-scalable=0;" />
    <link rel="stylesheet" media="screen" href="../../css/snippets.css" />
    <script type="text/javascript" src="../../js/jquery-1.4.2.min.js"></script>
    <script type="text/javascript" src="../../js/json2.js"></script>
    <script type="text/javascript" src="../../js/prowebapps.js"></script>
    <script type="text/javascript" src="webstorage-test.js"></script>
</head>
<body>
    <h1 class="fancy">Web Storage JSON Wrapper</h1>
    <ul id="items">
        <li class="header">Items in Storage (tap to remove)</li>
    </ul>
    <ul id="newitem">
        <li class="header">New Item</li>
        <li class="bordered"><input type="text" id="newtitle" placeholder="Title" /></li>
    </ul>
    <ul id="actions">
        <li><button id="add">Add</button></li>
        <li><button id="clear">Clear</button></li>
    </ul>
</body>
<html>
```

In the preceding code, there are four general items to take note of:

- Inclusion of the generic *snippets* stylesheet (`css/snippets.css`). As outlined in Chapter 1, this stylesheet forms part of the reusable code components that we will use and expand on over the course of the book. Full source of the stylesheet is viewable at the following URL: `http://sidelab.com/code/pawa/css/snippets.css`.

- Inclusion of `json2.js` so we can access JSON serialization and parsing.

- Inclusion of the `prowebapps.js` library. We will add some handy wrappers for saving to localStorage/sessionStorage, which will provide automatic serialization/deserialization of objects using JSON.

- Inclusion of `webstorage-test.js`, which will include the JavaScript code for this exercise.

Let's get on with coding. First, we'll add those storage wrapper functions to the `prowebapps.js` library. This is done by adding a `Storage` submodule to our existing PROWEBAPPS module:

```javascript
var module = {
    Storage: (function() {
        function getStorageScope(scope) {
            if (scope && (scope == "session")) {
                return sessionStorage;
            } // if

            return localStorage;
        } // getStorageTarget

        return {
            get: function(key, scope) {
                // get the storage target
                var value = getStorageScope(scope).getItem(key);

                // if the value looks like serialized JSON, parse it
                return (/^(\{|\[).*(\}|\])$/).test(value) ? JSON.parse(value) : value;
            },

            set: function(key, value, scope) {
                // if the value is an object, then stringify using JSON
                var serializable = jQuery.isArray(value) || jQuery.isPlainObject(value);
                var storeValue = serializable ? JSON.stringify(value) : value;

                // save the value
                getStorageScope(scope).setItem(key, storeValue);
            },

            remove: function(key, scope) {
                getStorageScope(scope).removeItem(key);
            }
        };
    })()

    ...
};
```

While we won't go into a detailed explanation of the preceding code, those of you who are interested will be able to see that we wrap the `getItem` and `setItem` methods of the HTML5 Storage interface into `get` and `set` static methods on the PROWEBAPPS.Storage module. We use some jQuery utility functions and regular expressions to determine if we need to use JSON to store/retrieve the data, and if so, then we do.

More important than how the preceding code works (which is relatively simple once you break it down) is how we will be able to use it. Basically, we now have three functions that permit more complex value storage at our disposal for interacting with the HTML5 Web Storage functionality:

- PROWEBAPPS.Storage.get(key, scope)
    - key is a string value used to identify the entry.
    - scope can be optionally specified as "session" (i.e., as a string) if you want to store to session storage instead of local storage.
- PROWEBAPPS.Storage.set(key, value, scope)
    - As per the get method, the key is a string value to identify the entry.
    - value is the data that we wish to save to Web Storage. (This can be a simple value, array, object, etc.). Arrays and objects are serialized using JSON and then stored as strings.
    - scope (optional) specifies whether the key value will be saved to session or local storage. Passing no value to this parameter means that the value will be saved to local storage.
- PROWEBAPPS.Storage.remove(key, scope)
    - key is a string value used to specify the entry that will be removed from storage.
    - The scope parameter (if supplied) will specify whether session or local storage should be used. If no value is supplied, then local storage is used by default.

Now that we have this functionality at our disposal, let's have a look at storing simple JavaScript objects and arrays using our PROWEBAPPS.Storage functions. We'll do this by creating our webstorage-test.js file, which will be used to power this little storage test application:

```
$(document).ready(function() {
    // read the data from local storage for the items
    var items = PROWEBAPPS.Storage.get("listitems");
    var loadTicks = new Date().getTime();

    function displayItems() {
        loadTicks = new Date().getTime();

        $("#items li[class!='header']").remove();
        if (items) {
            // create list items to display the current items
            for (var ii = 0; ii < items.length; ii++) {
                var itemAge = Math.floor((loadTicks - items[ii].created) / 1000);
                $("#items").append("<li>" + items[ii].title + " (created " + itemAge +
"s ago)</li>");
            } // for
        }
```

```
    else {
        $("#items").append("<li>No items</li>");

        // initialize the items array
        items = [];
    } // if..else
    } // displayItems

    // button click handlers go here
    displayItems();
});
```

The preceding code is very simple and is designed to retrieve an array of items (listitems) from localStorage and display them on the screen. With the code as it was before (without add or clear functionality defined), loading the page generates HTML output, as displayed in Figure 3–2.

Figure 3–2. *The Web Storage test application page*

As there are no items currently in storage (the PROWEBAPPS.Storage.get function currently returns null), we display "No items" on the screen. Let's implement the add and clear button click handlers to populate and save the array:

```
$("#add").click(function() {
    items.push({
        title: $("#newtitle").val(),
        created: new Date().getTime()
    });

    // save the items
    PROWEBAPPS.Storage.set("listitems", items);
    displayItems();
```

```
});

$("#clear").click(function() {
    items = null;
    PROWEBAPPS.Storage.remove("listitems");
    displayItems();
});
```

Once again, this is very simple code. In the case of the add handler, we push a new object onto the array using the title of the item and the current date time (represented in milliseconds), save the items to storage, and then refresh the display.

The clear handler is even simpler. We reset the items variable state back to null, remove listitems from local storage, and then update the display.

Local vs. Session Storage

As shown in the code previously, there is no difference between using localStorage and sessionStorage—not in terms of the actual interaction at least. In fact, the only real difference is the length of time the data is actually stored and what the data considers to be its owner.

In the case of local storage, the data is persistent and will not be removed unless it's requested to be removed by the user (e.g., by using the browser settings).

In the case of session storage, the data lasts only as long as the browsing context (which is usually terminated when the browser window closes). Additionally, browsers will maintain separate sessionStorage objects for separate windows or tabs; local storage, on the other hand, will be shared between windows and tabs.

> **NOTE:** In doing some detailed analysis of how multiple windows/tabs interact with Web Storage, it became clear that the implementation of the PROWEBAPPS.Storage module currently contains a flaw. It is currently possible for two windows to overwrite each other's changes in *localStorage*. In *sessionStorage*, however, there are never collisions.

For both localStorage and sessionStorage, data is stored on a per-origin basis. An origin refers to the site from which the page was loaded, and basically means that site B will not be able to access client-side data created by site A (which makes sense).

The Web SQL Database

Now that we have worked with the Web Storage API, it's appropriate that we get acquainted with Web Storage's cousin—the Web SQL Database. Given the more complicated nature of this storage API, we will cover it briefly here and then run through more concrete examples when we build our GeoMiner application later in the book.

The implementation of the Web SQL Database feels very much like interacting with a typical Ajax handler (the SQL aside), as interactions with the API are primarily asynchronous operations. Web workers (which only have sparse support on mobile browsers at the time of writing) also have access to a synchronous implementation — which is appropriate given their threaded execution context.

At a high level, we can summarize the HTML5 Web SQL Database implementation in about three methods:

- openDatabase: Used to open/create a database. This method takes five arguments:

  - databaseId: The ID of the database.

  - version: A string identifying the version of the database. This can be used to implement particular version-update scripts (more information on this is provided in Chapter 4).

  - description: A human-readable description of the database.

  - estimatedSize: The estimated size of the database (in bytes).

  - creationCallback: A callback that will be executed once the database has been opened/created (not implemented in all browsers).

- transaction/readTransaction: Used to open a transaction for the execution of one or more SQL statements. The transaction method is used for INSERT/UPDATE/DELETE operations, and the readTransaction is used for SELECT statements. This method only accepts one argument:

  - callback: The callback function that will be called when the transaction has been opened. When the callback is executed, it passes in a single argument for the transaction instance.

- executeSql: Used to run an SQL statement within a transaction. This method takes four arguments:

  - sqlText: The SQL statement to execute against the database.

  - sqlParameters: An array of values for the parameters included in sqlText statement. Parameters are specified in the SQL using a question mark (?).

  - completionCallback: A function callback that will be invoked when the SQL statement has been successfully executed. In the case of a SELECT statement, results will be returned as a second argument in the callback. A transaction argument is returned as the first argument in all cases if the callback is specified.

  - errorCallback: A callback that will be invoked if there are issues with the SQL statement or database.

While we won't go through the code in detail here, if you are interested in working through how our previous example of saving objects would look using the Web SQL Database instead of Web Storage, we have provided an example implementation at the following location: http://sidelab.com/code/pawa/snippets/03/webstorage-test-webdb.js.

Given the amount of material there is to cover, we will focus on implementing a local database reading and writing using the Web SQL Database API. This will be covered in the next example.

Saving To-Do List Items with a Client-Side Database

In this exercise, we will use the Web SQL Database API to save to-do list items to a client-side database for later use. We will work with the methods outlined previously to do this.

Begin by creating a submodule called TODOLIST.Storage in your JavaScript application code. This module will be responsible for handling interaction with the database for the application. It is important to encapsulate this functionality, as it gives you the option to use an alternative storage mechanism (e.g., the Web Storage API) at a later date without affecting the rest of the application code.

The following code should be added to the module definition in the todolist.js file (remember to include a comma if this isn't the last member of the module array):

```
Storage: (function() {
    // open/create a database for the application (expected size ~ 100K)
    var db = openDatabase("todolist", "1.0", "To Do List Database", 100 * 1024);

    // check that we have the required tables created
    db.transaction(function(transaction) {
        transaction.executeSql(
            "CREATE TABLE IF NOT EXISTS task(" +
            "   name TEXT NOT NULL, " +
            "   description TEXT, " +
            "   due DATETIME);");
    });

    return {
        saveTask: function(task, callback) {
            db.transaction(function(transaction) {
                transaction.executeSql(
                    "INSERT INTO task(name, description, due) VALUES (?, ?, ?);",
                    [task.name, task.description, task.due]
                );
            });
        }
    };
})()
```

At this stage, TODOLIST.Storage has only two functions:

- To create/open a client-side database called `todolist`, and to ensure that the required `task` table exists, creating it if required

- To save a to-do list item into the `task` table

We then create what might be called a DTO (data transfer object) or POJO (plain-old Java object) in other languages to capture the details of a to-do list item. In future exercises, we will refer to these as POJOs, since the acronym works almost as well for JavaScript as it does for Java.

As per the preceding Storage code, `Task` is added to the module definition of `todolist.js`:

```
Task: function(params) {
    params = jQuery.extend({
        name: "",
        description: "",
        due: null
    }, params);

    // initialize self
    var self = {
        id: null,
        name: params.name,
        description: params.description,
        due: params.due ? new Date(params.due) : null
    };

    return self;
}
```

> **NOTE:** While we have a preference for using POJOs to capture details about an object in our application, this isn't always the best way to go. You can see in the preceding case that `Task` adds very little extra value in this early stage. Personally, we find that architecting an application in this way provides some benefits once it reaches a certain size and complexity, but can feel like a waste of time initially.
>
> When it comes to actually saving `Task`, we'll provide an alternative implementation that will work without the POJO if that is your preference.

One final piece of supporting code is required and, if you have worked with jQuery and web apps before, you have probably built something like this yourself previously. To save yourself from writing the same code time and time again to extract form values from a form and map them into an object, you can use something like the following code to make that process more streamlined (given that you are able to use consistent naming for form fields, object properties, etc.).

The following code should be added to the module definition for the `prowebapps.js` file (remember, a trailing comma may be required depending on where you add the code in the module):

```
getFormValues: function(form) {
    var values = {};

    // iterate through the form values using jQuery
    jQuery(form).find(":input").each(function() {
        // get the name of the field
        var fieldName = this.name.replace(/^.*\[(\w+)\]$/, "$1");

        // set the value for the field
        values[fieldName] = this.value;
    });

    return values;
}
```

Now that all the building blocks are in place, let's go back and change the submit handler that was left blank when we finished Chapter 2 so that it contains some code that will actually save the to-do list item:

```
$("#taskentry").validate({
    submitHandler: function(form) {
        // get the values from the form in hashmap
        var formValues = PROWEBAPPS.getFormValues(form);

        // create a new item to save to the database
        var item = new TODOLIST.Task(formValues);

        // now create a new task
        TODOLIST.Storage.saveTask(item);
    },
    showErrors: function(errorMap, errorList) {
        // code from chapter 02
    }
});
```

Saving a new to-do item is now a simple three-step process:

1. Getting the values of the fields in the form as a JavaScript key/value pair array

2. Creating a new item from those form values

3. Asking the `Storage` module to save the item for us

Running this code on an Android handset or emulator is quite unsatisfying, as we haven't built our interface for displaying items yet. To get some confidence that this is actually working, let's have a look in Chrome, using the Chrome developer tools. As outlined in Chapter 1, a WebKit-based desktop browser is an invaluable tool when it comes to debugging mobile apps—my personal preference is Chrome.

So, we provide the form some data. As shown in Figure 3–3, I am going to give myself a to-do of mowing the lawn before the end of 2011 (it's not one of my strong points).

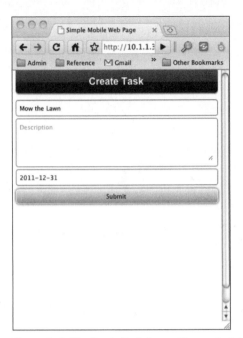

Figure 3–3. *The Create Task form with sample data displayed in Chrome*

On submitting the form, the data passes the validation checks that we set up in the last chapter and thus proceeds to save the data according to the logic that we set up in the submit handler. Having a look in the Storage tab in the developer tools, we can see that our data was indeed saved to the local database. Figure 3–4 shows the Chrome developer tools.

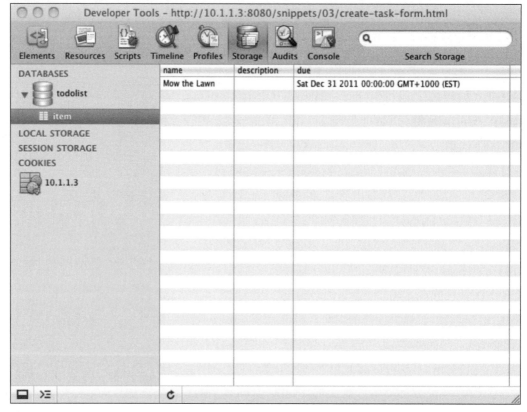

Figure 3–4. *The new task is saved, and can be seen using the Storage inspector in the Chrome developer tools.*

As promised, if you are not a fan of using POJOs and the like to encapsulate data moving around in your application, the submit handler code can be modified to the following:

```
$("#taskentry").validate({
    submitHandler: function(form) {
        // get the values from the form in hashmap
        var formValues = PROWEBAPPS.getFormValues(form);

        // now create a new to-do list item
        TODOLIST.Storage.saveTask(formValues);
    },
    showErrors: function(errorMap, errorList) {
        // code from chapter 02
    }
});
```

As it stands with the code in the Storage module, the date is saved as entered. Figure 3–5 shows that the database holds a value identical to what was entered, which indicates that this value is probably saved as a string.

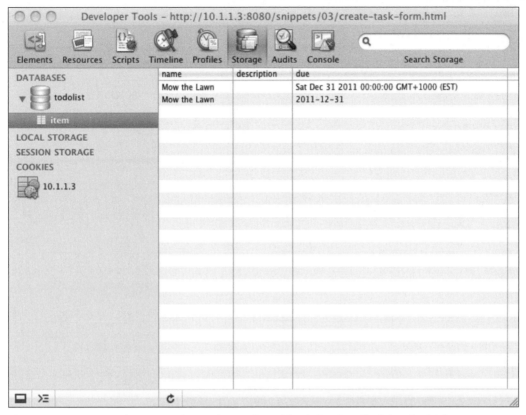

Figure 3–5. *The results of not converting a string to a Date object before inserting it into the database*

You can see the second entry has been added as is. In reality, this is also the case for the first entry too, as what is displayed here is simply the `toString` representation for a JavaScript `Date` object (as we converted the form value to a `Date` in the `Task` POJO).

> **CAUTION:** The preceding behavior is interesting, given that we explicitly defined the due field as a `DATETIME` type in our `CREATE TABLE` statement. While this won't cause any real issues in our application here, we think it is worth noting that with current implementations of the SQL Web Database you may need to test your data on read operations in addition to writes, as you may not be able to trust that the data in the database is of the type you expect.
>
> To confirm this behavior, try tweaking the code to see if you can actually push a string value into the due field. You will find that you can. This appears to be consistent with the way SQLite handles `DATETIME` columns. For more information, check out the following URL on the SQLite site: www.sqlite.org/datatype3.html.

Database Versioning and Upgrades

The HTML5 implementation of the Web SQL Database has already been quite well thought through, and provides a mechanism to apply version changes to our client-side databases when a new version of our application is deployed. This involves the use of the changeVersion method on an opened database. The method allows you to specify the old version, the new version, and a transaction callback to execute, in order to apply any updates required to move from one version to the next. Additionally, optional error and success callbacks can be supplied to monitor and respond to those particular response conditions.

For instance, in the next chapter we are going to add some functionality to our to-do list application to allow a user to mark items as complete. This is obviously a good idea, but the database is clearly lacking a place to store a completed flag or date. Time to fix that and create version 1.1 of our database.

The following code shows how we can replace our original openDatabase call in the TODOLIST.Storage module with one that can handle opening either version 1.1 or version 1.0 of the database, and upgrade version 1.0 appropriately:

```
var db = null;

try {
    db = openDatabase("todolist", "1.1", "To Do List Database", 100 * 1024);

    // check that we have the required tables created
    db.transaction(function(transaction) {
        transaction.executeSql(
            "CREATE TABLE IF NOT EXISTS task(" +
            "  name TEXT NOT NULL, " +
            "  description TEXT, " +
            "  due DATETIME, " +
            "  completed DATETIME);");
    });
}
catch (e) {
    db = openDatabase("todolist", "1.0", "To Do List Database", 100 * 1024);

    // check that we have the required tables created
    db.transaction(function(transaction) {
        transaction.executeSql(
            "CREATE TABLE IF NOT EXISTS task(" +
            "  name TEXT NOT NULL, " +
            "  description TEXT, " +
            "  due DATETIME);");
    });

    db.changeVersion("1.0", "1.1", function(transaction) {
        transaction.executeSql("ALTER TABLE item ADD completed DATETIME;");
    });
}
```

We'll be honest here and say that we're not huge fans of this implementation. It works, but we wonder how scalable it is when you are rolling out your 13th application update and corresponding database change. (Of course, one database change per app update would be very bad planning, but you get our point.)

Summary

We have explored two powerful mechanisms for storing data on the client side in this chapter. While not one of the shiniest toys in the HTML5 bag of tricks, it's certainly one of the game changers. Being able to store different types of data on the client side is going to create many opportunities for mobile web apps over the next few years.

In addition to the actual mechanics of Web Storage and the Web SQL Database, we also investigated ways of effectively encapsulating that and other functionality in web apps using the JavaScript module pattern. You can probably tell how important we think it is for building serious apps using JavaScript, but we promise we'll back off a little in the following chapters.

In the next chapter, we will finish our to-do list application by adding a view to display our to-do list items, and also a way to mark them as complete. At this point, we will go beyond single-page examples into a multiple-view/screen application. We will investigate ways to build this kind of functionality as well as briefly explore libraries that offer this functionality already.

Chapter 4

Constructing a Multipage App

Now that we have the ability to save tasks in our to-do list application, it's time to build our display screen and add the ability to complete tasks. This will bring our to-do list application to the point that it can actually be used for creating, viewing, and completing tasks.

With data now being saved to the client-side database, let's create a display screen so that we can keep track of all those things we have to do (sigh). We are going to be working toward building a display that shows the next five things that need to be done (in due date) order.

Once we have done this, we will be at a point where our to-do list application has multiple screens. While we could implement these using separate HTML pages, that would result in page loads that aren't required. This is best avoided, so we will implement some functionality that you will find in the likes of jQTouch (http://jqtouch.com) and iUI (http://code.google.com/p/iui) for creating a single HTML document that contains multiple application screens.

Single HTML File, Multiple App Pages

Before we get into building our main to-do list application page, let's work through adding some additional styles to our proui.css file to handle setting up divs for display and also showing a simple application menu at the base of the screen.

Firstly, let's look at what is required to correctly display only one page when the application page loads:

```
div.view {
    display: none;
    padding: 0 6px;
}

div#main {
```

```
    display: block;
}
```

This simple CSS sets all `div` elements with the class view to be hidden by default. The second style declaration simply says that, if we have a `div` with an ID of `main`, that should override the view class and display the block.

```
<div id="main" class="view">
    <h1>To Do List</h1>
    <p>Application Main Page</p>
</div>
<div id="add" class="view">
    <h1>Create Task</h1>
    <p>Add Form Goes Here</p>
</div>
```

The preceding HTML fragment would generate a display with a title bar showing "To Do List" and the text "Application Main Page." On page load, there would be no visibility of either the "Create Task" header or the "Add Form Goes Here" text.

Additionally, let's just make a simple change to the existing `proui.css` stylesheet styles to display the h1.`fancy` style if an h1 tag is contained within a `div` of class view:

```
h1.fancy, div.view h1 {
    background: -webkit-gradient(linear, left top, left bottom, color-stop(0.0,
#666666), color-stop(0.5, #3A3A3A), color-stop(0.5, #222222), color-stop(1.0, #000000));
    -webkit-box-shadow: 0 2px 1px #AAAAAA;
    -webkit-border-bottom-left-radius: 6px;
    -webkit-border-bottom-right-radius: 6px;
    font-size: 1.1em;
    color: white;
    padding: 10px 8px;
    margin: 0 0 6px 0;
    text-align: center;
}
```

In the to-do list application, we will create a bottom menu bar that will contain the action links that are relevant for the current view. This will meet the requirements of both items 1 and 2, and is consistent with native applications on Android.

> **NOTE:** We will be using the same screen real estate and UI styling to meet both of the preceding requirements for Android. If you have experience with other mobile platforms, however, then you will know these user interactions are often done differently depending on the platform. In that case, the location of action and back buttons will vary.
>
> Choosing an appropriate formatting style that is going to suit the majority of devices is difficult, which is why using a third-party UI suite is highly recommended. Unfortunately, at this time, most UI frameworks are geared toward an iPhone look and feel, and building an Android web app that feels like an iPhone app isn't really what we are after here.

We will get started by having a look at some CSS styling to create such an action bar:

```css
ul#menu {
    position: fixed;
    bottom: 0px;
    margin: 0;
    padding: 5px;
    list-style-type: none;
    background: -webkit-gradient(linear, left top, left bottom, color-stop(0.0,
#666666), color-stop(0.5, #3A3A3A), color-stop(0.5, #222222), color-stop(1.0,
#000000));;
    width: 100%;
}

ul#menu li {
    margin: 0;
    float: left;
    padding: 4px 10px 0 0;
}

ul#menu li a {
    color: white;
    font-weight: bold;
}
```

This CSS, when applied with the following menu list (inserted into the HTML just before our previous view declarations), will generate a display as per the one in Figure 4–1.

```html
<ul id="menu">
    <li><a href="#add">Add</a></li>
</ul>
```

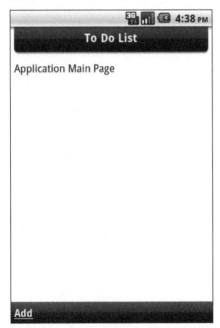

Figure 4–1. *Our application main view with an action menu bar*

While the preceding HTML fragment demonstrates how to construct the menu for display to the screen, it is not something that you would or should manually construct in HTML. Instead, we need an intelligent way to tell our application what the valid menu items for each screen are, and, additionally, what action should be taken for any given menu item.

Creating a View Manager

There are a variety of different approaches that could be used to prevent our having to write static HTML over and over again. For instance, we could use CSS classes as per the jQuery validation plug-in that was used in the previous chapter, and then build some JavaScript code to read the information out of the CSS classes and configure our application. In this particular case, however, we are going to write a ViewManager submodule for our prowebapps.js file that we will configure from our application JavaScript file.

The outline of the PROWEBAPPS.ViewManager module is shown here:

```
ViewManager: (function() {
    var views = {};
    var activeView = null;

    function switchView(oldView, newView) {
        // will switch views here
    } // switchView

    var subModule = {
        activate: function(viewId) {
            // save the old view
            var oldView = activeView;

            // if a view id has been specified, but doesn't exist in the views, check
for a div
            if (viewId && (! views[viewId]) && (jQuery("#" + viewId).get(0))) {
                subModule.define({
                    id: viewId
                });
            } // if

            // update the active view
            activeView = viewId ? views[viewId] : null;

            // update the associated ui elements
            switchView(oldView, activeView);
        },

        getActiveView: function() {
            return activeView ? jQuery("#" + activeView.id) : null;
        },

        define: function(args) {
            args = jQuery.extend({
                id: '',
                actions: []
```

```
        }, args);

            // if the id is specified, add the view to the list of defined views
            if (args.id) {
                views[args.id] = args;
            } // if
        }
    };

    return subModule;
})();
```

An application would then call PROWEBAPPS.ViewManager.define to define a new view with its associated actions (we'll see an example soon). The static function define allows us to register new views with the view manager, and activate sets the module variable activeView to match the specified view. We then make a call to switchView to update the UI elements based on the change in active view.

Expanding on the switchView stub, we implement the following private functions to implement changing the view:

```
function getViewActions(view) {
    var html = "";
    for (var ii = 0; view && (ii < view.actions.length); ii++) {
        html += "<li>" + view.actions[ii].getAnchor() + "</li>";
    } // for

    return html;
} // getViewActions

function getAction(view, actionId) {
    // extract the id portion from the action id
    actionId = actionId.replace(/^action_(\d+)$/i, "$1");

    // find the specified view in the active view and execute it
    for (var ii = 0; ii < view.actions.length; ii++) {
        if (view.actions[ii].id == actionId) {
            return view.actions[ii];
        } // if
    } // for

    return null;
} // getAction

function switchView(oldView, newView) {
    var ii, menu = jQuery("#menu").get(0);

    // switch the views using jQuery
    oldView ? jQuery("#" + oldView.id).hide() : null;
    newView ? jQuery("#" + newView.id).show().trigger("activated") : null;

    // if we have a menu, then update the actions
    if (menu) {
        // clear the menu and create list items and anchors as required
        jQuery(menu).html(getViewActions(activeView));

        // attach a click handler to each of the anchors now in the menu
```

```
        jQuery(menu).find("a").click(function(evt) {
            var action = getAction(activeView, this.id);
            if (action) {
                action.execute();
                evt.preventDefault();
            } // if
        });
    } // if
} // switchView
```

At this stage, the private `switchView` function has two purposes:

- To hide the current view if active, and show the new view. Also notice the call to the jQuery `trigger` method on the new element. We will be making use of that later in this chapter.

- To check for the presence of a #menu element. If it exists, populate it appropriately with links to the relevant actions for the active view. Once the menu has been built, the jQuery `click` function is used to handle finding and executing the action when a link is clicked.

Implementing View Actions

With the `ViewManager` functional, it is now just a matter of building some actions that the `ViewManager` can make use of. We can then integrate this new functionality into our to-do list app.

We will start with the `PROWEBAPPS.ViewAction` class:

```
ViewAction: function(args) {
    args = jQuery.extend({
        label: "",
        run: null
    }, args);

    var self = {
        id: actionCounter++,

        getAnchor: function() {
            return "<a href='#' id='action_" + self.id + "'>" + args.label + "</a>";
        },

        execute: function() {
            if (args.run) {
                args.run.apply(this, arguments);
            } // if
        }
    };

    return self;
}
```

This is a base class that knows how to display itself as an anchor tag, using the `getAnchor` method, and also has an `execute` method for executing the action. Additionally, note the reference to a variable called `actionCounter` that is being assigned to the id member of a new `ViewAction` object. This variable is defined within the scope of the PROWEBAPPS main module as such:

```
PROWEBAPPS = (function() {
    var actionCounter = 0;
    ...
})();
```

The variable will exist and maintain state for the life of the page/application, so we can use it as a counter for the actions and it will generate unique IDs for the anchors that are created. At no time, however, is the variable into global scope. This is one of the big attractions of using something like the module pattern in JavaScript code.

Let's now create a `PROWEBAPPS.ChangeViewAction` class that actually does something when it's executed:

```
ChangeViewAction: function(args) {
    // if the target is not defined, then raise an error
    if (! args.target) {
        throw new Error("Unable to create a ChangeViewAction without a target
specified.");
    } // if

    // prep the label to equal the target if not defined
    if (! args.label) {
        args.label = args.target;
    } // if

    return new module.ViewAction(jQuery.extend({
        run: function() {
            module.ViewManager.activate(args.target);
        }
    }, args));
}
```

At first glance the preceding code is a little confusing, but let's step through it and understand what is happening:

1. We first check to see that a target has been defined for the simple args object that has been passed to the class constructor; if not, an exception is raised.

2. If a label hasn't been defined in the constructor args, we assign the target value to the label to prevent displaying an empty anchor tag.

3. If all is well, we then create a new `PROWEBAPPS.ViewAction` and supply a run function handler. When the new `ViewAction` is subsequently executed, this function will be executed.

```
TODOLIST = (function() {
    // define the module
    var module = {
        ...
    };

    // define the main view
    PROWEBAPPS.ViewManager.define({
```

```
        id: "main",
        actions: [
            new PROWEBAPPS.ChangeViewAction({
                target: "add",
                label: "Add"
            })
        ]
    });

    return module;
})();
```

And *voila!* We are rewarded with a display that looks exactly like Figure 4–2. We guess this could be a little disheartening, but remember the following:

- It actually does something now.

- We are beginning to build up a pretty useful toolkit in the prowebapps.js file that will definitely make our lives easier—eventually.

Figure 4–2. *Clicking the Add link actually does something now.*

Note that we didn't define the "add" view, but the view still switched successfully. This is thanks to some code in the ViewManager.activate function that checks to see if a view actually does exist, regardless of whether it was explicitly defined or not.

Building the Application's Main Screen

Now that we have built some application code that will allow us to build more than just a simple application, we are ready to start building those separate screens. Let's start by building the main screen of our application.

For both the main screen and the to-do list task display, we'll begin by putting together a screen mockup (I'm a big fan of Inkscape [www.inkscape.org] for this kind of thing), and then building the display to match that layout. Figure 4–3 shows the mockup for the to-do list application home page.

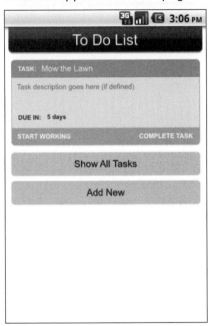

Figure 4–3. *To-do list application home page mockup*

The layout of the home screen is designed to be very simple. Rather than showing the complete lists of tasks, just the most important task is shown—in an attempt to stop us from getting distracted (trust me, I'm very distractable). Readers of the Lifehacker blog (http://lifehacker.com) may well be familiar with the technique.

The HTML for a static replacement for the main div is listed here:

```
<div id="main" class="view">
    <h1>To Do List</h1>
    <div class="task">
        <h3>Task: <span class="task-name">Mow the Lawn</span></h3>
        <p class="task-description">Task description goes here</p>
        <p class="task-due">
            <label>DUE IN:</label>
            <span class="task-daysleft">5 days</span>
        </p>
        <ul class="task-actions">
```

```
            <li class="right"><a href="#" class="task-complete">COMPLETE TASK</a></li>
            <li><a href="#" class="task-start">START WORKING</a></li>
        </ul>
    </div>
    <ul class="buttons">
        <li><a class="changeview" href="#alltasks">Show All Tasks</a></li>
        <li><a class="changeview" href="#add">Add New</a></li>
    </ul>
</div>
```

Notice here that we have a number of HTML elements that will end up displaying the actual task details once the application logic is written. For now, placeholder values are included.

Without any CSS to style this HTML (see Figure 4–4), the view looks pretty ordinary, so we add the following styles to the todolist.css file for the formatting of the task box, name, description, and so on:

```
div.task {
    margin: 8px 4px;
}

div.task h3 {
    border: 1px solid #ff6600;
    background: #ff7f2a;
    color: white;
    -webkit-border-top-left-radius: 5px;
    -webkit-border-top-right-radius: 5px;
    margin: 0;
    padding: 8px;
    font-size: 0.8em;
}

div.task p {
    margin: 0;
    background: #e6e6e6;
    border-left: 1px solid #b3b3b3;
    border-right: 1px solid #b3b3b3;
    padding: 8px;
}

p.task-due label {
    font-weight: bold;
    width: 70px;
    float: left;
}
```

Figure 4–4. *The main screen of our app is showing a distinct lack of style.*

Add the following for formatting the task actions that are displayed beneath the task details:

```
ul.task-actions {
    background: #b3b3b3;
    border: 1px solid #b3b3b3;
    color: white;
    padding: 8px;
    -webkit-border-bottom-left-radius: 5px;
    -webkit-border-bottom-right-radius: 5px;
    margin: 0;
    list-style-type: none;
}

ul.task-actions li a {
    color: white;
    text-decoration: none;
    font-weight: bold;
    font-size: 0.8em;
}

ul.task-actions li.right {
    padding: 4px 0 0 0;
}
```

Finally, we add a definition for elements matching the right class to float right:

```
.right {
    float: right;
}
```

While the task details area of the screen now looks like the mockup, there is still some work to do to show buttons instead of links—as shown in Figure 4–5. This is achieved by adding the following CSS to the `proui.css` file:

```
ul.buttons {
    margin: 4px 0 0 0;
    padding: 0;
    list-style-type: none;
}

ul.buttons li {
    margin: 4px 4px 10px 4px;
}

ul.buttons li a {
    display: block;
    background: -webkit-gradient(linear, left top, left bottom, color-stop(0.0,
#b3b3b3), color-stop(0.4, #666666), color-stop(1.0, #333333));
    color: white;
    text-decoration: none;
    padding: 8px;
    text-align: center;
    -webkit-box-shadow: 0 2px 2px #333333;
    -webkit-border-radius: 6px;
}
```

Figure 4–5. *Task elements styled*

With all the styles applied, this generates a static HTML screen, as shown in Figure 4–6. It's definitely starting to look the part.

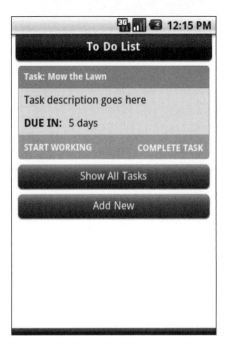

Figure 4–6. *The static HTML equivalent to our home screen mockup*

Tweaking ViewManager Functionality

Now that the display is ready, we can continue and update the application logic to make the home screen behave the way it should.

Let's start by getting rid of the Add link displayed in the global menu, which is displayed here because we have a view definition for the main view from our previous examples. The functionality is still useful, but not required on the Show All Tasks screen, so we'll modify the view definition by simply replacing main with alltasks for the view ID.

```
// define the all tasks view
PROWEBAPPS.ViewManager.define({
    id: "alltasks",
    actions: [
        new PROWEBAPPS.ChangeViewAction({
            target: "add",
            label: "Add"
        })
    ]
});
```

We'll also add some additional code to prowebapps.js to have the ViewManager submodule automatically add switching view handling to this and future button lists:

```
ViewManager: (function() {
    ...

    jQuery(document).ready(function() {
```

```
        jQuery("a.changeview").each(function() {
            jQuery(this).click(function(evt) {
                subModule.activate(this.href.replace(/^.*\#(.*)$/, "$1"));
                evt.preventDefault();
            }); // click
        });
    });

    return subModule;
})()
```

If you are not familiar with the jQuery each method, it calls the supplied callback for each element that matches the specified selector. At this stage, the callback will be fired twice (once for each of the buttons in the list), and a click event will be attached to the matching anchor. The handler for the click event calls the ViewManager.activate method to change to that view. We additionally call preventDefault on the event object to prevent the browser from attempting to navigate to the referenced named anchor. This stops the screen from scrolling back up to the top, which would reveal the URL bar (which is not what we want).

Home Screen Storage Requirements

From here we will write the code required to read the actual task data back out of the local database we created in the previous chapter. This is going to involve adding some additional methods to our storage wrapper. Once we have created the required methods for reading task data, we will add a method that will enable us to mark a task as complete.

> **NOTE:** Given some of the data typing we experienced in the previous chapter, we are going to have to implement things a little differently here. Normally, we would ask the SQL database to sort the tasks by their due date for us, but, as we are actually dealing with strings, that isn't going to be possible. There are ways you can use SQLite to do this, but it is quite complicated.

First, add a getTasks private function to the TODOLIST.Storage module:

```
function getTasks(callback, extraClauses) {
    db.transaction(function(transaction) {
        transaction.executeSql(
            "SELECT rowid as id, * FROM task " + (extraClauses ? extraClauses : ""),
            [],
            function (transaction, results) {
                // initialize an array to hold the tasks
                var tasks = [];

                // read each of the rows from the db, and create tasks
                for (var ii = 0; ii < results.rows.length; ii++) {
                    tasks.push(new module.Task(results.rows.item(ii)));
                } // for

                callback(tasks);
```

```
            }
        );
    });
} // getTasks
```

This function requests all the data stored in the `task` table of the database and populates an array with `Task` objects. This array is then passed through in the `getTasks` function call. The method is also written so that it accepts an optional parameter, `extraClauses`, which allows the function to add extra SQL clauses to the `SELECT` statement. This could include `WHERE` statements (as per the code following) or additionally `ORDER BY` statements that would then help to sort the tasks in a particular order.

> **CAUTION:** The reference here to `results.rows.item(index)` is not consistent with the current draft of the Web SQL database specification. It is, however, the behavior that is implemented in most browsers presently. While we would have expected that browsers would change to match the specification, the move by the W3C to deprecate the specification will probably mean that the functionality will remain as is.

Let's add some methods to the `Storage` module that will allow those using the module to access the saved tasks:

```
Storage: (function() {
    ...

    var subModule = {
        getIncompleteTasks: function(callback) {
            getTasks(callback, "WHERE completed IS NULL");
        },

        getTasksInPriorityOrder: function(callback) {
            subModule.getIncompleteTasks(function(tasks) {
                callback(tasks.sort(function(taskA, taskB) {
                    return taskA.due - taskB.due;
                }));
            });
        },

        getMostImportantTask: function(callback) {
            subModule.getTasksInPriorityOrder(function(tasks) {
                callback(tasks.length > 0 ? tasks[0] : null);
            });
        },

        ...
    };

    return subModule;
})()
```

Here we have added three methods:

- getIncompleteTasks: Used to return tasks that have not been marked as complete. Notice that we make use of the extraClauses parameter of the getTasks function to restrict the result set.

- getTasksInPriorityOrder: Used to return incomplete tasks in due date order. Note the use of the JavaScript Array.sort method here to sort the results. While we would normally implement this using an ORDER BY statement in our SQL call, some of the datetime mismatches make it simpler (but probably less efficient) to implement in JavaScript.

- getMostImportantTask: Used to return the first of our tasks from the getTasksInPriorityOrder method.

We now need to modify the saveTask method to allow us to update existing tasks, in addition to creating new tasks.

Additionally, the saveTask method is modified to support both creating new tasks and updating existing tasks:

```
saveTask: function(task, callback) {
    db.transaction(function(transaction) {
        // if the task id is not assigned, then insert
        if (! task.id) {
            transaction.executeSql(
                "INSERT INTO task(name, description, due) VALUES (?, ?, ?);",
                [task.name, task.description, task.due],
                function(tx) {
                    transaction.executeSql(
                        "SELECT MAX(rowid) AS id from task",
                        [],
                        function (tx, results) {
                            task.id = results.rows.item(0).id;
                            if (callback) {
                                callback();
                            } // if
                        }
                    );
                }
            );
        }
        // otherwise, update
        else {
            transaction.executeSql(
                "UPDATE task " +
                "SET name = ?, description = ?, due = ?, completed = ? " +
                "WHERE rowid = ?;",
                [task.name, task.description, task.due, task.completed, task.id],
                function (tx) {
                    if (callback) {
                        callback();
                    } // if
                }
            );
        } // if..else
    });
}
```

NOTE: If you haven't been working with JavaScript callbacks for long, it will take a little while to get used to the asynchronous behavior here. In very simple terms, we need to move away from linear thinking. Instead of thinking, "A occurs, then B occurs, and then C occurs," we should think, "A occurs, we initiate B, C occurs, B's ready, so it completes." It definitely takes some getting used to.

We are almost at the point where we can actually replace some of those placeholder values on the main screen with real data. Before we do that, though, let's quickly tweak our Task class to include a getDaysDue method to report the number of days until the task is due. We'll also add a complete method that will allow us to mark the task as complete:

```
Task: function(params) {
    params = jQuery.extend({
        id: null,
        name: "",
        description: "",
        due: null
    }, params);

    // initialize self
    var self = {
        id: params.id,
        name: params.name,
        description: params.description,
        due: params.due ? new Date(params.due) : null,
        completed: null,

        complete: function() {
            self.completed = new Date();
        },

        getDaysDue: function() {
            return Math.floor((self.due - new Date()) / MILLISECONDS_TO_DAYS);
        }
    };

    return self;
}
```

The MILLISECONDS_TO_DAYS constant is defined privately in the TODOLIST module:

```
TODOLIST = (function() {
    var MILLISECONDS_TO_DAYS = 86400000;

    ...
});
```

Wiring Up the Home Screen

With the required methods added to the TODOLIST.Storage module, and a UI to display our task information, we are now ready to start bringing those pieces together. Thankfully, this is made simple given jQuery's event system and the trigger call we implemented earlier. Essentially, we need to bind to listen for the activated event, and then do something in response to that event occurring. We will implement the bind handler and code that is called as a result in three places. First, we modify the document.ready event listener to attach event handlers to various views (just the main view at this stage) and then activate the main view on load of the application:

```
$(document).ready(function() {
    ...

    // bind activation handlers
    $("#main").bind("activated", TODOLIST.activateMain);

    // initialize the main view
    PROWEBAPPS.ViewManager.activate("main");
});
```

Next, we implement the TODOLIST.activateMain module function that is invoked when the activated event is received for the #main element:

```
activateMain: function() {
    TODOLIST.Storage.getMostImportantTask(function(task) {
        if (task) {
            // the no tasks message may be displayed, so remove it
            jQuery("#main .notasks").remove();

            // update the task details
            showTaskDetails("#main .task", task);

            // attach a click handler to the complete task button
            jQuery("#main .task-complete").unbind().click(function() {
                jQuery("#main .task").slideUp();

                // mark the task as complete
                task.complete();

                // save the task back to storage
                TODOLIST.Storage.saveTask(task, module.activateMain);
            });
        }
        else {
            jQuery("#main .notasks").remove();
            jQuery("#main .task").slideUp().after("<p class='notasks'>You have no tasks
to complete</p>");
        }
    });
}
```

You can see in the preceding code that we make the call to our TODOLIST.Storage.getMostImportantTask function and pass through a callback to receive the most important task that has been found in the database. Based on whether a task was found or not (the database could be empty), we then either update the contents of the main task or hide the contents and let the user know there are no tasks to complete.

The code also attaches an event handler to the Complete Task link (note the jQuery unbind to prevent multiple event calls) to handle completing the task. Thanks to the work we have put into the Storage module, wiring up the completion handler takes minimal code.

Both in this code sample and the one following, a couple of CSS classes are used. You can decide how you want them to look and add something to the application stylesheet (todolist.css) according to your tastes.

Finally, we create a private function, showTaskDetails, to do the work of updating an HTML div designed for displaying task details with the actual values:

```
function showTaskDetails(selector, task) {
    var container = jQuery(selector),
        daysDue = task.getDaysDue();

    // update the relevant task details
    container.find(".task-name").html(task.name);
    container.find(".task-description").html(task.description);

    if (daysDue < 0) {
        container.find(".task-daysleft")
            .html("OVERDUE BY " + Math.abs(daysDue) + " DAYS").addClass("overdue");
    }
    else {
        container.find(".task-daysleft")
            .html(daysDue + " days").removeClass("overdue");
    } // if..else
} // showTaskDetails
```

This yields the various displays, as shown in Figure 4–7 (depending on your data).

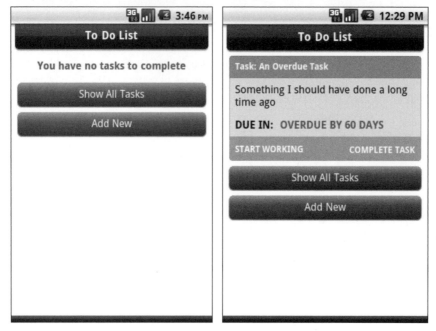

Figure 4–7. *The main screen display based on data that is available*

Congratulations, the main page of the application is now complete. This, combined with the task-adding functionality that we explored in previous chapters, allows us to create tasks and keep track of important ones. We will need to build the show-all-tasks screen as well so that we can access the other tasks.

Before we do that, though, it's time we take a little break and have you cut some code (see Exercise 4–1).

EXERCISE 4–1: INTEGRATING THE ADD FORM AS AN EXTRA SCREEN

You now have the required pieces to take the code we created in the last chapter in the `create-task-form.html` file and integrate it into the `todolist.html` file. Additionally, with only a small amount of JavaScript, you should be able to return the user to the application main screen once they have successfully created a new task.

There are a few things we haven't created yet (such as having a back action automatically added), but we will be completing that in the next section, and this will automatically be made available in your Add view.

Building the All Tasks Screen

Once again, we will start with a mockup of the screen (displayed in Figure 4–8). The screen, as you might expect, shows a list of all the outstanding tasks, with the due date.

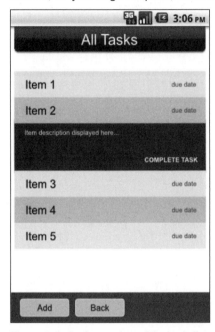

Figure 4–8. *Design mockup of the to-do list main screen*

Based on what's displayed in the preceding mockup, we are pretty much covered in terms of our Storage methods, as we can both get tasks in priority order and complete tasks. This, then, is simply going to be a UI and wiring exercise.

It would be great if the back button were automatically displayed for any screen that isn't the main screen of the application. It will be worth adding some additional code to the PROWEBAPPS.ViewManager module to provide us with that functionality.

It's time to implement the UI. This will involve the following:

1. Implementing the basic HTML layout in the todolist.html file.

2. On activation of this screen, reading the current items from the database and generating a list of those items.

3. Handling a user tapping on an individual item. This will show the details (and the complete task link) for that item, hiding the previously selected item. Some nice jQuery transitions (slideUp, slideDown) will look good here.

4. Finally, handling a user marking a task as complete. This will be an exercise for you.

First is the HTML layout. There isn't much required here as most of the display for this screen will be dynamically generated using JavaScript:

```
<div id="alltasks" class="view">
    <h1 class="fancy">All Tasks</h1>
    <ul id="tasklist">
    </ul>
</div>
```

From here we move on to reading the current items from the database and populating the display. This involves some application code to handle activation of the #alltasks div. We create the handler method in the TODOLIST module (we put it right after the activateMain function added before):

```
activateAllTasks: function() {
    TODOLIST.Storage.getTasksInPriorityOrder(function(tasks) {
        // update the current tasks
        currentTasks = tasks;

        populateTaskList();

        // refresh the task list display
        jQuery("ul#tasklist li").click(function() {
            toggleDetailsDisplay(this);
        });

        jQuery("ul#tasklist a.task-complete").click(function() {
            // complete the task
            alert("complete the task");
        });
    });
}
```

You can see that this code updates a variable called currentTasks, and then calls a function called populateTaskList, and finally attaches event handling to the newly created list items (assuming there are tasks). If a list item is clicked, the toggleDetailsDisplay function is called to display the description and complete button for that task.

The currentTasks variable should be created in the TODOLIST module scope so that any code that would like to access this variable can do so:

```
TODOLIST = (function() {
    ...

    // define an array that will hold the current tasks
    var currentTasks = [];

    // define the module
    var module = {
        ...
    };

    return module;
})();
```

We then create our populateTaskList function as a private function in the TODOLIST module scope:

```
function populateTaskList() {
    function pad(n) {
        return n<10 ? '0'+n : n;
    }

    var listHtml = "",
        monthNames = ["JAN", "FEB", "MAR", "APR", "MAY", "JUN", "JUL", "AUG", "SEP",
"OCT", "NOV", "DEC"];

    // iterate through the current tasks
    for (var ii = 0; ii < currentTasks.length; ii++) {
        var dueDateHtml =
            "<ul class='calendar right'>" +
                "<li class='day'>" + pad(currentTasks[ii].due.getDate()) + "</li>" +
                "<li class='month'>" + monthNames[currentTasks[ii].due.getMonth()] +
"</li>" +
                "<li class='year'>" + currentTasks[ii].due.getFullYear() + "</li>" +
                "</ul>";

        // add the list item for the task
        listHtml += "<li id='task_" + currentTasks[ii].id + "'>" + dueDateHtml +
            "<div class='task-header'>" + currentTasks[ii].name + "</div>" +
            "<div class='task-details'>" +
                currentTasks[ii].description + "<br />" +
                "<a href='#' class='task-complete right'>COMPLETE TASK</a> " +
            "</div>" +
            "</li>";
    } // for

    jQuery("ul#tasklist").html(listHtml);
} // populateTaskList
```

The preceding code populates the ul#tasklist with the HTML required to display both the task name, due date, description, and complete task link. Let's take a peek at how that looks. With a couple of tasks in the database, it renders a display like the one shown in Figure 4–9.

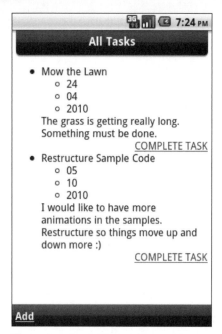

Figure 4–9. *The All Tasks display with no style applied. What did we do before CSS?*

It's pretty obvious that the screen needs to have some style applied, and it's probably appropriate that we do that now before implementing any more JavaScript (otherwise we won't be able to tell when something is selected). The following CSS will give us a result similar to the mockup:

```
ul#tasklist {
    margin: 0;
    padding: 0;
    list-style-type: none;
}

ul#tasklist > li {
    padding: 0;
    margin: 0;
    clear: both;
    background: #ececec;
}

ul#tasklist > li:nth-child(2n) {
    background: #cccccc;
}

ul#tasklist .task-header {
    padding: 19px 0px 17px 10px;
}

ul#tasklist .task-details {
    clear: both;
    background: #333333;
```

```
        color: white;
        padding: 8px;
        display: none;
}

ul#tasklist .task-details a {
        color: white;
        text-decoration: none;
        font: bold 0.8em Arial;
}
```

While most of this is common CSS, note the bold CSS3 selector for the list items within #tasklist. This selector matches every second list item in the task list, and thus an alternative background color is applied. There are quite a few additional CSS selectors available in the CSS3 selectors specification (www.w3.org/TR/css3-selectors/#selectors), so it's well worth keeping an eye on what's going on in that space. While we won't go through them in detail here, we would definitely encourage you to visit the link at the W3C site and experiment with them in your own applications.

We also apply some extra styles to make our date look like a nice little calendar:

```
ul.calendar {
        -webkit-border-radius: 4px;
        -webkit-box-shadow: 0 0 2px #333333;
        background: -webkit-gradient(linear, left top, left bottom, color-stop(0.0,
#F8F8F8), color-stop(1.0, #AAAAAA));
        margin: 6px 6px 6px 0;
        padding: 0 6px;
        list-style-type: none;
}

ul.calendar li {
        margin: 0;
        padding: 0;
        text-align: center;
        font-weight: bold;
        font-size: 0.7em;
}

ul.calendar li.day {
        font-size: 0.85em;
        padding: 1px 0 0 0;
}
```

With the stylesheet applied, our screen should look something like the one in Figure 4–10.

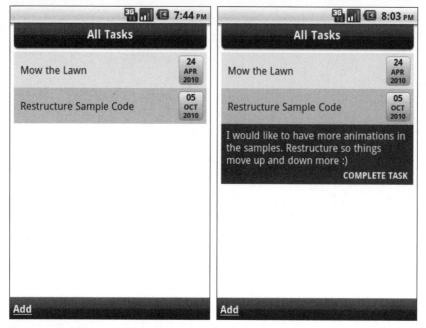

Figure 4–10. *With some CSS applied, it's starting to look the part.*

So we are almost there. We just need to go back and add the required JavaScript to toggle the display of the task description and complete the task link:

```
function toggleDetailsDisplay(listItem) {
    // slide up any active task details panes
    jQuery(".task-details").slideUp();

    // if the current item is selected, implement a toggle
    if (activeItem == listItem) {
        activeItem = null;
        return;
    }

    // in the current list item, toggle the display of the details pane
    jQuery(listItem).find(".task-details").slideDown();

    // update the active item
    activeItem = listItem;
} // toggleDetailsDisplay
```

EXERCISE 4–2: FINISHING OFF THE ALL TASKS SCREEN

We're going to go on ahead and implement those extensions to the PROWEBAPPS.ViewManager module to support automatically adding a Back link for screens other than the application main screen. If you wouldn't mind finishing off the All Tasks screen, that would be fantastic.

From here, all that really needs to be done is to implement the complete-task functionality—but that should be pretty simple given we did it on the main screen. You could also add some additional CSS to show that a task is overdue (as per the mockup).

Implementing the View Stack

If you haven't noticed already, it's pretty frustrating that, when we hit a particular screen in our application, the only way to get back to the previous screen is to refresh the page. This isn't going to cut it, so it's time to do something about it.

The first thing that is required will be to implement some kind of view or screen stack. We need a mechanism that will allow us to keep track of which screens have preceded this one. The best place to implement this functionality will be in the switchView private function in the PROWEBAPPS.ViewManager module. Let's modify that function now:

```
function switchView(oldView, newView) {
    var ii, menu = jQuery("#menu").get(0);

    // if the old view is assigned, then push it onto the stack
    updateViewStack(oldView, newView);


    ...
} // switchView
```

As you can see, we have added a call to a new function called updateViewStack passing through the old and the new view. The implementation of updateViewStack is quite simple, and is used to determine whether our movement from the oldView to the newView should change the state of the stack.

```
function updateViewStack(oldView, newView) {
    // first let's determine if we should push onto the stack
    var shouldPush = oldView && (
        (viewStack.length === 0) ||
        (newView && (viewStack[viewStack.length - 1].id != newView.id))
    );

    // if we should push onto the stack, then do so, otherwise pop
    if (shouldPush) {
        viewStack.push(oldView);

        // if the back action does not exist yet, then create it
        if (! backAction) {
            backAction = new module.ViewAction({
                label: "Back",
                run: function() {
```

```
                        subModule.activate(viewStack[viewStack.length - 1].id);
                }
            });
        } // if
    }
    else if (oldView && newView && (viewStack.length > 0)) {
        viewStack.pop();
    } // if..else
} // updateViewStack
```

In the preceding code, the shouldPush variable is initialized based on the presence of having being passed an oldView, and the view stack being either empty or having the last item in the stack being something other than the newView we are transitioning to. If we are transitioning back to the view that is the most recent view that was pushed to the stack, then it will be popped off as a result.

With the view stack in place, the back action can be used to take the user back to screens that they were on previously without needing to be told in each and every case what that screen was. This in turn is going to save a lot of effort coding in the long term.

NOTE: The backAction ViewAction is initialized in the preceding function as opposed to variable definitions of the module (which you can see towards the top of the module definition). This is not because I am a massive *lazy-loading* fan (not creating variables until they are needed), but, rather, it is because of the way I have implemented the module pattern.

In JavaScript, a variable cannot be referenced until the definition of that variable is complete— which is fair enough. If we try to reference the ViewAction class of the PROWEBAPPS module (using module.ViewAction), it fails. If we create it later, once the definition is complete, everything's fine.

If you encounter this situation, it may be worth considering refactoring your code to define modules/classes that are required in a module definition as a separate, private module/class and then including it in the exported module by using a simple assignment.

To make use of our newly created stack, we are going to need to modify the getViewActions and getAction private functions in the ViewManager module. Here is a section of the ViewManager module that highlights the required changes:

```
ViewManager: (function() {
    var views = {},
        activeView = null,
        viewStack = [],
        backAction = null;

    function getViewActions(view) {
        var html = "";
        for (var ii = 0; view && (ii < view.actions.length); ii++) {
            html += "<li>" + view.actions[ii].getAnchor() + "</li>";
        } // for
```

```
        // if the view stack is active, then add a back action
        if (viewStack.length > 0) {
            html += "<li>" + backAction.getAnchor() + "</li>";
        } // if

        return html;
    } // getViewActions

    function getAction(view, actionId) {
        // extract the id portion from the action id
        actionId = actionId.replace(/^action_(\d+)$/i, "$1");

        if (backAction && (backAction.id == actionId)) {
            return backAction;
        } // if

        // find the specified view in the active view and execute it
        for (var ii = 0; ii < view.actions.length; ii++) {
            if (view.actions[ii].id == actionId) {
                return view.actions[ii];
            } // if
        } // for

        return null;
    } // getAction

    ...
})()
```

You can see that two additional variables have been added for the viewStack and the backAction. Additionally, the getViewActions and getAction functions are modified to properly handle the back action behavior. In the case of getViewActions, the function checks whether the viewStack contains any items, and, if it does, includes the backAction in the actions that will be displayed for the current view. The changes to the getAction method provide the function with a mechanism for providing the backAction handler even though it hasn't been explicitly defined.

One final piece of the puzzle remains. We require a method in the PROWEBAPPS.ViewManager module that will allow us to initiate going back manually:

```
ViewManager: (function() {
    ...

    var subModule = {
        ...

        back: function() {
            if (backAction) {
                backAction.execute();
            } // if
        },

        ...
    };

    return subModule;
})()
```

This method will be called in instances where you have completed a screen and need to return the user to the previous screen. For instance, we need to change the function call `PROWEBAPPS.ViewManager.activate("main")` to `PROWEBAPPS.ViewManager.back()` in our submit handler for the task entry form to make sure the application flows correctly.

And with that, we are done. More can be done to the application itself to polish it up, but there are good bones to work with here. There are a number of possible extensions that could be made to the application to enhance it from this point, so please feel free to try anything that interests you.

Summary

In this chapter, we explored one way of implementing a view manager useful for building a multipage web app that operates correctly on an Android device. This included looking at different ways of navigating through an application and implementing some intelligence to create appropriate navigation controls.

We also finished having a look at the Web SQL Database API by implementing the code required to retrieve items from our database and display them in the app.

By now, you should be relatively comfortable with the JavaScript module pattern, and be able to implement it in your own applications if you choose to.

In the next chapter, we will go through how we can synchronize the data in our To Do List with an online data store. This will enable us to create other clients (such as a desktop web application) that can view the data we are collecting in our mobile app.

Chapter 5

Synchronizing with the Cloud

In this chapter, we will explore using a variety of hosted (or cloud) services that are available to us for synchronizing our tasks from our to-do list with online storage. Although offline storage is a very handy and powerful feature, we cannot deny the fact we are in a connected world. Data should be shared and made available online. To achieve this, all the data we are collecting locally has to be synchronized with an online solution.

What you will learn in this chapter is how to use leading-edge technologies, such as NoSQL cloud-hosted solutions, which are storage systems that don't rely on the classic relational form, and instead provide a new way to deal with storing data. We currently have a lot of solutions that encapsulate the complexity of these new technologies for you and let you focus on the core development of your application.

But that's not all—using an online storage framework provides a way of hosting your mobile web application in the cloud, making your application available for the entire world. While native applications live inside a device, mobile web applications need to be *hosted*. That is, their pages are served from a remote location—a server that communicates with the mobile native browser. While you could host your applications on one of the many classic web-hosting providers that are available, in this chapter we look at a powerful and affordable alternative cloud-hosting solution. This solution will permit you to host both your storage mechanism and the application itself.

Exploring Online Storage Options

At present, the options for synchronizing locally stored data with centralized storage in the cloud are somewhat limited. This situation is slowly changing, though, and in the future we may well be spoiled for choice. For the purposes of this chapter, however, our primary need is something that works well from the client side, and in particular with JavaScript; for that reason, JSON (JavaScript Object Notation) will be the format we'll use to both transmit and store the data. JSON is also useful because it's the most common data interchange format (besides XML) in web-based architectures in which the client side relies heavily on JavaScript. Let's take a look at the requirements for a suitable online data synchronization store that will ensure that our offline data will be mirrored on the Web (and thus accessible to other people).

Online Synchronization Store Requirements

What exactly are we looking for in an online storage solution? A solution that would serve us well for a general synchronization solution will require the following features:

- Avoiding a complex and somewhat old-school three-tier architecture (front end, back end, and database)

- Some flavor of user authentication

- A supporting JavaScript library that makes synchronizing data stored on the device a snap

Additionally, given that we want to focus on giving users of our application the best experience possible, our online storage solution shouldn't take another whole person/team to create or maintain. It should be both simple and scalable.

Bearing the requirement of simplicity in mind, we will explore the features just outlined in a little more depth.

Avoiding a Three-Tier Architecture

Classic web applications are based on three-tier architecture, made up of:

- A front-end layer, containing the HTML pages, styles, and other assets

- A back-end layer, hosted by an application server (such as Tomcat or JBoss for enterprise Java solutions, or IIS for .NET applications)

- A database provider, such as MySQL, Oracle, or Microsoft SQL Server

This kind of architecture requires mastering at least three different kinds of development skills: front-end, server-side, and database skills. This is far beyond the scope of this book, as we want to put the focus on building web applications—especially on the front-end aspects. Furthermore, modern frameworks allow us to abstract much of this formerly problematic business logic and storage.

User Authentication

Our mobile application as we have built it now works very well for a user running it from a single device. Having all the information contained within storage on a single device, however, is not a great solution. If instead that information is going to be stored on the

Internet somewhere, we need some identity information attached to it so we can retrieve it from a second or third device.

Because we are building a web-based application, not a native application, we are not able to use the unique IMEI (International Mobile Equipment Identity) number of the device, or any other low-level information. This is because mobile web browsers have no access to this information. Fortunately, there are many options available on the web side to manage your identity. That identity could be many things—an OpenID (see http://openid.net), a Google account, or a Twitter account, to name but a few. It should, however, not be a new account that people have to create for this particular application and then again for another application, as this does not constitute a reusable (and thus efficient) solution.

A JavaScript Synchronization Library

Ideally, we are looking for a solution that can take our locally stored data and do some convention-based synchronization processing to push our data in the cloud. Once this data is online, we would then be able to use it from a desktop application, or maybe a tablet running either Android or Chrome.

At this stage, offerings in this space are especially hard to find, as cross-platform web apps are pretty new on most people's radars. Another option is to write your own synchronization library. This shouldn't be too difficult, as our needs are quite simple, and you have already seen in the previous chapter how to communicate with an offline database.

Possible Synchronization Solutions

One solution that does a good job of covering our needs is jsonengine (see http://code.google.com/p/jsonengine). The following are some of its most valuable features:

- It runs on Google App Engine (a cloud-based solution).

- It requires no back-end scripting.

- It provides identity management using the Google account mechanism and OpenID.

- Besides being a data storage solution, it's also possible to host and serve the application code from within jsonengine itself.

As the name suggests, jsonengine uses the JSON format to store its data. This is useful, since our application is heavily based on JavaScript, and it's easy to manipulate JSON objects using the JSON2 library.

Additionally, jsonengine provides a robust mechanism for inserting data via a REST (http://en.wikipedia.org/wiki/Representational_State_Transfer) API. The API endpoints provide the ability to read, insert, update, and delete data using standard HTTP methods (GET, POST, PUT and DELETE respectively).

Getting Started with Google App Engine

A jsonengine instance is best hosted on Google App Engine (http://appengine.google.com/), which deserves a short introduction. Google App Engine is Google's cloud-computing technology. It virtualizes web applications across multiple servers and data centers. In simple terms, that means that your application is not running in one single physical place (like a data center in Silicon Valley), but is replicated all around the world using Google's impressive data center coverage.

Google App Engine is a Platform-as-a-Service (PaaS) solution, and differs from the other cloud-computing services (such as Amazon Web Services). The main difference is that Google App Engine provides a complete set of services and tools based on conventions rather than configuration, which allows applications to be deployed very quickly. Another advantage of Google App Engine is its pricing model—it's free up to a certain level of used resources.

> **NOTE:** PaaS is like any other type of hosting service, except that, instead of providing you with a blank, "wildcard" server, it offers a predefined set of services and hardware solutions. It encapsulates a lot of complexity and configuration tweaks for you. The catch is that you'll have less freedom, and you'll have to follow the solution provider's guidelines.

So, before you can use jsonengine, you have to set up Google App Engine. The first thing you have to do is download the Google App Engine framework, so you can test and deploy your application locally before putting it into the cloud. Google App Engine proposes two different kinds of framework:

- A Python-based SDK
- A Java-based SDK

As jsonengine is based on Java, we are going to use the Java-based version. Don't worry if you don't have any knowledge about Java—it won't be necessary. We simply need to deploy jsonengine, so you won't have to do anything to configure or implement it.

Let's start by installing Google App Engine. First, download the binaries, which you can find here:

http://code.google.com/appengine/downloads.html

Then follow the installation instructions here:

http://code.google.com/appengine/docs/java/gettingstarted/installing.html

An additional useful guide for installing the App Engine SDK can be found on the jsonengine site:

http://code.google.com/p/jsonengine/wiki/HowToInstall

Deploying jsonengine Locally

Deploying a jsonengine instance is very easy: just download the provided WAR archive and deploy it using the following Google App Engine command:

```
dev_appserver location/to/you/war/folder
```

This will start the Google App Engine server locally, open your favorite browser, and go to `http://localhost:8080/samples/bbs.html`. You should now be able to see the jsonengine's sample application.

That's all! Now that you have an up-and-running, ultra-scalable online storage solution, we can go back to our to-do application to start implementing the synchronization process.

Since jsonengine is a web application, not just a storage solution, it can serve web content, making it ideal for the mobile web application we're building. All the code we've implemented (HTML, JavaScript, and CSS) can be hosted inside jsonengine's instance.

Take a look at the jsonengine's distribution. It has a `war` folder containing a classic web application structure (CSS, JS, etc.). If you have all your resources inside the right folders, with a single command from the App Engine SDK, you can actually deploy your application—which is pretty neat. When you deploy your application, the `war` folder is packaged in a WAR archive. (A WAR archive is simply the enterprise version of a JAR (Java archive format); it functions just like a ZIP file.)

Let's perform a quick test to ensure that jsonengine does indeed serve web assets in addition to JSON data. Take the sample code from Chapter 4 and paste it in your `war` folder. This should result in the following folder structure:

```
JSONEngine—
|- war—
   |- css—
      |- proui.css
   |- js
      |- jquery-1.4.2.min.js
      |- jquery.validate.js
      |- json2.js
      |- prowebapps.js
   |- snippets—
      |- 04—
         |- todolist.html
         |- todolist.css
         |- todolist.js
```

Browse to `http://localhost:8080/snippets/04/todolist.html`, and you will see your application running.

Since we're building a mobile web application, you should also try it on the Android emulator. As discussed in Chapter 1, the Android emulator is unable to communicate with a webserver on your machine via the *localhost* address. As such, we will need to instruct the AppEngine development server to bind to other network addresses on our machine (by default, the Google App Engine local server binds to the localhost address).

Fortunately, though, the dev_appserver command comes with an option parameter to make the server listen on all the IPs (0.0.0.0) of your local machine.

Stop your server and restart it by adding the following parameter -a 0.0.0.0 right after your command and before the path to your war folder. Once you have done this, you will be able to access the application from the emulator or mobile device by using the IP of your local machine.

> **NOTE:** If you have Mongoose running in the background, the AppEngine development server will not be able to bind to the alternative address. In this case, simply close down the Mongoose server and then start the AppEngine dev server again.

At the end of this chapter, you'll see how to deploy the application on the cloud; it's not very complicated and it can be done in one single command. The deployed online application will have the exact same behavior as on your local server—there is nothing to configure and it's definitively a huge time-saver.

Choosing a Suitable Synchronization Mode

Ideally, data synchronization is bidirectional, which means that, for example, system A creates/updates records that will be reflected on system B, which can also update/create data. However, that brings a lot of data integrity issues. For example, what if system A is updating a record that system B is deleting? With a legacy storage system like Oracle or MySQL, you can use locks, rollbacks, and other similar features to deal with these kinds of issues. But now we are using a quite different and innovative approach, and to keep things on a reasonable easy level we will choose a simple but still powerful synchronization mode.

We will use a one-way synchronization, in which the offline database will be the master and the online storage will be the slave. That means that each new record will always be stored initially in the offline database, and will be synchronized with the online storage only after the user decides to do so. Inserting new records directly into jsonengine will be impossible.

To illustrate this, let's imagine the following use case: our to-do web application has become popular and is being used by a famous scientist who's collecting data in the middle of the jungle. All day long, the data is stored offline, but, when the scientist returns to his headquarters at the end of the day, he wants to share his collected information with the other scientists working in the main office in Amsterdam. His colleagues have read-only permissions, but there are also batch processes that will output very interesting statistics for all scientists around the world.

Sending Your Offline Data to jsonengine

As jsonengine expects input in JSON format, we have to convert our offline SQL data to JSON format. The global flow is quite simple:

1. Select all the offline records.

2. Parse them to JSON format.

3. Send them to jsonengine.

Selecting all the database records is something we have already done before, so we can copy and paste an existing function, clean it up, add some JSON conversion goodness, and finally send the data to our online storage service, as follows:

```
function synchronizeOnline(callback) {
    db.transaction(function(transaction) {
        transaction.executeSql(
            "SELECT rowid as id, * FROM task ",
            [],
            function (transaction, results) {
                var tasksSynchronized = 0;

                // initialise an array to hold the tasks
                // read each of the rows from the db, and create tasks
                for (var ii = 0; ii < results.rows.length; ii++) {
                    var task = new module.Task(results.rows.item(ii)),
                        taskJson = JSON.stringify(task);

                    $.post("/_je/tasks", {_doc:taskJson,_docId:task.id}, function() {
                        // once the post has completed, increment the counter
                        tasksSynchronized += 1;

                        // and check to see if we have finished the sync operation
                        if (callback && (tasksSynchronized === results.rows.length)) {
                            callback(tasksSynchronized, true);
                        } // if
                    });
                } // for

                // fire the callback and provide information on the number
                // of tasks that were updated
                if (callback) {
                    callback(results.rows.length, false);
                } // if
            }
        );
    });
}
```

Let's focus on the for loop, where the interesting stuff happens. Firstly, we use the JSON library to serialize a Task object that we have retrieved from the database to a JSON string. Next, we use the jQuery **post** function to send that serialized data (using a POST request) to jsonengine for storage.

You can see that our post call takes three arguments:

- The first argument is the url that we are making the POST request to. In this case, our storage URL is the same as our application; we just prefix it with _je (for "JSON storage")—this is simply a jsonengine convention.

- Our next argument contains the data that we are sending through the jsonengine. For jsonengine to be able to save our data effectively, it needs two things:

  - A document (_doc)—this is the data that is going to be stored.

  - A document id (_docId)—the unique key of our document that we are storing. As jsonengine is smart enough to detect whether the provided _docId already exists, and will either create a new record or update the existing record.

- Finally, we supply a success callback for the post function and this is called once the request has been successfully completed.

What is happening here? First, we're using jQuery's post function. This is one of jQuery's most powerful functions when we have to deal with network communication. This function will perform a HTTP POST request, and of course we pass an array of parameters: ("/_je/tasks", {_doc:taskJson,_docId:task.id}, success callback).

The first parameter is the URL to which we are posting our request. In this case, our storage URL will be the same as our application; we just prefix it with _js (for "JSON storage")—this is simply a jsonengine convention.

The second parameter, {_doc:taskJson,_docId:task.id}, is more jsonengine specific. It's a nested parameter's map. _doc defines the name of our storage record, and it can be compared to a database table name. The value we provide is the freshly JSON-converted string; in jsonengine terms, it's called the *JSON document*. Then, _docId represents the unique key of our record. As you can see, we are using the index of our for loop because it's the same index as the ID of each of the offline task's entries.

> **NOTE:** Where does jsonengine store the submitted JSON strings? It's using Google App Engine's data store. As Google's online storage solution, Google App Engine takes care of all the distribution, replication, and load balancing of data. In fact, jsonengine is just an abstraction layer above the data store to perform the storage of JSON documents transparently.

Updating the User Interface for Online Synchronization

We have now enhanced our custom library with a function to synchronize the offline data with an online storage solution, but in order to test it we need to add some user interaction. Therefore, we have to work on our user interface layer and see how we can bind a back-end function to a visually interactive action. Let's add a button called "Synchronize" to the main screen:

```
<ul class="buttons">
    <li><a class="changeview" href="#alltasks">Show All Tasks</a></li>
    <li><a class="changeview" href="#add">Add New</a></li>
    <li class="changeview"><a href="#" class="synchronize">Synchronize</a></li>
</ul>
```

Now we have to bind the click event to our new synchronizeOnline() function:

```
activateMain: function() {
    TODOLIST.Storage.getMostImportantTask(function(task) {
        if (task) {
            // the no tasks message may be displayed, so remove it
            jQuery("#main .notasks").remove();

            // update the task details
            showTaskDetails("#main .task", task);

            // attach a click handler to the complete task button
            jQuery("#main .task-complete").unbind().click(function() {
                jQuery("#main .task").slideUp();

                // mark the task as complete
                task.complete();

                // save the task back to storage
                TODOLIST.Storage.saveTask(task, module.activateMain);
            });

            jQuery("#main .synchronize").unbind().click(function() {
                TODOLIST.Storage.synchronizeTasks();
            });
        }
        else {
            jQuery("#main .notasks").remove();
            jQuery("#main .task").slideUp().after("<p class='notasks'>You have no tasks
to complete</p>");
        }
    });
}
```

Then we simply expose the **synchronizeOnline** function through the **Storage** submodule as the **synchronizeTasks** function:

```
Storage: (function() {
    ...

    var subModule = {
        ...
        synchronizeTasks: synchronizeOnline,
        ...
    };

    return subModule;
})()
```

Refresh your application, and you will see your updated user interface, as shown in Figure 5–1.

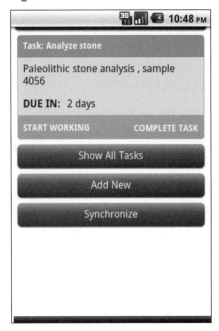

Figure 5–1. *Adding a Synchronize button*

We can now just click the Synchronize button, and all the offline data will be flushed into a modern and ultra-scalable JSON storage system! That's nice, but so far we don't have any feedback about this process—it happens all under the hood. To remedy that, let's display an info banner once the synchronization process is done.

First, we add an "info" div element just before the button stack:

```
...
<div id="info"></div>
<ul class="buttons">
<li><a class="changeview" href="#alltasks">Show All Tasks</a></li>
    <li><a class="changeview" href="#add">Add New</a></li>
    <li class="changeview"><a href="#"    class="synchronize">synchronize</a></li>
</ul>
```

Then add some styling for this `div`:

```
#info {
    margin: 8px 6px 2px 6px;
    padding: 6px 14px;
    background: -webkit-gradient(linear, left top, left bottom, color-stop(0.0,
#71D90F), color-stop(0.7, #529E0B));
    -webkit-border-radius: 4px;
    color: white;
    display: none;
}
```

Notice the `display:none` attribute, which ensures that the `div` won't be visible until we explicitly want it to be displayed.

To display the notification message, let's make a change to our **activateMain** function to show some information once the synchronization process has been initiated:

```
activateMain: function() {
    TODOLIST.Storage.getMostImportantTask(function(task) {
        if (task) {
            ...

            jQuery("#main .synchronize").unbind().click(function() {
                TODOLIST.Storage.synchronizeTasks(function(updateCount) {
                    $("#info")
                        .html("Completed : " + updateCount + " task(s) have been
synchronized !")
                        .show();
                });
            });
        }
        ...
    });
}
```

All we're doing here is updating the info `div` HTML. Now, when the synchronization process completes, the info banner will be displayed, as shown in Figure 5–2.

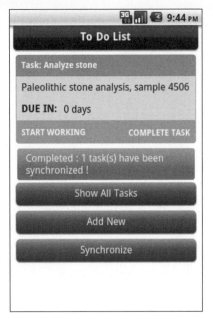

Figure 5–2. *Visual synchronization feedback*

Now that we're sure our synchronization process is working, we need a client interface that will read the data from our online storage solution.

Making a Desktop Interface

One of the benefits of building a web-based application is that you can easily provide access to your data in different web-based formats—for example, tablet devices and more standard desktop browsers. First, let's focus on the latter and see how we can connect our storage solution to a "regular" desktop web application.

Creating a desktop interface from an existing mobile interface is far simpler than trying to create a mobile interface from an existing desktop web application. To see evidence of this, look at the way the various mobile application interfaces have affected the user interfaces of their various big brothers. The recent revisions to the Twitter web interface are an example of how mobile user interface paradigms can affect desktop interfaces to create a better user experience (see http://twitter.com).

As we have one-way synchronization only, the desktop application will be read-only (and, because building a desktop interface is not really in the scope of this book, we'll keep it minimal). If we go back to the example of our scientist collecting data, consider the desktop application as a reporting tool for his colleagues all around the world who want to keep informed about his latest findings.

What you'll learn in this section is that building a mobile web application relying on robust and standard web technologies allows you to extend its features to other web-based engines, and especially to a desktop web interface, like the browser you use on your laptop or desktop system.

The first thing we have to do is to retrieve the data we stored on our cloud-based storage solution.

Querying a jsonengine Instance

You've already seen how easy it is to insert data using the REST API. Likewise, making a query will also be done through the REST API, using the HTTP GET method. First, we have to create a new HTML page—let's call it todolist-readonly.html.

```html
<!DOCTYPE HTML PUBLIC "-//W3C//DTD HTML 4.01 Transitional//EN"
"http://www.w3.org/TR/html4/loose.dtd">
<html>
<head>
<meta http-equiv="Content-Type" content="text/html; charset=UTF-8" />
<title>Tasks page</title>
<link rel="stylesheet" media="screen" href="todolist-readonly.css" />
<script type="text/javascript" src="../../js/jquery-1.4.2.min.js"></script>
<script type="text/javascript">
// get all the posts and show them
$(function() {
    $.get("/_je/tasks", { sort: "_createdAt.desc" }, function (result) {
        var rowsHtml = '';

        for (var ii = 0; ii < result.length; ii++) {
            rowsHtml += '<tr>' +
                '<td>' + result[ii].name + '</td>' +
                '<td>' + result[ii].description + '</td>' +
                '<td>' + result[ii].due + '</td>' +
            '</tr>';
        } // for

        $('#taskTable tbody').html(rowsHtml);
    });
});
</script>
</head>
<body>
<h1>Current tasks stored in jsonengine</h1>
<table id="taskTable">
    <thead>
        <tr>
            <th>Name</th>
            <th>Description</th>
            <th>Due</th>
        </tr>
    </thead>
    <tbody />
</table>
</body>
</html>
```

The interesting part here is the JavaScript function that is called when the page is loaded. We are using jQuery's `get` function—the syntax is almost the same as the `post` function, but we are now passing sorting parameters. The result is an array of JSON documents. A JSON document is a JSON string representation of a `Task` instance. We just have to iterate through the array and update a HTML table to add a new row.

In this particular instance, we are first collecting all the new rows in a string and then replacing the body of the table (`tbody`) using a single call using the jQuery `html` function. While we could just as easily have appended each row as we found it, we increase the speed of our application by trying to do updates to the HTML as few times as possible. While it's not something that you would notice in a small page like this, it is a good habit to get into.

With the HTML page complete, we will also add some very basic styling to the `todolist-readonly.css` stylesheet:

```
table, td {
    border: 1px solid #666666;
    width: 100%;
}

td {
    width:33%;
    padding: 2px;
}
```

Then navigate to your freshly made page, and you should see something like Figure 5–3.

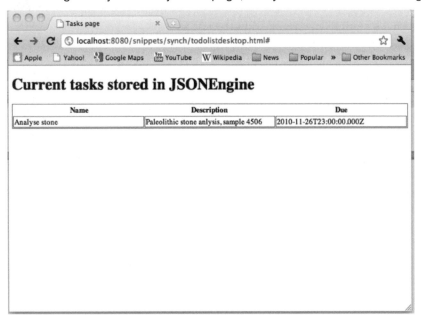

Figure 5–3. *The desktop application showing the synchronized tasks*

As you can see, all the data inside the offline database is now available online—at least on the server, that is; we haven't yet uploaded our application to the cloud. Before doing that, we have to add some security to the storage solution; if we leave it as it is, everybody will have access to the desktop web page. Fortunately, jsonengine comes with a security admin page where you can set the access level for your storage documents, as shown in Figure 5–4.

Figure 5–4. *The jsonengine security admin page*

Here, we can add our JSON "tasks" document and set the read level to "protected," so that users will only be able to view the data if they are connected with their Google or OpenID accounts.

Deploying Your Application on the Cloud

OK, it's time to go live so that the whole world will be able to use your mobile application. But first you will need a Google account (or Gmail account). Once you have that, you can access Google App Engine by logging in at https://appengine.google.com. From there, you can create a new application, and choose an application identifier—which will also be the URL to access your app—and a title. Before you upload our application, you must be sure that the application identifier matches the one that is defined in your local application. To do this, open the `war/web-ing/appengine-web.xml` file and check this line:

```
<application>jsonengine</application>
```

Replace `jsonengine` with the application ID you chose just before. Now you're ready to deploy your application—go to the `bin` folder of your Google App Engine SDK and type the following command (on Windows):

```
appcfg.cmd update location/to/you/war/folder
```

On the Mac and Linux, type the following:

```
appcfg.sh update location/to/you/war/folder
```

Enter your Google username and password at the prompts. If the upload process is successful, you will see the message "Update completed successfully." That's it! Our application is in the cloud—navigate to your page: `http://my-app-id.appspot.com/snippets/05/todolist-readonly.html`.

Summary

We have achieved some interesting things so far: we have a mobile web application with powerful features that can store data offline and synchronize it with an online environment. Synchronizing offline data for a mobile app with a powerful online storage mechanism is a very new and innovative concept.

What we need now are some features to compete with native applications. In the next chapter, we'll add some tasty user interface elements and deal with offline conditions.

Chapter 6

Competing with Native Apps

It's quite impressive that we can produce powerful and scalable mobile web applications just using HTML, CSS, and JavaScript. However, so far we haven't achieved the look and feel that we would with a native application. Also, if our Internet connection goes down, our application will probably stop working, despite the fact that we're using a local database.

In this chapter, you will learn how to go a step further in polishing your web app, first by adding user interface enhancements. We'll use CSS3's amazing animation and transition capabilities, and we'll also use robust and popular JavaScript libraries. Next, we'll add geolocation and offline support using the latest HTML5 specifications and the Chrome browser. At the end of this chapter, we will have a fully standalone application that will be very similar to a native application.

Adding Lightweight Animations and Native-Like Layouts

One of the big differences between native and web applications is that web applications often lack the great-looking user interfaces that native apps can offer. The good news is that technologies like HTML5, CSS3, and JavaScript can now offer solutions that compete with native technologies—for example, providing native browser animation features and ensuring that specific visual elements have a fixed position, such as a top bar menu.

One of these new technologies, CSS3, adds a lot of improvements, including shadows, rotations, and gradients. But for this part we will focus on two very interesting features: CSS transitions and CSS animations.

Adding a Simple Loading Spinner

In the previous chapter, we implemented an online synchronization function. The only visual feedback we had was an info banner telling us the process was successful. But what about during the process itself? For example, if we have thousands of records to synchronize, it will take some time before this process is done. In this case, it would be nice to have some visual feedback during the synchronization, like a loading spinner.

In the old-fashioned way, you would use a semitransparent animated GIF and control it with some JavaScript. The downside of this approach is that it requires an extra resource with a limited number of frames (to keep the image size as small as possible), which reduces the smoothness of the animation; and, because the image is semitransparent with its hardcoded foreground and background color, you also add a dependency to the application's color chart. If you decide to change the background color of your application, you also have to generate your animated GIF again.

For these reasons, we won't use an image; instead, we'll "draw" and animate the spinner using CSS3 animations and transitions. The spinner will consist of 12 bars rotating around an axis and fading out. Let's first define the main spinner style:

```
div.spinner {
                position: absolute;
                top: 50%;
                left:70%;
                margin: -100px 0 0 -100px;
                height: 54px;
                width: 54px;
                text-indent: 250px;
                white-space: nowrap;
                overflow: hidde;
}
```

Then we define the inner div style. Here, we set the common styles that will be shared by all the bars. Basically, we create a bar by styling a div, playing with the corner radius and shadow properties. We also attach an animation to a bar—a fade animation that will be defined later.

```
div.spinner div {
    width: 12%;
    height: 26%;
    background: #000;
    position: absolute;
    left: 50%;
    top: 50%;
    opacity: 0;
    -webkit-animation: fade 1s linear infinite;
    -webkit-border-radius: 50px;
    -webkit-box-shadow: 0 0 3px rgba(0,0,0,0.2);
  }
```

Finally, we define the 12 bars that will be used in the animation, increasing the rotation angle for each of them by 30 degrees using the -webkit-transform:rotate attribute. The fade effect, combined with a different start delay using the -webkit-animation-delay attribute for each bar, will create the illusion of a rotation effect.

```
div.spinner div.bar1 {
              -webkit-transform:rotate(0deg) translate(0, -142%);
              -webkit-animation-delay: 0s;
              }
div.spinner div.bar2 {
              -webkit-transform:rotate(30deg) translate(0, -142%);
              -webkit-animation-delay: 0.9176s;
              }
[..]
div.spinner div.bar12 {
              -webkit-transform:rotate(330deg) translate(0, -142%);
              -webkit-animation-delay: -0.0833s;
              }
```

We also define our fade animation:

```
@-webkit-keyframes fade {
    from {opacity: 1;}
    to {opacity: 0.25;}
  }
```

Before we try out the spinner, let's introduce some new CSS3 selectors:

- `-webkit-animation`: Defines the name of your animation, which will be declared in a separate style block starting with `@-webkit-keyframes`. Notice the values that follow the name of the animation: we have a duration value, a transition-timing function that defines how the animation should proceed over the duration (here we are using a linear function, but there are a lot of different options—ease-in, ease-out, etc.), and finally a value defining the animation's frequency (the animation will run infinitely in our case).

- `-webkit-transform`: Can transform any HTML element. Its possible values are translate, rotate, and scale. Notice that you can chain transform values like we did in the previous code sample—we first rotate the `div` and translate it to the upper-left corner to make it rotate around an axis.

- `-webkit-animation-delay-count`: Defines the delay before your animation starts. This is useful when you want to chain a lot of different animations, like our 12 bars.

> **NOTE:** A linear transition function will time your animation equally over the duration you provide; for example, if you are moving an image by 200 pixels with a duration of 2 seconds, after 1 second your image will have moved by 100 pixels. But maybe there are situations where you want to have another type of timing, like rotating an image very slowly in the beginning and finishing with a fast rotation.

To be able to test our loading spinner, we have to add a `div` containing all the bars' `div`s on the main page:

```
<div id="spinner">
                <div class="bar1"></div>
                <div class="bar2"></div>
                <div class="bar3"></div>
                <div class="bar4"></div>
                <div class="bar5"></div>
                <div class="bar6"></div>
                <div class="bar7"></div>
                <div class="bar8"></div>
                <div class="bar9"></div>
                <div class="bar10"></div>
                <div class="bar11"></div>
                <div class="bar12"></div>
</div>
```

Refresh your application and you will see the loading spinner, as shown in Figure 6–1.

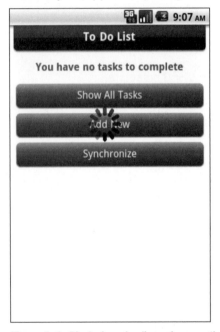

Figure 6–1. *Displaying a loading spinner on the main view*

This is a good first step, but we only want to see the spinner when we are synchronizing—not all the time, even if it's a beautiful spinner. It should appear at the moment we press the Synchronize button and disappear when we show the info banner displaying that the process was successful. To do this, we update the main spinner style with display:none; and we control the container visibility with some JavaScript.

The best place to hook in is probably the synchronizeOnline function; we set the visibility of the spinner container to true when entering the function and revert it to false just before we exit the function:

```
function synchronizeOnline () {
            $("spinner"). .show();
            [...]
            $("spinner"). .hide();
}
```

That's all we have to do. Notice the handy jQuery's hide and show functions, which encapsulate some CSS manipulation for us.

Adding Scrollable Content

As our tasks list continues to grow, it will end up not fitting on the screen anymore. Of course, the browser will natively insert a vertical scrollbar, but, when you scroll down, your top bar containing the title will disappear. Remember, we are competing with native apps, and this kind of behavior is not exactly what we are hoping for.

Fortunately, there is a JavaScript library that will help us fix this visual problem: iScroll (http://cubiq.org/iscroll). This piece of JavaScript can make a particular container scrollable. Once your script is imported into your page, you just have to declare a scrollable instance variable: myScroll = new iScroll('scroller');.

Let's see how we can integrate this in our application. The only part where we need this is in the All Tasks screen, so let's see how we can refactor this element:

```
<div id="alltasks" class="view">
    <h1 class="fancy">All Tasks</h1>
            <div id="wrapper">
                <div id="scroller">
                                    <ul id="tasklist"></ul>
                </div>
            <div>
</div>
```

Notice here that the scrollable div is wrapped by another div that will have a fixed size. Here is the CSS of the wrapper div:

```
#wrapper {
    position:relative;
    z-index:1;
    width:auto;
     overflow:hidden;
}
```

You may wonder why we are not setting the height, since the wrapping container must have a fixed height. That's because we will set the height programmatically, ensuring it will be correct whatever the screen size is. That brings us to the JavaScript part—we just have to fire up an iScroll instance and set the height. We put that in the ready function because it has to be initialized when the page loads.

```
$(document).ready(function() {
        [..]
        myScroll = new iScroll('scroller', {desktopCompatibility:true});
        var wrapperH = window.innerHeight - 35;
        document.getElementById('wrapper').style.height  = wrapperH;
});
```

Be sure you have enough tasks in your application and browse to All Tasks view, as shown in Figure 6–2; you should now be able to scroll your tasks without the title bar scrolling along.

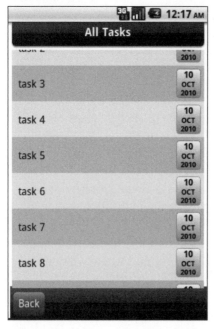

Figure 6–2. *Adding a scrollable div with fixed header and footer*

Sprucing Up the Action Bar

We are getting pretty close to a native application look and feel, but the action bar at the bottom could be a bit nicer, and should also be present on the start page; that will reinforce the feeling that we are staying on the same page whatever we do.

Let's start by adding the action bar on the main page by tweaking the ViewManager:

```
// define the alltasks view
   PROWEBAPPS.ViewManager.define({
                  id: "main",
               actions: [
                  new PROWEBAPPS.ChangeViewAction({
                  target: "alltasks",
                label: "All tasks",
                className: "alltasks"
                     }),
                  new PROWEBAPPS.ChangeViewAction({
                     target: "add",
                     label: "Add",
                     className: "add"
                  }),
                  new PROWEBAPPS.ViewAction({
                     target: "synchronize",
                     label: "Synchronize",
```

```
                                className: "synchronize"
                            })
                        ]
                });
```

The refactoring is pretty simple: the action bar is rendered when the action stack is not null; also, instead of defining an action stack for the alltasks view, we define an action stack for the main view. Notice that the synchronize action is using ViewAction, not ChangeViewAction, because we don't want to switch to another view when we activate this action. As you can see, we also introduce a new property—className. Here it's only relevant for the synchronize action because the click handler function is bound to the element's class name.

The action bar is not rendered on the main view; we can remove all the buttons as they have moved to the action bar. The actions are rendered now like old-fashioned web links; we can easily style them so that they appear as buttons.

```
ul#menu li a {
    display: block;
    background: -webkit-gradient(linear, left top, left bottom, color-stop(0.0,
#b3b3b3), color-stop(0.4, #666666), color-stop(1.0, #333333));;
    color: white;
    text-decoration: none;
    padding: 8px;
    text-align: center;
    -webkit-box-shadow: 0 2px 2px #333333;
    -webkit-border-radius: 6px;
}
```

Refresh your page and you should see our native-like application, as shown in Figure 6–3.

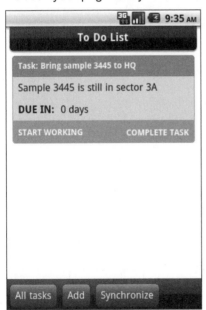

Figure 6–3. *Restyling the action bar*

Making Your Application Location-Aware

One of the things that make mobile applications unique is that they can detect and make use of your current physical location. One of the most famous applications that use this information is *foursquare*, an app that allows people to "check into" particular places and share this information with others.

For a long time, these kinds of features were only possible with native applications, which had access to lower-level hardware such as the GPS sensor. Again, W3C's HTML5 team came up with a revolutionary proposal by allowing the browser to access the GPS of your device and expose it through a JavaScript library. In other words, mobile web applications can now be location-aware, thus bridging a huge gap between native and web-based applications. This topic will be central to the discussion in this chapter.

> **NOTE:** For a long time, mobile web applications didn't have access to low-level hardware, such as the camera or the GPS sensor. However, things are changing—the browser is a native application and has access to low-level hardware APIs, and can expose them to web applications by providing extra JavaScript functions. For the moment, only a few low-level APIs are exposed (e.g., Geolocation and DeviceOrientation events) Camera and contact list access are still unavailable, but with the growing popularity of mobile web applications, it's likely that such access will be added in the future.

The W3C Geolocation API Specification

The entry point of the W3C Geolocation API is a simple JavaScript function with its callback function:

```
navigator.geolocation.getCurrentPosition(showMap);

function showMap(position) {
        // handle position variable
  }
```

This will be sufficient to retrieve our current location; the callback function `showMap` takes a `position` parameter that contains all the information we need to make our application location-aware. Tables 6–1 and 6–2 outline the `Position` object and its associated `Coordinates` object.

Table 6–1. *The Position Object*

Property Name	Type
coords	Coordinates
timestamp	DOMTimestamp

Table 6–2. *The Coordinates Object*

Property Name	Type
longitude	double
latitude	double
altitude	double
accuracy	double
altitudeAccuracy	double
heading	double
speed	double

That may seem like a lot of information, but for now we are really interested in only two attributes: longitude and latitude, which will be enough to determine our geolocation and eventually display it on a map. So, position.coords.longitude and position.coords.latitude are the properties we want to handle.

Let's take advantage of the local storage feature discussed previously, and store our position on the browser side when we start our application so we will be able to access this information whenever we want. First, we have to retrieve our location—let's do that inside the ready function and store the location in the callback function:

```
$(document).ready(function() {
                [..]
                navigator.geolocation.getCurrentPosition(
            function storePosition(position) {

localStorage.setItem('longitude',position.coords.longitude);

localStorage.setItem('latitude',position.coords.latitude);
                            $("#geolocation")
                        .html("Your position : " + position.coords.latitude +
                ","+ position.coords.longitude)
                            .css("display","block");
            });
});
```

Notice that at the end of the function we manipulate the geolocation DOM element; this will be an information banner displayed on the main screen that shows our current position. So we also add a geolocation div element on the main screen:

```
<div id="geolocation"> </div>
```

Next, we apply some styling:

```
#geolocation {
    margin: 8px 6px 2px 6px;
    padding: 6px 14px;
```

```
    background: -webkit-gradient(linear, left top, left bottom, color-stop(0.0,
#71D90F), color-stop(0.7, #529E0B));
    -webkit-border-radius: 4px;
    color: white;
    display: none;
}
```

Start your application, and a pop-up will ask permission to share your location. After accepting, you should see the screen shown in Figure 6–4.

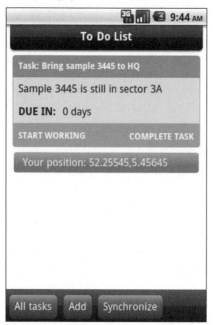

Figure 6–4. *Displaying your geolocation*

Now that we are sure our location has been retrieved and stored offline, we can enhance our Task object with the new data. This will be very simple—we just have to change the structure of our Task table by adding two columns: longitude and latitude. And once we save a new task, we just have to retrieve the geoinformation from our local storage. Let's start by updating our database structure:

```
// open/create a database for the application (expected size ~ 100K)
    var db = null;

    try {
        db = openDatabase("todolist", "1.2", "To Do List Database", 100 * 1024);

        // check that we have the required tables created
        db.transaction(function(transaction) {
            transaction.executeSql(
                "CREATE TABLE IF NOT EXISTS task(" +
                " name TEXT NOT NULL, " +
                " description TEXT, " +
                " due DATETIME, " +
                " completed DATETIME, " +
```

```
                                                              "  longitude
REAL, " +
                                                              "  latitude
REAL";");
        });
    }
    catch (e) {
        db = openDatabase("todolist", "1.1", "To Do List Database", 100 * 1024);

        // check that we have the required tables created
        db.transaction(function(transaction) {
            transaction.executeSql(
                "CREATE TABLE IF NOT EXISTS task(" +
                "  name TEXT NOT NULL, " +
                "  description TEXT, " +
                "  due DATETIME, " +
                "  completed DATETIME);");
        });

        db.changeVersion("1.1", "1.2", function(transaction) {
            transaction.executeSql("ALTER TABLE task ADD longitude REAL;");
                                        transaction.executeSql("ALTER
TABLE task ADD latitude REAL;");
        });
    }
```

This should remind you of what we did in Chapter 3 to update an existing database.
Here we try to open the updated database with its two new columns. If it fails, we can
fall back in the catch section and manually alter the existing database.

Next, we refactor our saveTask function:

```
saveTask: function(task, callback) {
                db.transaction(function(transaction) {
                    // if the task id is not assigned, then insert
                    if (! task.id) {
                        transaction.executeSql(
                            "INSERT INTO task(name, description, due,longitude,latitude)
VALUES (?, ?, ?, ?, ?);",
                            [task.name, task.description,
task.due,parseFloat(localStorage["longitude"]),parseFloat(localStorage["latitude"])],
                            function(tx) {
                                transaction.executeSql(
                                    "SELECT MAX(rowid) AS id from task",
                                    [],
                                    function (tx, results) {
                                        task.id = results.rows.item(0).id;
                                        if (callback) {
                                            callback();
                                        } // if
                                    }
                                );
                            }
                        );
                    }
                    // otherwise, update
                    else {
                        transaction.executeSql(
```

```
                                "UPDATE task " +
                                "SET name = ?, description = ?, due = ?, completed = ?,
longitude = ?, latitude = ? " +
                                "WHERE rowid = ?;",
                                [task.name, task.description, task.due, task.completed,
parseFloat(localStorage["longitude"]),parseFloat(localStorage["latitude"]), task.id],
                                function (tx) {
                                    if (callback) {
                                        callback();
                                    } // if
                                }
                            );
                    } // if..else
                });
        }
```

Our application is now totally location-aware; each task is bound to a location. In the
next chapters, you will see how to combine this information with maps and process your
location against other locations.

Running Your Application Offline

With all of the design work we've done, it would be hard for the average user to tell
whether our application is native or web-based. However, there is still one big
difference: cut off your Internet connection (or put your device in airplane mode) and
refresh your application, and you'll probably get a "page not found" error. What we need
now is a way of running our application offline!

Again, the new HTML5 standard will come to the rescue with its *offline application
cache*. This new HTML5 feature will cache for us on the client side all the static
resources: HTML, images, CSS, and JavaScript. The next time the user navigates to
your application, the browser will use its cache instead of retrieving the files from the
server, regardless of the connection status.

The Offline Cache Manifest File

How does it work? Offline caching relies on the *cache manifest* file that is hosted on the
web server. It's a simple text file document containing all the resources that have to be
cached. The first important thing is the content type of this file. It has to be served with
the MIME type text/cache-manifest. So, let's see how we can configure Google App
Engine (discussed in the previous chapter) to set the right MIME type for our cache file.
Extra MIME types definition are specified in the web.xml file that you will find under your
war/web-inf folder:

```
<?xml version="1.0" encoding="utf-8"?>
<web-app xmlns="http://java.sun.com/xml/ns/javaee" version="2.5">
    [...]
    <mime-mapping>
        <extension>manifest</extension>
        <mime-type>text/cache-manifest</mime-type>
    </mime-mapping>
</web-app>
```

By adding these parameters, Google App Engine will take care of setting the right content type for files with a `manifest` extension. Now that the server is configured, it's time to create our cache manifest file. Create an empty text file called `cache.manifest` that starts with this line: `CACHE MANIFEST`. We will place this file at the root of the web application (i.e., directly under the `war` folder).

The next step is to list all the resources we want to cache—for us that will be the following:

- `snippets/06/todolist.html`
- `snippets/06/css/proui.css`
- `snippets/06todolist.css`
- `js/jquery-1.4.2.min.js`
- `js/jquery.validate.js`
- `js/prowebapps.js`
- `snippets/06/iscroll.js`
- `snippets/06/todolist.js`

These are all the static resources we need to run the application; we just have to add them to the cache manifest file (all except the `todolist.html` file, which will be cached implicitly):

```
CACHE MANIFEST
css/proui.css
snippets/06/todolist.css
js/jquery-1.4.2.min.js
js/jquery.validate.js
js/prowebapps.js
snippets/06/iscroll.js
snippets/06/todolist.js
```

The paths are relative to the location of the manifest file, but you could also use the absolute paths. Now we finally have to declare the manifest file in our application, which we do by adding an attribute inside the HTML tag of the application page:

```
<html manifest="cache.manifest">
```

That's it! The application is ready to be cached the next time we will access it (online, of course). To check out that the files are correctly cached, we will use Chrome's web console:

```
Creating Application Cache with manifest http://localhost:8080/cache.manifest
Application Cache Checking event
Application Cache Downloading event
Application Cache Progress event (0 of 7) http://localhost:8080/snippets/06/todolist.css
Application Cache Progress event (1 of 7) http://localhost:8080/js/jquery-1.4.2.min.js
Application Cache Progress event (2 of 7) http://localhost:8080/js/prowebapps.js
Application Cache Progress event (3 of 7) http://localhost:8080/snippets/06/todolist.js
Application Cache Progress event (4 of 7) http://localhost:8080/js/jquery.validate.js
Application Cache Progress event (5 of 7) http://localhost:8080/snippets/06/iscroll.js
Application Cache Progress event (6 of 7) http://localhost:8080/css/proui.css
```

```
Application Cache Progress event (7 of 7)
Application Cache Cached event
```

If you turn off your Internet connection now, the application will still work because the browser will retrieve the files from the local cache instead of the server. Going back to our scientist example from Chapter 5, the scientist will now be able to use his application everywhere he wants, even if he plans collecting data on the moon!

But what happens if a resource file is modified? The offline cache mechanism uses a byte-to-byte comparison between the remote and cached manifest, so any change will be detected.

Exploring Hidden Offline-Caching Features

The offline-caching file also provides two other useful features: keywords NETWORK and FALLBACK. NETWORK can define resources that will always skip the cached resources and will always try to retrieve them from the server. FALLBACK comes in handy when you want to supply an alternative cached resource to a resource that always has to be retrieved online when your connection is down.

To illustrate this feature, let's imagine that we want an icon showing whether we are online or offline, as in Figure 6–5.

Figure 6–5. *The "online" and "offline" icons*

We update our `cache.manifest` file as follows:

```
CACHE MANIFEST
css/proui.css
snippets/06/todolist.css
js/jquery-1.4.2.min.js
js/jquery.validate.js
js/prowebapps.js
snippets/06/iscroll.js
snippets/06/todolist.js
FALLBACK:
online.png offline.png
```

Here we are saying that `online.png` should never be cached; however, if we don't have a connection, we provide a fallback file, `offline.png`, defined by the FALLBACK keyword. (Note the trailing : for both keywords, which is required.) Let's try it out and add this icon to our application. Regarding the cache manifest file, we just have to reference the Check icon in our page; showing the X icon will be handled by the caching mechanism.

Add the icon to the main view :

```
<div id="main" class="view">
        <h1>To Do List</h1>
        <img src="online.png" height="25" width="25"/>
        [...]
  </div>
```

Refresh your application and you should see something similar to Figure 6–6.

Figure 6–6. *Application in online mode*

Turn off your Internet connection and refresh your page, and you should see something like Figure 6–7.

Figure 6–7. *Application in offline mode*

Detecting Your Connection Status

Beyond its caching capabilities, HTML5's offline-caching feature can provide some extra utilities to deal with offline mode. But these usually involve some more advanced use cases where offline caching will not be enough. For instance, when you are offline, the synchronize function is quite useless, and it would be better if you could hide the Synchronize button in this case.

Let's see how we could implement that. First, we must be able to detect whether we're online or not when we start the application. This may sound quite simple, but is actually more complicated than it seems. HTML5 has specified a feature that enables a web application to check the connection status: `navigator.online`, which should return a Boolean value. Unfortunately, Chrome doesn't support this feature yet, and we have to use a workaround to simulate this behavior.

> **NOTE:** The HTML5 specification defines that the browser should be able to detect its connection status by using the JavaScript function `navigator.online`. This function returns a Boolean value that can be used to used to change your application behavior for offline vs. online scenarios.
>
> Unfortunately, this feature is still not supported on the current Android browsers—but it will be in the next release. Even better, though, the browser that ships with Android 2.2 Froyo gives you more details about your connection type and speed. That gives you the option to adapt your resources depending on your bandwidth. For more details, see
> `http://davidbcalhoun.com/2010/using-navigator-connection-android`.

What we are going to do is make an HTTP request to a site, and, if we don't receive an answer after a configurable timeout, we can consider that we are offline. For some strange reasons, Ajax's jQuery function doesn't trigger a timeout event or an error event when you have no connection—for these reasons, we have to work around this by using jQuery's Timers plug-in; after tweaking it a bit, we should end up with something like this:

```
$('#synhcronize').oneTime(3000, function(){
    $('#synhcronize').css("display","block");
});

$.ajax({ url:'http://query.yahooapis.com/v1/public/yql?"+
        "q=select%20*%20from%20html%20where%20url%3D%22"+
        encodeURIComponent(url)+
        "%22&format=xml'&callback=?',
            dataType: 'jsonp',
            timeout: 3000,
            complete: function() {
                    $('#messages').stopTime();
            }
});
```

We start by binding a timer to the Synchronize button. After three seconds, it will call the function defined inline. This function masks the button after determining that there is no connection available.

At the same time, we fire a simple YQL query (`developer.yahoo.com/YQL`) using an Ajax call, and, if the call is completed and successful, then we stop the timer and the button will stay visible.

Summary

You saw in this chapter that the look and feel of web-based applications can, in fact, compete with native applications. CSS3 and HTML5 are really beginning to break new ground in these areas. In this chapter, you learned how to enhance the user interface by adding animations and complex layouts, and you also learned how to deal with situations where no connection is available by implementing mechanisms that make web applications behave like native ones.

In the next chapter, we'll focus on one of the features just introduced: working with location information—commonly called location-based services.

Chapter 7

Exploring Interactivity

In previous chapters, we explored building an Android web app similar to any desktop web app. Our experience of mobile development so far has been catering for a smaller display and taking advantage of some of the HTML5 API features implemented in mobile WebKit.

In this chapter, we will take a slight break from building complete mobile web apps and explore interactivity through touch events and the HTML5 canvas. Throughout the chapter, we will look at:

- Touch events and where they are both similar to and different from mouse events for desktop browsers

- HTML5 canvas drawing and animation, including some simple best practices when working with canvas and animation

- Some more advanced animation techniques, such as how to produce more realistic animation through various techniques

- Some of the current things to watch out for when working with the canvas on Android, which also includes differences in the way the canvas behaves between different versions of the Android OS

Introduction to the HTML5 Canvas

The HTML5 canvas is an extremely cool addition to the tools that you have at your disposal for building web applications in general. The canvas element provides web developers a way to integrate a custom drawing area into their HTML layouts. This can be particularly useful and gives developers the ability to do more with their pages, whether that be adding some interactivity or displaying a graph.

While not all browsers include support for the canvas tag, Android's WebKit browser does. This gives us the opportunity to explore using it in our applications, and possibly even writing simple games for Android purely using web technologies. While Flash (www.adobe.com/products/flashplayer) is normally the tool of choice for writing simple games for the Web, the HTML5 canvas and JavaScript do provide a compelling alternative. And with cross-platform mobile support for Flash currently limited, this makes the canvas worth investigating.

We will do that now by first having a look at some of the simple operations that can be completed using the canvas.

In this first example, we will use the canvas to simply draw a line from the top-left corner of the display to the bottom right. First is the simplecanvas.html file:

```html
<html>
<head>
    <title>Simple Canvas Demo</title>
    <meta name="viewport" content="width=device-width; user-scalable=0;" />
    <link rel="stylesheet" href="../../css/proui.css" />
    <script type="text/javascript" src="../../js/jquery-1.4.2.min.js"></script>
    <script type="text/javascript" src="../../js/prowebapps.js"></script>
    <script type="text/javascript" src="simplecanvas.js"></script>
</head>
<body>
    <canvas id="simple"></canvas>
</body>
</html>
```

Nothing much to talk about here, apart from the presence of the canvas tag, which by itself does absolutely nothing. It's time to look at the simplecanvas.js file that goes along with our HTML:

```javascript
(function() {
    var canvas = null,
        context = null;

    function resetCanvas() {
        canvas = document.getElementById("simple");

        // set the canvas height to the window height and width
        canvas.width = window.innerWidth;
        canvas.height = window.innerHeight;

        // get a reference to our drawing context
        context = canvas.getContext("2d");

        // now draw the line
        drawLine();
    } // resetContext

    function drawLine() {
        context.beginPath();
        context.moveTo(0, 0);
        context.lineTo(canvas.width, canvas.height);
        context.stroke();
    } // drawLine

    $(window).bind("resize", resetCanvas).bind("reorient", resetCanvas);

    $(document).ready(function() {
        window.scrollTo(0, 1);
```

```
        resetCanvas();
    });
})();
```

Even here, there really isn't anything very complicated going on. Once you strip away the additional code to handle window resizing and so forth, the code does three things to draw the line:

- It gets a reference to the canvas and sizes the canvas to match the window size. This is done when we capture a window resize event or the device orientation changes (thanks to our previous work in Chapter 1).

- It gets a reference to the 2d context of the canvas. To achieve this, we use the getContext method of a canvas object.

- It draws the line. This involves flagging to the canvas that we are going to draw a path with the beginPath method. We then use the moveTo method to move to the top-left corner (moving draws nothing), and then follow that with the drawTo method to draw to the bottom-right corner. Finally, we tell the canvas to draw a line along the path we defined, using the stroke method.

The result is displayed in Figure 7–1.

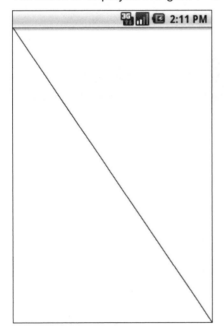

Figure 7–1. *The canvas used to draw a diagonal line in the Android browser*

Drawing Interactively to the Canvas

Now that we at least know how to create a simple canvas, let's look at how we can do that interactively to create some unique mobile web apps. While jumping in and working with touch events would be great, it's worth taking a little time to investigate how this is done using mouse events first—given that this is probably more familiar to us.

Once we have the interactivity built using mouse events in a desktop browser, we will then explore how similar functionality would be implemented using touch events. By working with mouse events in the first instance and then moving to touch events, we will gain an understanding of some important differences between mobile interactivity and desktop interactivity.

Interactivity: The Way of the Mouse

Start by copying the previous `simplecanvas.html` file to a new HTML file called `mousecanvas.html`, and change the script tag to reference `mousecanvas.js` instead of `simplecanvas.js`.

Next, let's create our `mousecanvas.js` file. We'll start with the `simplecanvas.js` file as a base and make modifications so that we are drawing in response to the mouse events rather than once when the document loads.

```
(function() {
    var canvas = null,
        context = null,
        buttonDown = 0;

    function resetCanvas() {
        canvas = document.getElementById("simple");

        // set the canvas height to the window height and width
        canvas.width = window.innerWidth;
        canvas.height = window.innerHeight;

        // get a reference to our drawing context
        context = canvas.getContext("2d");
    } // resetContext

    $(window).bind("resize", resetCanvas).bind("reorient", resetCanvas);

    $(document).ready(function() {
        window.scrollTo(0, 1);
        resetCanvas();

        document.body.addEventListener("mousedown", function(evt) {
            if (buttonDown === 0) {
                context.moveTo(evt.pageX, evt.pageY);
            } // if

            ++buttonDown;
        }, false);
```

```
    document.body.addEventListener("mousemove", function(evt) {
        if (buttonDown > 0) {
            context.lineTo(evt.pageX, evt.pageY);
            context.stroke();
        } // if
    }, false);

    document.body.addEventListener("mouseup", function(evt) {
        --buttonDown;
    }, false);
  });
})();
```

To test this code, run it using an HTML5-compatible desktop browser. As mentioned in previous chapters, Chrome is a good choice, as it is based on WebKit and has some excellent tools support. Figure 7–2 shows a sample drawing after mouse interaction.

NOTE: You may be wondering why we are running code in a desktop browser when this is a book on mobile development. Well, in the preceding example, we are working with mouse events, so a desktop browser is required. Additionally, as you begin to work more with mobile web app development, you will find desktop browsers are an important part of your development process. There is little or no development tools support on mobile browsers at this stage, so it's important not to forget your desktop-based WebKit browser as an important part of your development tool set.

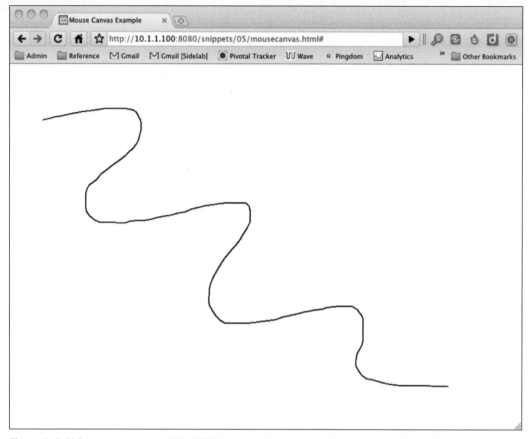

Figure 7–2. *Using mouse events and the HTML5 canvas allows tragic artists to express themselves.*

While the preceding code works well enough in a browser, it does absolutely nothing useful on an Android device—unless of course you consider being able to scroll the title bar that we hid back into view useful.

Interactivity: The Way of Touch

In transitioning to using touch events, let's first take a look at the event-naming conventions, as displayed in Table 7–1.

Table 7–1. *How Touch Events Relate to Respective Mouse Events*

Interaction Style	Start Event	"Continue" Event	End Event
Mouse	mousedown	mouseover	mouseup
Touch	touchdown	touchmove	touchup

The naming of these functions gives us a clue to the differences between working with touch and mouse events. Both mouse and touch events have "down" and "up" events to signify that interaction has started and ended, respectively.

The primary difference, however, is between the mouseover and touchmove events. A touch event has no concept of hovering, and thus we have no touchover event, so it is replaced with the touchmove event, signifying that a touch event has started and the touch points are changing. This is an important point to note, as familiar web concepts such as "hover states" have no effect on mobile devices, so it's important to consider alternative mechanisms to provide feedback to your app users.

We will now create our touchcanvas.html and touchcanvas.js files. As per the mouse canvas example, the HTML file is very simple, so just make a copy of the previous mousecanvas.html file and tweak the references.

Our touchcanvas.js file is more or less a replacement of the mouse event handlers with the relevant touch event handlers:

```
(function() {
    var canvas = null,
        context = null;

    function resetCanvas() {
        canvas = document.getElementById("simple");

        // set the canvas height to the window height and width
        canvas.width = window.innerWidth;
        canvas.height = window.innerHeight;

        // get a reference to our drawing context
        context = canvas.getContext("2d");
    } // resetContext

    $(window).bind("resize", resetCanvas).bind("reorient", resetCanvas);

    $(document).ready(function() {
        window.scrollTo(0, 1);
        resetCanvas();

        document.body.addEventListener("touchstart", function(evt) {
            context.beginPath();
            context.moveTo(evt.touches[0].pageX, evt.touches[0].pageY);

            evt.preventDefault();
        }, false);

        document.body.addEventListener("touchmove", function(evt) {
            context.lineTo(evt.touches[0].pageX, evt.touches[0].pageY);
            context.stroke();
        }, false);

        document.body.addEventListener("touchend", function(evt) {
        }, false);
    });
})();
```

With the preceding code implemented, you should be able to draw using touch on your Android device and simulate touch events in the emulator. Figure 7–3 shows an example.

Figure 7–3. *More advanced drawings are possible given the intuitive nature of the touch interface.*

The primary differences between this code and the `mousecanvas.js` file are:

- With mouse events, mouse button information is included to signify whether the left, right, or other button was pressed. When it comes to touch events, we have no concept of varying buttons, and as such there is no need to monitor button states. Given this situation, the `touchstart` handler has no code to do this, and the `touchend` event handler does nothing and could quite simply be removed.

- References to `evt.pageX` and `evt.pageY` are replaced with references to the `touches` array of the event object. In our example, we reference `evt.touches[0].pageX` and `evt.touches[0].pageY` to get the screen coordinates of the first touch.

- The `touchstart` handler makes a call to the `preventDefault` method of the event object to tell the browser not to take any further action with this event. Without this call, the browser will initiate scrolling on the window; this is not desirable behavior, as it would interfere with our attempts to draw in the canvas area.

With the touch canvas example complete, you should now have a basic understanding of how to use both the HTML5 canvas and touch interactivity to create some simple interactive mobile web apps. Time now to take this further.

> **NOTE:** In the last few chapters, we have been exploring components of the emerging HTML5 spec. As such, it might be natural to expect that touch is part of that specification; however, it isn't.
>
> A separate W3C working group has been set up for standardizing touch interaction, so over time we would expect the way we implement touch interfaces to change slightly as the different organizations working with touch interfaces come to agree on a standard implementation.
>
> If you are interested, the URL for the working group is
> `www.w3.org/2010/07/touchinterface-charter.html`.

Implementing Canvas Animation

This next section is focused on exploring animation using the HTML5 canvas and how simply that can be implemented. We will have a look at a couple of different examples of animation using the canvas, using a mix of animation using both simple drawings and images. In each of these examples, simple touch events will be used to drive the samples.

In addition to the animations, we will also explore the impact that device DPI (or dots-per-inch) has on working with images in the canvas. This is probably one of the more frustrating parts of using HTML5 on Android, as its effects differ between different versions of the operating system; however, we will look into some strategies for working around the problem.

Creating an Animation Loop

If you've worked with JavaScript in the past, you will be familiar with both the `setTimeout` and `setInterval` functions. These functions allow a block of JavaScript to execute after *n* milliseconds or every *n* milliseconds, respectively. In the case of animation, we want a recurring event, so we will be using the `setInterval` method.

Again, for this example, we only need the barest of HTML files, so create a new HTML file called `drops.html` and a corresponding JavaScript file (you know the drill). We will work through a few animation examples in this chapter, and each example will be structured in a similar manner to the example that follows. Our first animation example implements a simple animation loop that simulates raindrops in the browser.

Here is the initial code for `drops.js`:

```
(function() {
    var canvas = null,
        context = null,
        drops = [];

    function resetCanvas() {
```

```
    ...
} // resetContext

function animate() {
    ...
} // animate

$(window).bind("resize", resetCanvas).bind("reorient", resetCanvas);

$(document).ready(function() {
    window.scrollTo(0, 1);
    resetCanvas();

    document.body.addEventListener("touchstart", function(evt) {
        // add the new drop
        drops.push({
            size: 2,
            maxSize: 20 + (Math.random() * 50),
            x: evt.touches[0].pageX,
            y: evt.touches[0].pageY
        });

        // prevent screen scrolling
        evt.preventDefault();
    }, false);

    setInterval(animate, 40);
});
})();
```

The code is structured in a similar fashion to previous examples, with the resetCanvas function used to handle both initialization and resizing the canvas appropriately.

We have implemented the touchstart handler to add new "drops" to our drops array, defining an initial size and a randomly generated maximum size, and capturing the x and y coordinates of the touch position.

We then have the animation loop, which is implemented in the animate function and created by using the setInterval call. We have defined a delay of 40 milliseconds, which equates to approximately 25 frames of animation per second.

Drawing a Frame of Animation

Before we have a look at the actual animate function implementation, first we will have a look at the things that we should do in a single pass of drawing our animation. To try to explain this clearly, we have broken the process down into six simple steps:

1. *Save the canvas context.* Saving the canvas context saves information about the current canvas state, which can be restored later. This is particularly important when you are writing code that you want to integrate with other canvas-drawing code. Without saving and restoring canvas state, it would be quite possible to effect the other draw code that is making similar changes.

2. *Clear the background*. The first step in drawing an animation frame usually involves clearing the background from what has been drawn in the previous frame. As you become more comfortable with drawing to the canvas, however, you may want to limit doing this to squeeze more performance out of your animations. For what we are doing here, though, clearing the background is ideal.

3. *Adjust canvas parameters*. Before drawing to the canvas, you may want to change parameters such as stroke or fill style, and also colors.

4. *Draw the animation frame*. Draw the animation frame using the various canvas methods provided. We'll look at an example shortly that touches on a few elements of this, but, for further information, the Mozilla Developer Center Canvas Tutorial is an excellent resource (https://developer.mozilla.org/en/Canvas_tutorial).

5. *Perform animation loop logic*. It is likely that, to effect any kind of animation, you will need to update variable values, perform calculations, and so on. Generally, within the animation loop is an effective place to perform this kind of logic.

6. *Restore the canvas state*. Once the animation loop has been completed, restore the canvas state to prevent modifications that have been made to the canvas within the loop (such as changes to fill or stroke style) being used in other parts of the application.

> **NOTE:** While some would suggest that saving and restoring the canvas state is optional depending on your implementation, our advice would be to implement the logic at least in the first instance, as it is the best chance you have of making your code reusable within another application. If for some reason (such as performance optimization) it becomes necessary to remove the state-saving and restoring steps, then do so with care.

A Working Example

With an understanding of the steps that are required in a single pass of the animate function, let's now have a look at the code:

```
function animate() {
    context.save();
    try {
        // clear the drawing surface
        context.clearRect(0, 0, canvas.width, canvas.height);

        // set a stroke style
        context.strokeStyle = "rgba(68, 221, 255, 0.5)";
        context.lineWidth = 4;

        // iterate through the drops and draw them to the canvas
        var ii = 0;
```

```
        while (ii < drops.length) {
            // draw the drop
            context.beginPath();
            context.arc(drops[ii].x, drops[ii].y, drops[ii].size, 0, 2 * Math.PI,
false);
            context.stroke();

            // increase the size of the drop
            drops[ii].size += 2;

            // if the drop has exceeded its max size, then remove it
            if (drops[ii].size > drops[ii].maxSize) {
                drops.splice(ii, 1);
            }
            // otherwise, on to the next drop
            else {
                ii++;
            } // if..else
        } // while
    }
    finally {
        context.restore();
    } // try..finally
} // animate
```

The code in the `animate` function creates an animation that will produce a result similar to that shown in Figure 7–4.

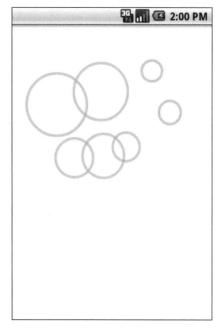

Figure 7–4. *A snapshot of the animation created by our drops.js file*

Looking at the preceding code, we can see that all of the items that were outlined previously have been covered:

- The context.save method is called to save the canvas state as per step 1. We then open a try..finally block to implement steps 2 through 5.

- The first call in the inner block is then calling the context.clearRect method to clear the canvas background. This covers step 2 in our process, but, as mentioned earlier, in some cases you may want to remove this to optimize performance.

- We then move to step 3, which is adjusting the canvas parameter for drawing the display. In our sample, we are adjusting the strokeStyle and lineWidth parameters of the canvas context. Additionally, note our use of the CSS3 rgba function to specify the strokeStyle (see www.w3.org/TR/css3-color/#rgba-color for more info on the rgba function). The rgba function allows us to provide the red, green, blue, and finally alpha values for the color of the stroke (or fill). This provides us with the ability to create semitransparent lines and fill, which can provide some visually appealing effects.

- Then step 4—we draw. In the case of our example, steps 4 and 5 are very much intermingled, which is probably something that will occur in many implementations. Our draw code here is simply drawing circles for each of the drops on the display, but you will probably notice that a simple circle function is nowhere in sight. Instead, we use paths. At first glance, this is a little disconcerting—but don't worry, you will get used to using paths, and we cover this in a little more detail soon.

- Step 5 then follows; as mentioned, this is mixed fairly tightly with step 4, as we are both drawing and updating multiple drops when we are drawing a single frame of animation. In our code, the size of the drop is increased, and, if it reaches a certain size, then it is removed from the drops that we will draw.

- Finally, we break out of the try block in the try..finally loop and execute the finally section. The finally section always executes, and in this case it restores the canvas state as per step 6.

A Quick Overview of Canvas Paths

You will notice as you work with the canvas that it is a fairly low-level API. Different people have different opinions on this, and, while the HTML5 standard is far from locked down, it is likely that it will remain this way.

One example of the low-level nature of the canvas involves the extensive use of paths rather than higher-level abstractions (such as circles, ellipses, etc.). As shown in the previous code sample, drawing a circle involved the following code:

```
context.beginPath();
context.arc(drops[ii].x, drops[ii].y, drops[ii].size, 0, 2 * Math.PI, false);
context.stroke();
```

This is a good example of how paths are used:

1. We tell the canvas context that we are starting to work with a path by calling the beginPath method.

2. We then perform the relevant path-drawing operations to create the shape(s) we require. In the preceding example, we use the arc method to draw a circle, but we could also use the lineTo or rect methods to draw lines and rectangles also.

3. Once all the path-drawing operations have been completed, either the stroke or fill methods of the canvas context are called to draw or fill the specified path.

While it takes a bit of getting used to, having access to low-level path operations allows for very flexible implementations in your code. It isn't for everyone, though, and JavaScript libraries such as fabric.js (see http://github.com/kangax/fabric.js) can definitely simplify the process of working with the canvas if you are interested.

> **NOTE:** As previously mentioned, this chapter is meant to serve as an introduction to what can be achieved using the HTML5 canvas, and we suspect that you could write an entire book on the topic. As such, it takes significantly more than a small section of the book to explain path operations in any depth. For further information and a solid tutorial on the topic, we would once again recommend the Mozilla resources on the topic:
> https://developer.mozilla.org/en/Canvas_tutorial/Drawing_shapes.

Now armed with a basic understanding of an animation loop and how you can use the HTML5 canvas and touch to create simple interactive web apps, we'll have a look at some more complicated examples.

Drawing Images: Accounting for Device DPI

Over the next few examples, our goal will be to show a car animating across the screen. At the same time, we will be exploring the impact of device DPI on various versions of the Android OS, and some strategies that can be used to deal with this.

To get started, once again create an HTML file to contain the application, but with a minor difference this time:

```
<html>
<head>
    <title>Simple Car Animation</title>
    <meta name="viewport" content="target-densitydpi=device-dpi; width=device-width;
user-scalable=0;" />
    <link rel="stylesheet" href="../../css/proui.css" />
    <script type="text/javascript" src="../../js/jquery-1.4.2.min.js"></script>
    <script type="text/javascript" src="../../js/prowebapps.js"></script>
    <script type="text/javascript" src="car.js"></script>
</head>
<body>
    <canvas id="main"></canvas>
```

```
</body>
</html>
```

In Chapter 2, we looked at the various values that can be specified in the `viewport` meta tag. Here is an example where setting the `target-densitydpi` actually makes a difference to what is displayed in the browser. Figure 7–5 illustrates the difference between specifying and not specifying the `target-densitydpi` setting when using a high DPI device.

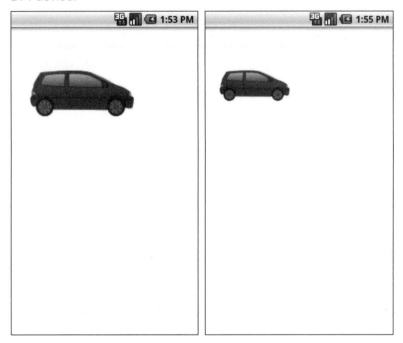

Figure 7–5. *The difference between including and not including the target-densitydpi (on the left, there is no setting; on the right, it is included)*

Since a `target-densitydpi` setting has not been included in the `viewport` meta tag, the emulator has automatically scaled up the image. This isn't really what is desired, as this can make the car start to look a little pixelated.

Once the device is instructed to use the **device-dpi**, it no longer scales, and the quality of the image is improved. There is still more work to do regarding device pixel ratios in our JavaScript, but that's a start.

Speaking of JavaScript, here is our `car.js` file:

```javascript
(function() {
    var canvas = null,
        context = null,
        car = null,
        carX = 0,
        endPos = null;

    function resetCanvas() {
```

```
    ...
} // resetContext

function animate() {
    context.save();
    try {
        if (endPos && car && car.complete) {
            // clear the drawing surface
            context.clearRect(0, 0, canvas.width, canvas.height);

            // draw the car
            context.drawImage(car, carX - car.width, endPos.y - car.height);

            // draw an indicator to highlight the difference between the car and
            context.beginPath();
            context.arc(carX, endPos.y, 5, 0, Math.PI * 2, false);
            context.fill();

            // increment the car x
            carX += 3;

            // if the car x is greater than the end pos, then remove it
            if (carX > endPos.x) {
                endPos = null;
            } // if
        } // if
    }
    finally {
        context.restore();
    } // try..finally
} // animate

$(window).bind("resize", resetCanvas).bind("reorient", resetCanvas);

$(document).ready(function() {
    window.scrollTo(0, 1);
    resetCanvas();

    document.body.addEventListener("touchstart", function(evt) {
        endPos = {
            x: evt.touches[0].pageX,
            y: evt.touches[0].pageY
        };

        carX = 0;

        // prevent screen scrolling
        evt.preventDefault();
    }, false);

    // load our car image
    car = new Image();
    car.src = "car.png";

    setInterval(animate, 40);
});
})();
```

In the first version of this file, we included a marker to help us understand the impact of device DPI when rendering images. To gain an understanding of how this works, run an emulator using an Android OS 2.1 AVD image with a high-resolution screen DPI skin (something like WVGA800—see Chapter 1 for details on how to do this). This will allow us to compare positioning in an emulator running in medium DPI vs. high DPI mode.

> **NOTE:** You may be wondering why a specific version of the Android emulator is required to demonstrate the difference between a standard resolution and a high-resolution display. This is due to some differences in behavior between different versions of the Android OS, and it is explained in more detail soon.

Figures 7–6 and 7–7 illustrate the difference between the two device pixel ratios and the impact on drawing images.

Figure 7–6. *A device pixel ratio of 1 means that both our marker and image are drawn at the position of the touch.*

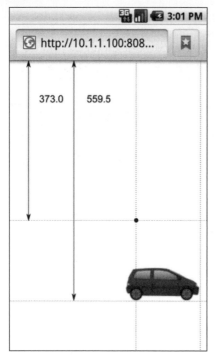

Figure 7–7. *A device pixel ratio of 1.5 shows that images require adjustment. Guidelines have been added.*

Not surprisingly, the position at which the screen was touched and the end position of the car differ by a factor of 1.5, while the marker is drawn right where it's meant to be. For this reason, when we are drawing images to the canvas, we will need to apply some scaling to ensure that those images appear in the correct location.

The following code demonstrates the adjustments required to display the image in the correct location:

```
// draw the car
context.drawImage(car,
          (carX / window.devicePixelRatio) - car.width,
          (endPos.y / window.devicePixelRatio) - car.height);

// draw an indicator to highlight the difference between the car and
context.beginPath();
context.arc(carX, endPos.y, 5, 0, Math.PI * 2, false);
context.fill();
```

With this code modification made, the car image is drawn in the correct location and appears at a position in line with the marker.

> **NOTE:** For the moment, if you are targeting 2.1 as an application platform we would recommend that you look at including appropriate `windowDevicePixel` ratio tweaks (plus some browser detection code). If you feel comfortable targeting 2.2 and above only, then you are able to let the Android browser deal with things rather than have to account for this behavior yourself.
>
> Additionally, if you are working on an Android 2.2 development platform, then adjust the sample code in this chapter, removing any instance that we divide by the `window.devicePixelRatio`.

A Tale of Three Androids

One of the primary criticisms of Android to date has been around the fragmentation of the OS versions that are "in the wild." This a problem primarily because different versions of the OS may do something different from another version—yielding unexpected results. While this can be frustrating to work with as a developer, it is worth persevering, as you are ultimately writing code that will work (with minor modification) on any mobile device with a WebKit browser.

We find ourselves in that situation when we compare the techniques required to position images in high DPI devices for versions of Android up to and including 2.1 with those required for versions 2.2 and beyond. Figure 7–8 illustrates the difference in image positioning when compensating for `devicePixelRatio` the same way across three different versions of the Android OS. In each of the images, the touch start position was the center of the screen, but you can see the resulting image position in 2.2 no longer requires the compensation applied for previous versions.

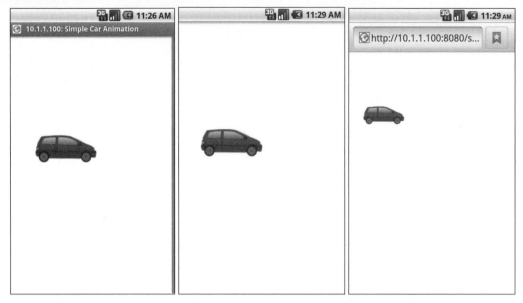

Figure 7–8. *Android 1.6, 2.1, and 2.2 (shown from left to right) compensate for device DPI differently.*

In reality, Android OS version 2.2 (code-named Froyo) implements the functionality correctly. This is great, as having to compensate for devicePixelRatio in JavaScript once an appropriate viewport meta tag is supplied definitely feels like double handling.

With the need to support more versions of Android than just 2.2, though, we need to implement a method of detection that will provide information on how the current device is rendering images to the canvas. This information can then be used to determine whether we need to apply adjustments in the code.

NOTE: Ideally, we would have loved to include the code to demonstrate effective detection in this chapter. Unfortunately, however, neither simple browser detection (www.quirksmode.org/js/detect.html) nor feature detection (https://developer.mozilla.org/en/Browser_Feature_Detection) techniques are effective at determining whether our offsets should be applied. We have started a GitHub fork of the excellent Modernizr project (www.modernizr.com) to look at providing suitable detection for this situation. So, if you are looking to work with the HTML5 canvas on Android, we would recommend checking out the following repository: http://github.com/sidelab/Modernizr.

Once suitable detection has been implemented, details on how to implement the technique will be described on the project wiki: http://github.com/sidelab/Modernizr/wiki.

Advanced Animation Techniques

Our previous animation examples have been a good introduction to implementing simple animation with the HTML5 canvas, but the animations obviously weren't smooth. In this section, we will investigate techniques that will help to make the animation smoother and more believable.

Creating Realistic Movement in Animations

In both of the previous examples, we implemented very primitive techniques for animating our display. For instance, the car animation loop simply incremented the x position of the car by 3 pixels each time the function was called. Did anyone think that looked believable? No, we didn't think so. Let's fix that first of all.

To do this, we will use *easing* to smooth the start or end of the animation (or both). For instance, applying some appropriate easing to our animation would make the car appear to accelerate up to speed or brake to a stop.

As this isn't a book specifically focused on animation, we won't go into depth on what is involved in creating an easing effect nor attempt to write code from the ground up. Rather, we will use some of Robert Penner's existing easing equations (see `www.robertpenner.com/easing`) to create a more realistic effect of motion for our car. These equations were first written for Flash, but have a look in the source of many of the JavaScript libraries that implement easing animation and you will find a reference to Robert's excellent work.

It's likely we will make use of these easing equations again, so let's add them to our `prowebapps.js` file:

```
PROWEBAPPS = (function() {
    ...

    var module = {
        ...

        Easing: (function() {
            var subModule = {
                Linear: function(t, b, c, d) {
                    return c*t/d + b;
                },

                Sine: {
                    In: function(t, b, c, d) {
                        return -c * Math.cos(t/d * (Math.PI/2)) + c + b;
                    },

                    Out: function(t, b, c, d) {
                        return c * Math.sin(t/d * (Math.PI/2)) + b;
                    },

                    InOut: function(t, b, c, d) {
                        return -c/2 * (Math.cos(Math.PI*t/d) - 1) + b;
```

```
                }
              }
          };

          return subModule;
      })(),

      ...
  };

  ...

  return module;
})();
```

In the preceding code, we added two of the many easing functions available in Penner's work. Each of these easing functions takes four parameters:

- t: The elapsed time for the animation

- b: The beginning value, or the value we are easing from

- c: The change value, or the difference between the end value and the start

- d: The duration of the animation

So, by way of example, the following would tell us what the value should be if we were easing from 0 to 500, 600 milliseconds in, for a 2-second animation:

```
newValue = PROWEBAPPS.Easing.Linear(600, 0, 500, 2000);
```

And if we were easing from 1100 to 1700 at the same point in time:

```
newValue = PROWEBAPPS.Easing.Linear(600, 1100, 600, 2000);
```

If that doesn't make complete sense yet, don't worry—it will by the time we have a few examples down. Let's integrate the easing code into our car animation sample. We would suggest creating a separate JavaScript file so that you can do a side-by-side comparison.

Here's the sample code for `car-easing.js`:

```
(function() {
    var ANIMATION_DURATION = 1000;

    var canvas = null,
        context = null,
        car = null,
        endPos = null,
        animationStart = 0;

    function resetCanvas() {
        ...
    } // resetContext

    function animate() {
        context.save();
```

```
        try {
            if (endPos && car && car.complete) {
                // determine the elapsed time
                var elapsedTime = new Date().getTime() - animationStart,
                        carX = PROWEBAPPS.Easing.Linear(
                                elapsedTime,
                                0,
                                endPos.x,
                                ANIMATION_DURATION) - car.width;

                // clear the drawing surface
                context.clearRect(0, 0, canvas.width, canvas.height);

                // draw the car
                context.drawImage(car, carX, endPos.y - car.height);

                // if the car x is greater than the end pos, then remove it
                if (elapsedTime > ANIMATION_DURATION) {
                    endPos = null;
                } // if
            } // if
        }
        finally {
            context.restore();
        } // try..finally
    } // animate

    $(window).bind("resize", resetCanvas).bind("reorient", resetCanvas);

    $(document).ready(function() {
        window.scrollTo(0, 1);
        resetCanvas();

        document.body.addEventListener("touchstart", function(evt) {
            endPos = {
                x: evt.touches[0].pageX / window.devicePixelRatio,
                y: evt.touches[0].pageY / window.devicePixelRatio
            };

            // capture the animation start tick count
            animationStart = new Date().getTime();

            // prevent screen scrolling
            evt.preventDefault();
        }, false);

        // load our car image
        car = new Image();
        car.src = "car.png";

        setInterval(animate, 40);
    });
})();
```

We'll quickly go through the notable sections of this code:

- The "constant" `ANIMATION_DURATION` is used to set the time that the animation will run for.

- Each time the `animate` function is called, and when the animation is first triggered (in the `touchstart` event handler), we use a call to `new Date().getTime()` to determine the current time in milliseconds. In the context of the `animate` function, we use that figure to determine how much time has elapsed since the animation started.

- The calculation of the `carX` variable has changed to use the `PROWEBAPPS.Easing.Linear` function. This variable can now be declared locally in that function. The `Linear` easing function doesn't actually perform any easing. Once we have validated our modifications, we will drop in the `Sine` easing functions to replace the `Linear` easing.

- Determining that the animation has reached its final value is now done based on a comparison between `elapsedTime` and the animation duration. This is done as some easing functions return higher values than the destination on the way to the end value (sounds confusing, but you'll see).

Running this sample should display the car animating, but still show an animation that doesn't look any smoother—the car still stops very abruptly. Let's fix that now. Replace the reference to `PROWEBAPPS.Easing.Linear` with `PROWEBAPPS.Easing.Sine.Out`, and you should see the car image slow down as it approaches the x coordinate of your touch start point.

NOTE: The majority of Penner's easing equations come in three variants: *In*, *Out*, and *InOut*. The In variant will apply the easing at the beginning of the animation, and, in the case of our car, this means it will start slow and then speed up. *Easing out* means that values will have easing applied as the animation approaches its final value, which is exactly what we want with our car—for it to slow to a stop. An InOut easing function applies easing at both the start and end of the animation. We'd recommend playing around with the different variants to get a feel for how they work.

ADDING AN ADDITIONAL EASING FUNCTION TO PROWEBAPPS

As mentioned previously, we really only implemented one of Penner's easing functions for our animation, and there are many more useful easing functions in his library. It is a reasonably simple exercise to take another of his existing samples from ActionScript and port it to JavaScript and into the `prowebapps.js` file. One that would look good with the car animation (and a personal favorite of mine) would be the "Back Out" easing function.

The Back Out easing function is a good pick for this particular situation as the effect is to slightly overshoot the actual animation end point, and then slowly reverse back to the target point. In the case of a car, this looks quite believable. We don't think you'll be disappointed with whichever additional easing function(s) you may choose. Trust us, it's hard to stop applying easing to your animations once you start.

Canvas Transformations and Animation

It is impressive how powerful the HTML5 canvas is, and what can be achieved with it using minimal code can definitely give you a buzz. In this next section, we will introduce some transformation operations that we can use to provide additional animation to our car.

Before we get into that, though, we'll have a look at a simple example to get an overview of how transformations operate. There are a number of different transformation operations that are available to you when using the canvas; however, since this isn't a book on the HTML5 canvas specifically, we will only touch on two operations that we require to expand on our sample:

- `translate`: The `translate` method shifts the origin of the canvas to the specified position. By default, the origin (0,0) of the canvas refers to the top-left corner, but that can be changed using the `translate` method.

- `rotate`: The `rotate` method rotates the canvas around the origin. Used in combination with the `translate` method, it can do some very cool things.

NOTE: Once you start using transformation operations, you won't want to have to reverse changes to the context state all the time. This is why we recommended getting into the habit of using the `save` and `restore` methods of the canvas, as they will prevent you from having to keep track of the various transformations and state changes you make.

For more information on canvas transformations and the importance of the `save` and `restore` methods, we highly recommend the Mozilla Developer Center's information on the topic, at `https://developer.mozilla.org/en/Canvas_tutorial/Transformations`.

Let's take a look at what we can do with `translate` and `rotate` methods in a simple example. Create another HTML file for this example, `rotation.html`, and base it on one of our earlier examples. Then create a `rotation.js` file and include that in the HTML:

```
(function() {
    var canvas = null,
        context = null,
        angle = 0;

    function resetCanvas() {
        ...
    } // resetContext

    function animate() {
        context.save();
        try {
            // clear the drawing surface
            context.clearRect(0, 0, canvas.width, canvas.height);

            // set the origin of the context to the center of the canvas
            context.translate(canvas.width * 0.5, canvas.height * 0.5);

            // rotate the canvas around the origin (canvas center)
            context.rotate(angle);

            // draw a rectangle at the specified position
            context.fillStyle = "#FF0000";
            context.fillRect(-30, -30, 60, 60);

            // increment the angle
            angle += 0.05 * Math.PI;
        }
        finally {
            context.restore();
        } // try..finally
    } // animate

    $(window).bind("resize", resetCanvas).bind("reorient", resetCanvas);

    $(document).ready(function() {
        window.scrollTo(0, 1);
        resetCanvas();

        setInterval(animate, 40);
    });
})();
```

While transformations can sound difficult, the preceding is very simple code and should produce a result similar that displayed in Figure 7–9.

Figure 7–9. *A rotating animation can be created simply by using various canvas transformation operations.*

Just quickly, we will walk through the code from this implementation of the `animate` function:

1. The `translate` method is called shortly after the canvas is cleared, and we set the origin of the canvas to the center of the canvas.

2. The `rotate` method is then called, passing in the angle of rotation (in radians) that should be applied.

3. Next, a canvas `fillStyle` is specified, and the `fillRect` method is called to draw a solid-red square at the center of the canvas.

4. The value of the `angle` variable is then incremented for the next time the square is drawn.

When working with transformations on the canvas, it is important to remember a few things:

- The `translate` method *shifts the origin of the canvas*, which means that both of your subsequent transformation operations and any draw operations are now made relative to the point you translated to.

- Calling `context.save()` prior to performing the translation, and then using `context.restore()` after, will help to make using transformations manageable. Although not always appropriate, having the origin shift back to a constant point after transformation operations will make your draw code easier to manage and keep track of.

Transformations and Our Car Animation

Getting back to our car animation, we're sure you can think of a way that we might be able to use rotation to make our animation more believable again. That's right, let's make those wheels turn. Obviously, we will require a separate wheel image to be able to apply the rotation to it, and not the rest of the car. Luckily, we have one.

Create a new HTML file for this demo, called wheelie.html, and a corresponding wheelie.js file for the code:

```
(function() {
    var ANIMATION_DURATION = 3000;

    var canvas = null,
        context = null,
        car = null,
        wheel = null,
        endPos = null,
        endAngle = 0,
        wheelOffset = 0,
        animationStart = 0;

    function resetCanvas() {
        ...
    } // resetContext

    function drawWheel(x, y, rotation) {
        if (wheel && wheel.complete) {
            context.save();
            try {
                // translate and rotate around the wheel center
                context.translate(x, y);
                context.rotate(rotation);

                // draw the wheel image (taking into account the wheel image size)
                context.drawImage(wheel, -wheelOffset, -wheelOffset);
            }
            finally {
                context.restore();
            } // try..finally

        } // if
    } // drawWheel

    function animate() {
        context.save();
        try {
            if (endPos && car && car.complete) {
                // determine the elapsed time
                var elapsedTime = new Date().getTime() - animationStart,
                    carX = PROWEBAPPS.Easing.Back.Out(
                                elapsedTime,
                                0,
                                endPos.x,
                                ANIMATION_DURATION) - car.width,
                    wheelAngle = PROWEBAPPS.Easing.Back.Out(
```

```
                                elapsedTime,
                                0,
                                endAngle,
                                ANIMATION_DURATION);

                // clear the drawing surface
                context.clearRect(0, 0, canvas.width, canvas.height);

                // draw the car
                context.drawImage(car, carX, endPos.y - car.height);

                // draw the wheels at the appropriate position
                drawWheel(carX + 17, endPos.y - 10, wheelAngle);
                drawWheel(carX + 99, endPos.y - 10, wheelAngle);

                // if the car x is greater than the end pos, then remove it
                if (elapsedTime > ANIMATION_DURATION) {
                    endPos = null;
                } // if
            } // if
        }
        finally {
            context.restore();
        } // try..finally
} // animate

function startCar(destX, destY) {
    endPos = {
        x: destX,
        y: destY
    };

    // calculate the end angle based on the end x position
    endAngle = (endPos.x / window.innerWidth) * 8 * Math.PI;

    // capture the animation start tick count
    animationStart = new Date().getTime();
} // startCar

$(window).bind("resize", resetCanvas).bind("reorient", resetCanvas);

$(document).ready(function() {
    window.scrollTo(0, 1);
    resetCanvas();

    document.body.addEventListener("touchstart", function(evt) {
        startCar(
            evt.touches[0].pageX / window.devicePixelRatio,
            evt.touches[0].pageY / window.devicePixelRatio);

        // prevent screen scrolling
        evt.preventDefault();
    }, false);

    // load our car image
    car = new Image();
    car.src = "car.png";
```

```
        wheel = new Image();
        wheel.src = "wheel.png";
        wheel.onload = function() {
            wheelOffset = wheel.width * 0.5;
        };

        setInterval(animate, 20);
    });
})();
```

The result is shown in Figure 7–10. Walking through the functionality of this code, we can see the following significant details:

- We add a drawWheel function that is responsible for rotating the canvas around a particular point and then drawing the wheel image so that it is centered on that point. We use the same technique that we used in the earlier rotation sample—we translate the origin of the canvas to the center point where the wheel was drawn, apply the rotation, and then call drawImage to draw the wheel image at the appropriate position.

- Inside the animate function, we calculate the angle that we should rotate the wheel by. We do this by applying the same tween function that we are using to animate the x position of the car image. This means that the wheels move in sync with the car. The example uses the PROWEBAPPS.Easing.Back.Out, but, if you chose not to implement any additional easing equations, you can obtain the required source code from the GitHub repository, at http://github.com/sidelab/prowebapps-code/blob/master/js/prowebapps.js. Alternatively, feel free to use one of the easing equations implemented earlier if that is preferred.

- The drawWheel function is called twice in the animate function—once for each wheel.

- In startCar (which is essentially the functionality that used to be contained within the touchstart handler), a variable called endAngle is initialized. This variable is used in the wheel-easing calculation, and is set relative to the distance of the x position that we are sending the car to. By calculating this value relative to the end position of the car, the wheels move at a speed appropriate for the distance that the car has to move.

- Finally, the wheel image is loaded after the car image. For the wheel image load, we attach an onload handler so the wheelOffset can be calculated for an accurate wheel-imaging position in the drawWheel function.

Figure 7–10. *Animating the wheels provides a convincing animation.*

NOTE: As per previous notes regarding strange behavior in Android 2.1 and canvas drawing, the rotated wheel does not appear correctly for that version. Every other version of Android is fine. While we have shown you some techniques on how to combat the oddities of 2.1 in your application code, if it is possible, then it would be wise to recommend users use Android 2.2 or greater for any web applications that make use of the HTML5 canvas.

The adoption of Android 2.2 is accelerating, and since we initially wrote the contents of this chapter (at which time 2.1 was the dominant version) 2.1 now runs second in usage to 2.2 (as at January 4, 2011 Android 2.2 is installed on 51.8 percent of devices, and 2.1 is now at 35.2 percent). You can keep an eye on Android OS version distribution ratio at the following url: http://developer.android.com/resources/dashboard/platform-versions.html.

While we considered removing the content on the "tweaks" that were required to deal with the inadequacies of 2.1, we felt that content still offered value to those of you who might have to deal with 2.1 during your mobile web application development. If you are in that group, then our thoughts are with you—good luck.

Summary

In this chapter, we covered a lot of material and samples focused on the HTML5 canvas, and looked at how we can use a combination of touch events and animation to create some interactive demos. Hopefully, by exploring some of the functionality that is available with the HTML5 canvas, you have seen some potential for using this interactivity in your own applications or simple mobile games.

We will work with the canvas again before the end of the book, but in the next chapter we will start to explore mobile mapping and location-based services. This will provide a basis for building a mobile game that uses elements of mapping, interactivity, and geolocation. There is a lot to learn, but it's going to be a lot of fun doing it.

Chapter 8

Location-Based Services and Mobile Mapping

The focus of the next four chapters will be on location-based services and building a geosocial game utilizing data from the geosocial network Gowalla (http://gowalla.com). If the terms *location-based service* and *geosocial network* mean little to you now (or if you've never heard of Gowalla), don't worry—they will be explained very soon.

As far as coding in this chapter, we will be looking at a couple of different mobile-friendly mapping APIs (Google Maps and Tile5) and how to render a simple map using them. We will then go deeper into the Google Maps API and look at how to display markers and interact with the map. While it would be great to do this with both Google and Tile5, we really need to focus on a single solution to get through all the content. Additionally, Google presently provides one of the most robust mapping solutions for mobile, so it makes sense to use its API in this book.

Location-Based Services

The term *location-based service* is generally used to define an information service that provides data based on geographical position (see http://en.wikipedia.org/wiki/Location-based_service for more information). Location-based services have risen in popularity recently and will continue to do so as more consumers acquire location-aware mobile devices.

One excellent example of using a location-based service is searching for an ATM (automated teller machine) that is close to your current location. Figure 8–1 shows an example of the native Google Maps application on Android showing that kind of information.

Figure 8–1. *Google Maps providing nearby ATM locations is one example of a location-based service.*

Another example is an application called Urbanspoon (www.urbanspoon.com), which offers information on restaurants, including user reviews. A mobile screen capture from the Urbanspoon application "Near Me" feature is shown in Figure 8–2.

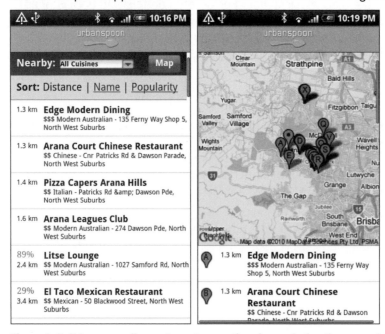

Figure 8–2. *Urbanspoon offers restaurant suggestions for nearby locations, complete with user ratings.*

An interesting point about the Urbanspoon application is that, while the application is deployed as a native app, both of the results screens shown here were pulled down from the Web and embedded into the native application using a WebView (see `http://developer.android.com/reference/android/webkit/WebView.html`). This is a similar technique to what we will be looking at in the next chapter using PhoneGap (see `http://phonegap.com`), and is an excellent way to deploy an application to the Android marketplace while still using web technologies for building most of the application.

There are many more examples of location-based applications available both on the Web and in the Android marketplace.

Geosocial Networking

Geosocial networks (see `http://en.wikipedia.org/wiki/Geosocial_networking` for more info) have started to evolve over the last couple of years; they're essentially a result of the combination of location-based services and social networks (see `http://en.wikipedia.org/wiki/Social_network` for more on social networks). The current geosocial networks have far fewer participants than the leading social networks, but with the rollout of Facebook Places (`www.facebook.com/places`) geosocial networking is starting to hit the online mainstream.

Geosocial networking currently revolves around the concept of *check-ins*. A check-in is basically where a user tells the geosocial network that they are at a particular place, spot, or venue (different geosocial networks use different terminology). In addition to registering that they are at a particular place, a user can also perform other actions that are associated with the venue. Depending on the social network, tips, tasks, or photos can be left by a user for others on the geosocial network to see.

A very interesting part of geosocial networks is the way in which the real world and virtual world interact. For instance, most social networks give rewards to users for regular check-ins or for having the most check-ins for a particular place (Foursquare calls the person with the most check-ins the mayor). Some businesses that have registered as places in the geosocial networks can then use those geosocial rewards to provide discounts to regular customers. This in turn incentivizes geosocial network users to regularly visit and check into venues, and also to participate in the geosocial network.

Figure 8–3 shows the screen captures from two major geosocial networks: Foursquare and Gowalla.

Figure 8–3. *Foursquare and Gowalla are two of the larger geosocial networks.*

A core concept in geosocial networks is that the locations (places, spots, or venues) are user contributed. For instance, if while using Foursquare you went to a new restaurant and wanted to check in there, but couldn't find it in the list of places, you could create it, which would allow both you and others to check in at that location. Using this technique, a geosocial network with an active community can quickly gather a large list of places.

Hopefully that provides some background information on both location-based services and geosocial networking. Let's now get back to coding using some maps.

Mobile Mapping

While there are quite a few different JavaScript mapping APIs available, very few of those have been optimized for (or even work on) mobile devices. At the time of writing, the primary thing that is lacking in most of the existing mapping APIs is touch support for mobile devices. Thankfully, this is not the case with the Google Maps API, so we will be able to run through some sample code using that API.

In this section, we will have a look at implementing mobile maps for both Google Maps and a fairly new HTML5 mapping API called Tile5 (www.tile5.org). For both APIs, we will walk through the process of displaying a simple map, and then we will go on with the Google API to work through some samples in more detail.

Displaying a Map with Google Maps

Getting started with Google Maps is very simple. The following code sample (adapted from the Google Maps V3 JavaScript Tutorial, at
`http://code.google.com/apis/maps/documentation/javascript/tutorial.html`)
demonstrates just how easy it is:

```html
<!DOCTYPE html>
<html>
<head>
    <title>Simple Google Map | Pro Web Apps</title>
    <meta name="viewport" content="width=device-width; initial-scale=1.0; maximum-
scale=1.0; user-scalable=0;" />
    <link rel="stylesheet" media="screen" href="../../css/proui.css" />
    <style type="text/css">
      html { height: 100% }
      body { height: 100%; margin: 0px; padding: 0px }
    </style>
    <script type="text/javascript" src="../../js/jquery-1.4.2.min.js"></script>
    <script type="text/javascript" src="../../js/prowebapps.js"></script>
    <script type="text/javascript"
src="http://maps.google.com/maps/api/js?sensor=false"></script>
    <script type="text/javascript">
    function initMap() {
        // set the map size to be window height less the header
        $("#map_canvas").height($(window).height() - $("#main h1").outerHeight() - 20);

        // initialize the map initial position to near Sydney Australia
        var latlng = new google.maps.LatLng(-34.397, 150.644);

        // configure the default options
        var myOptions = {
            zoom: 8,
            center: latlng,
            mapTypeId: google.maps.MapTypeId.ROADMAP
        };

        // create the map, attaching it to the map_canvas element
        var map = new google.maps.Map(
            document.getElementById("map_canvas"),
            myOptions);
    }
    </script>
</head>
<body onload="initMap()">
    <ul id="menu">
    </ul>
    <div id="main" class="view">
        <h1>Google Map Test</h1>
        <div id="map_canvas"></div>
    </div>
</body>
</html>
```

The preceding code sample demonstrates just how little JavaScript is required to get a simple map displayed in a web app. Essentially, it is a three-step process:

1. Include the Google Maps API in your web application. The required script is located at `http://maps.google.com/maps/api/js`, and takes a `sensor` parameter. In the sample, we passed through a value of false for the `sensor` parameter, but, if we had detected the user's location using the Geolocation API as we did in Chapter 6, we would have needed to pass this value through as `true`.

2. Define a function to initialize the map. This function's primary purpose is to create a new instance of a `google.maps.Map` class. The constructor takes two arguments: first, the `div` that will contain the map once the map is created; and, second, an object of options that influence the map initialization. In the preceding sample, the map was instructed to go to zoom level 8, positioned at a latitude and longitude near Sydney, Australia, and showing the map with a "Road Map" style.

3. Finally, hook the function (`initMap`) up to the `onload` event of the document body.

Once that is all done (and combined with our standard boilerplate template), a screen similar to Figure 8–4 will be displayed.

Figure 8–4. *Displaying a mobile-friendly Google map is a simple exercise.*

Tile5: An Alternative HTML5 Mapping API

While in most cases the Google Maps API is the best choice for your application, there are times where it just isn't an option—perhaps due to licensing restrictions (you may want to display advertising other than Google ads) or a particular client's needs. One example of this would be a client that wants to use its own mapping server for maps—it's more common than you might think.

Tile5 (`http://tile5.org`) is an open source JavaScript library being developed to provide a mobile device-friendly mapping solution that can support multiple map providers. Presently, the majority of mapping APIs tie you to a particular map provider (OpenLayers—`http://openlayers.org`—is a notable exception on the desktop). For some users, this restriction is completely acceptable, while other users regularly need to work with different mapping services, and having to change between APIs can be quite frustrating. This is where Tile5 on mobile, and OpenLayers on the desktop, come into their own.

As Tile5 is targeted at modern smartphone devices (at the time of writing, Android support is in progress but not yet stable), it is able to make extensive use of HTML5. While, at this stage, the use of HTML5 only provides an experience comparable with other non-HTML5 mapping APIs, we are likely to see hardware-accelerated HTML5 canvas implementations soon, and that is going to make things very exciting.

The following code sample shows the equivalent code required to display a simple map using Tile5 in a similar fashion to the previous example using Google Maps. For this example, Tile5 connects to the CloudMade (`http://cloudmade.com`) mapping servers, which serve image tiles generated from OpenStreetMap data. If you aren't already familiar with the OpenStreetMap (`http://openstreetmap.org`) initiative, then it's definitely worth taking a look at. In their own words, it is "a free editable map of the whole world." Essentially, as users we have the ability to add and update information on the map. In the same way that Wikipedia is an encyclopedia that is maintained by people all over the world, OpenStreetMap is a street map and atlas with many maintainers.

```
<!DOCTYPE html>
<html>
<head>
    <title>Simple Tile5 Map | Pro Web Apps</title>
    <meta name="viewport" content="width=device-width; initial-scale=1.0; maximum-
scale=1.0; user-scalable=0;" />
    <link rel="stylesheet" media="screen" href="../../css/proui.css" />
    <style type="text/css">
      html { height: 100% }
      body { height: 100%; margin: 0px; padding: 0px }
    </style>
    <script type="text/javascript" src="../../js/jquery-1.4.2.min.js"></script>
    <script type="text/javascript" src="../../js/prowebapps.js"></script>
    <script type="text/javascript"
src="http://www.tile5.org/jsapi/0.9.1/tile5.js"></script>
    <script type="text/javascript"
src="http://www.tile5.org/jsapi/0.9.1/tile5.osm.js"></script>
```

```
        <script type="text/javascript"
src="http://www.tile5.org/jsapi/0.9.1/tile5.cloudmade.js"></script>
        <script type="text/javascript">
        function initMap() {
            // set the map size to be window height less the header
            $("#map_canvas")
                .attr('height', ($(window).height() - $("#main h1").outerHeight() - 20))
                .attr('width', $(window).width() - 15);

            var map = new T5.Map({
                container: 'map_canvas',
                provider: new T5.Geo.Cloudmade.MapProvider({
                    apikey: "13077497529148b0a40f1bf71728d125"
                })
            });

            map.gotoPosition(new T5.Geo.Position(-34.397, 150.644), 8);
        }
        </script>
</head>
<body onload="initMap()">
    <ul id="menu">
    </ul>
    <div id="main" class="view">
        <h1>Tile5 Map Test</h1>
        <canvas id="map_canvas"></canvas>
    </div>
</body>
</html>
```

The implementation of this sample is very similar to the previous Google Maps example:

1. The Tile5 library files are included from the Tile5 site. First, the core `tile5.js` library is included, and this provides the generic functionality for mapping. We then include two additional files, `tile5.osm.js` and `tile5.cloudmade.js`, which provide the code required to talk to CloudMade and other OpenStreetMap-based services.

2. A function is defined to initialize the map. In Tile5, this involves first creating a `T5.Map` instance and informing it of the HTML5 canvas element that it will attach to, and also informing the provider that will be used to supply the map tiles. Once a map instance is created, the `gotoPosition` method is called, instructing Tile5 to draw a map at a particular latitude and longitude for a zoom level.

3. As per the Google example, the `initMap` function is called in response to the body onload event.

This generates a screen like the one shown in Figure 8–5.

Figure 8–5. *The Tile5 mapping API provides an HTML5-based mobile mapping solution.*

While Tile5 is showing a lot of promise, it still hasn't reached a point where Android support has been fully implemented and tested. Even though HTML5 has been used, there are still certain nuances that require tweaking to ensure the library behaves well on both iOS and Android; and up until now the primary focus has been iOS compatibility. For this reason, the application that we will build over the next few chapters will be built using Google's more mature API. As the Tile5 library matures, however, it is likely to provide one of the best alternatives to Google Maps for Android web apps.

> **NOTE:** The Tile5 library is a product being actively developed by Sidelab (www.sidelab.com). As I (Damon Oehlman) am the founder of Sidelab in addition to one of the authors of this book, I think it's only fair to be open as to my involvement.

Adding Markers to a Google Map

One of the main reasons that you will have for implementing a map is to draw attention to nearby locations. Earlier in the chapter, we considered the specific example of showing nearby ATMs on a map, and in this and other situations placing graphical markers are an excellent way of communicating this.

The code to add a marker to the map is also very simple, as demonstrated in the following code sample. With the following code, simply replace the initMap function in the previous sample with the updated function contents:

```
<script type="text/javascript">
function initMap() {
    // set the map size to be window height less the header
    $("#map_canvas").height($(window).height() - $("#main h1").outerHeight() - 20);

    // initialize the map initial position to Sydney Australia
    var latlng = new google.maps.LatLng(-34.397, 150.644);

    // configure the default options
    var myOptions = {
        zoom: 8,
        center: latlng,
        mapTypeId: google.maps.MapTypeId.ROADMAP
    };

    // create the map, attaching it to the map_canvas element
    var map = new google.maps.Map(
        document.getElementById("map_canvas"),
        myOptions);

    // create a new marker to and display it on the map
    var marker = new google.maps.Marker({
        position: latlng,
        map: map
    });

    // capture touch click events for the created marker
    google.maps.event.addListener(marker, 'click', function() {
        alert('marker clicked');
    });
}
</script>
```

The preceding code performs two functions:

1. First, a new marker is defined by creating an instance of a google.maps.Marker class. This is initialized by providing both the position of the marker and the map the marker will be added to. Once created, the marker will appear on the map.

2. Next, we add an event listener to respond to click events for that marker. In the preceding samples, we simply displayed an alert to confirm that the event had fired.

Once this has been completed, screens similar to the ones shown in Figure 8–6 will be displayed.

Figure 8–6. *Adding a marker to the Google map draws attention to a location.*

We'll next have a look at something more intelligent than just showing an alert when the marker is clicked.

Showing Marker Detail

If you have had experience building desktop web applications and sites that incorporate Google Maps, then you will probably already be thinking ahead to displaying an info window for the marker. While this is very simple to do, it isn't a typically good fit for mobile maps, as demonstrated in Figure 8–7.

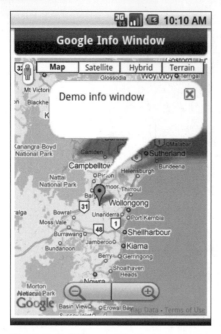

Figure 8–7. *While great for desktop mapping apps, the info window isn't well suited to mobile web apps.*

While not required, if you are interested in seeing the results for yourself, here is the code that corresponds to the screenshot displayed in Figure 8–7:

```
function initMap() {
    // set the map size to be window height less the header
    $("#map_canvas").height($(window).height() - $("#main h1").outerHeight() - 20);

    // initialize the map initial position to Sydney Australia
    var latlng = new google.maps.LatLng(-34.397, 150.644);

    // configure the default options
    var myOptions = {
        zoom: 8,
        center: latlng,
        mapTypeId: google.maps.MapTypeId.ROADMAP
    };

    // create the map, attaching it to the map_canvas element
    var map = new google.maps.Map(
        document.getElementById("map_canvas"),
        myOptions);

    // create a new marker to and display it on the map
    var marker = new google.maps.Marker({
        position: latlng,
        map: map
    });

    // create a simple info window
    var infowindow = new google.maps.InfoWindow({
```

```
        content: 'Demo info window'
    });

    // capture touch click events for the created marker
    google.maps.event.addListener(marker, 'click', function() {
        infowindow.open(map,marker);
    });
}
```

While it is all well and good to talk about how not to display marker detail, obviously this doesn't help us build a mobile web app that includes mobile mapping. So let's have a look at some alternative possibilities:

- We could take the user to a detail page for that marker as soon as it's tapped.

- We could try to create a smaller custom info window that takes up less screen real estate and doesn't require a Close button—the window would automatically close when another pin has been tapped.

- We could rework the interface to display marker detail at either the top or the bottom of the display, and perhaps provide a More Details button to take the user to the full detail page for the marker.

Given these options, the third one is probably the best, so we will go with that option and see what can be done to restructure the interface and provide a foundation to move forward with our application build.

A Mobile-Optimized Mapping UI

In this next section, we will work through the process of creating a UI for mapping that is optimized for a mobile device. All the building blocks that we require are supplied in the Google Maps toolbox. It's just a case of being a little more selective with what we use than we might ordinarily be with a desktop application.

A Mapping UI Mockup

Before we get into the code for our mobile mapping UI, we will begin by putting together a UI mockup, as we did for our to-do list application in Chapter 4. This is displayed in Figure 8–8.

Figure 8–8. *A mockup of our optimized UI for mobile mapping*

There are six primary components to the interface:

1. The application title bar. We have gone back to the simple title style for this application as it is better suited to work with a full-screen map, and we really don't want to waste pixels with such limited screen real estate.

2. The currently selected marker title. This bar is displayed when a marker is tapped, and shows the title of the tapped marker. The active marker is shown in element 4. Depending on the application, tapping the actual marker title could be used to take the user to a detailed information page for the selected marker. In this case, the title should probably be underlined to indicate that it is also a link.

3. Marker change selection navigation controls. These navigation controls are included to provide an alternative mechanism for navigating through the markers. Instead of having to tap individual markers, the navigation controls can be used to move through the markers and change the active marker selection.

4. The active marker. This is the marker that was most recently tapped or that has been navigated to with the navigation controls.

5. An inactive marker. Inactive markers are displayed in gray, while the active marker is displayed in blue.

6. The zoom controls. These are provided by the Google Maps API for Android, as Android does not support multitouch events in the web browser at present. If you were to load the display on an iPhone, the zoom controls would not be displayed; however, other devices with a similar single-touch limitation would be likely to display the controls also.

No work will be required on our part to have these zoom controls display, but it is important to remember that they are displayed at the base of the map, and thus that part of the screen is accounted for.

> **NOTE:** The preceding UI has been designed with fingers in mind. When designing a mobile UI, it is important to remember that your users will not be using the pixel-accurate selection of a mouse cursor. Rather, they will be using their fingers, which at their most accurate probably have a contact surface of about 10 pixels. If, as in the preceding mapping interface, it is possible that tappable elements will be in close proximity to one another (the markers in our case), think about providing alternative UI mechanisms to avoid causing your users frustration.

Coding a Boilerplate Mobile Mapping UI

With a clear understanding of the application UI that we want to create, let's now take a look at the code that is required to pull the interface together.

First, here's the HTML code that is required:

```html
<!DOCTYPE html>
<html>
<head>
<meta name="viewport" content="initial-scale=1.0, user-scalable=no" />
<link rel="stylesheet" media="screen" href="mapapp.css" />
<script type="text/javascript" src="../../js/jquery-1.4.2.min.js"></script>
<script type="text/javascript" src="mapapp.js"></script>
<script type="text/javascript" src="http://maps.google.com/maps/api/js?sensor=false">
</script>
<script type="text/javascript">
function initialize() {
    var latlng = new google.maps.LatLng(-34.397, 150.644);

    MAPAPP.init(latlng, 8);
    MAPAPP.addMarker(latlng, 'Test Marker', 'Some test content');
} // initialize
</script>
</head>
<body onload="initialize()">
<h1 class="simple floating">Mapping App Boilerplate</h1>
<div id="map_canvas" style="width:100%; height:100%"></div>
<div id="marker-nav">
    <img src="../../img/navigation-arrow.png" class="left disabled" />
    <span class='marker-title'>Test Text</span>
    <img src="../../img/navigation-arrow.png" class="right" />
</div>
```

```
<div id="marker-detail" class="child-screen">
    <div class='content'>Some Test Content</div>
    <button class='close'>Close</button>
</div>
</body>
</html>
```

The preceding HTML is simply a modified version of the HTML that we used before to demonstrate a simple Google Maps interface. We have, however, moved the inline CSS and JavaScript into separate files and wrapped the JavaScript in a module called MAPAPP. This means the previous body of the initialize function is now largely encapsulated within the MAPAPP.init function. In this case, the initialize function simply initializes the map at the specified position (and zoom level) and then adds a simple test marker.

To get the actual page displaying in a similar way to our mockup (Figure 8–8), we also need to create a mapapp.css stylesheet that will contain our required CSS rules:

```
/* apply the standard css recommended in GMaps tutorial */
html {
    height: 100%
}

body {
    height: 100%;
    margin: 0px;
    padding: 0px;
    overflow: hidden;
    font-family: Arial;
}

#map_canvas {
    height: 100%
}

/* title styles */
h1.simple {
    font-size: 0.9em;
    padding: 8px 4px 4px 8px;
    background: #333333;
    color: #AAAAAA;
    border-bottom: 2px solid #AAAAAA;
    margin: 0 0 4px 0;
}

h1.floating {
    position: absolute;
    width: 100%;
    z-index: 100;
}

/* marker navigation bar */
#marker-nav {
    /* set general color and style */
    background: rgba(33, 69, 123, 0.8);
    color: white;
```

```
    font-weight: bold;
    text-shadow: 1px 1px 1px rgba(50, 50, 50, 0.85);
    text-align: center;

    /* initialize positioning and layout */
    position: absolute;
    top: 20px;
    z-index: 90;
    width: 90%;
    margin: 0 2%;
    padding: 18px 3% 10px;

    /* add the 'mandatory' border radius */
    border: 2px solid rgba(255, 255, 255, 0.2);
    -webkit-border-radius: 12px;
}

/* marker navigation elements styling */
#marker-nav img.left {
    float: left;
    -webkit-transform: rotate(180deg);
}

#marker-nav img.right {
    float: right;
}

#marker-nav img.disabled {
    opacity: 0.25;
}

#marker-nav span.has-detail {
    text-decoration: underline;
}
```

The preceding code can essentially be broken down into four sections:

1. First, we have the recommended core CSS from the basic Google Maps Hello World tutorial. This code sets the containing elements and the map container to fill the device screen. Note that additional CSS instruction has been added here (overflow: hidden) to assist with displaying detail views later in the chapter. By applying the overflow: hidden CSS, we can hide elements offscreen and not have scrollbars show for the window.

2. Next, we provide some CSS that instructs an h1 header element with the class of simple to be rendered using an absolute position and appear with the look and feel of the simple header style that we defined back in Chapter 2. Note also that a z-index CSS rule has been specified to instruct the h1 element to display above the map. Without this instruction, the header would not be visible.

3. We then apply some look-and-feel styling for the #marker-nav element. Once again, absolute positioning is used to ensure that the navigation bar plays nicely with the Google map, which is set to occupy the entire screen. Note the use of percentage positioning in the width, padding, and margin CSS rules. Using percentages here provides the best possible chance of our mapapp template working with varying screen sizes.

4. Finally, we have some CSS rules for displaying the navigation buttons and having them align correctly inside the navigation menu. Additionally, here we see the webkit-transform CSS3 rule being used (as in Chapter 6 for the loading spinner) to enable us to reuse the same basic navigation arrow image but display it rotated 180 degrees.

All that is required to complete the display is to incorporate the very simple JavaScript Google Maps display logic from earlier into its own file, mapapp.js, and wrap this using the JavaScript module pattern so we can build a larger application on it.

```javascript
MAPAPP = (function() {
    // initialize constants
    var DEFAULT_ZOOM = 8;

    // initialize variables
    var map = null,
        markers = [];

    function addMarker(position, title, content) {
        // create a new marker to and display it on the map
        var marker = new google.maps.Marker({
            position: position,
            map: map,
            title: title
        });

        // add the marker to the array of markers
        markers.push(marker);

        // capture touch click events for the created marker
        google.maps.event.addListener(marker, 'click', function() {
            // update the navbar title using jQuery
            $('#marker-nav .marker-title').html(marker.getTitle());
        });
    } // addMarker

    var module = {
        addMarker: addMarker,

        init: function(position, zoomLevel) {
            // define the required options
            var myOptions = {
                zoom: zoomLevel ? zoomLevel : DEFAULT_ZOOM,
                center: position,
                mapTypeControl: false,
                streetViewControl: false,
                mapTypeId: google.maps.MapTypeId.ROADMAP
```

```
        };

        // initialize the map
        map = new google.maps.Map(
            document.getElementById("map_canvas"),
            myOptions);
    }
};

return module;
})();
```

In the preceding code, we separate the previously combined functionality into two functions: APPMAP.init and APPMAP.addMarker. This will give us an excellent base from which to implement the extended functionality in the next section (adding multiple markers and viewing marker detail).

With that last piece of the initial boilerplate code in place, an interface similar to the one displayed in Figure 8–9 should be displayed. The only real difference between the preceding JavaScript and the earlier samples is that this one uses jQuery to update the navbar title with the title of the marker in response to the marker being clicked.

Figure 8–9. *With everything going to plan, our actual layout will be displayed much like our mockup.*

Implementing UI Navigation in the Boilerplate

With the interface laid out as required, we will now flesh out other parts of our application interface. First, we will make some simple modifications to the HTML to include a child view div that will provide us with the ability to select a marker, tap the marker title, and get more information on that location.

The modifications to the mapapp.html are as follows:

```
<!DOCTYPE html>
<html>
...
<div id="marker-nav">
    <img src="../../img/navigation-arrow.png" class="left disabled" />
    <span class='marker-title'>Test Text</span>
    <img src="../../img/navigation-arrow.png" class="right" />
</div>
<div id="marker-detail" class="child-screen">
    <div class='content'>Some Test Content</div>
    <button class='close'>Close</button>
</div>
</body>
</html>
```

The marker-detail div is added just before the end of the body tag, and just after the marker-nav div that we created earlier. Making these changes to the HTML will break the map display, and the following additional CSS rules are required to bring everything back to displaying correctly. Add the following CSS to the end of the mapapp.css file:

```
div.child-screen {
    background: rgba(255, 255, 255, 0.75);
    width: 100%;
    height: 100%;
    left: 100%;
    top: 0px;
    position: absolute;
    z-index: 91;
}

div.child-screen .content {
    margin: 50px 10px 0;
}

div.child-screen button.close {
    height: 30px;
    position: absolute;
    bottom: 10px;
    left: 10px;
    right: 10px;
    display: block;
}
```

Notice that the CSS rules specify that a div of class child-screen will be displayed with absolute positioning and have a height and width of 100%. This means that these div elements, like the map, will take up the entire screen when displayed. What stops this screen from displaying when the HTML is first rendered is the absolute left position specified at 100% (shown in bold).

This works in conjunction with the `overflow: hidden` CSS from the previous code to hide the `div` off the right side of the map until we need it.

When we require the `child-screen div` to display, we dynamically set the left position of the `div` to `0px`. In terms of visual styling, we apply a background fill using the `rgba` CSS function to display a slightly transparent white background. This provides a nice visual effect, in which the map is still slightly visible under the child screen that has been activated. The z-index of 91 places it above the HTML elements on the map screen, but beneath the `h1` title.

Finally, make the following modifications to the `mapapp.js` file to properly activate the navigation flow:

```
MAPAPP = (function() {
    // initialize constants
    var DEFAULT_ZOOM = 8;

    // initialize variables
    var map = null,
        mainScreen = true,
        markers = [],
        markerContent = {};

    ...

    function activateMarker(marker) {
        // update the navbar title using jQuery
        $('#marker-nav .marker-title')
            .html(marker.getTitle())
            .removeClass('has-detail')
            .unbind('click');

        // if content has been provided, then add the has-detail
        // class to adjust the display to be "link-like" and
        // attach the click event handler
        var content = markerContent[marker.getTitle()];
        if (content) {
            $('#marker-nav .marker-title')
                .addClass('has-detail')
                .click(function() {
                    $('#marker-detail .content').html(content);
                    showScreen('marker-detail');
                });
        } // if
    } // activateMarker

    function addMarker(position, title, content) {
        // create a new marker to and display it on the map
        var marker = new google.maps.Marker({
            position: position,
            map: map,
            title: title
        });
```

```
        // save the marker content
        markerContent[title] = content;

        // add the marker to the array of markers
        markers.push(marker);

        // if the first marker, activate automatically
        if (markers.length === 1) {
            activateMarker(marker, content);
        } // if

        // capture touch click events for the created marker
        google.maps.event.addListener(marker, 'click', function() {
            // activate the clicked marker
            activateMarker(marker);
        });
    } // addMarker

    function initScreen() {
        // watch for location hash changes
        setInterval(watchHash, 10);

        // next attach a click handler to all close buttons
        $('button.close').click(showScreen);
    } // initScreen

    function showScreen(screenId) {
        mainScreen = typeof screenId !== 'string';
        if (typeof screenId === 'string') {
            $('#' + screenId).css('left', '0px');

            // update the location hash to marker detail
            window.location.hash = screenId;
        }
        else {
            $('div.child-screen').css('left', '100%');
            window.location.hash = '';
        } // if..else

        scrollTo(0, 1);
    } // showScreen

    function watchHash() {
        // this function monitors the location hash for a reset to empty
        if ((! mainScreen) && (window.location.hash === '')) {
            showScreen();
        } // if
    } // watchHash

    var module = {
        addMarker: addMarker,

        init: function(position, zoomLevel) {
            ...

            // initialize the screen
```

```
        initScreen();
      }
   };

   return module;
})();
```

In the preceding code, the showScreen function does most of the legwork. When it is passed a string parameter (which it checks for using the JavaScript typeof operator), it uses jQuery to bring that HTML element into view by adjusting its left position. This works in conjunction with the previously defined CSS to bring in and hide separate views in the main application viewing area. To the end user, this provides a similar experience to what we coded in the earlier to-do list application. In this case, however, we are using absolute positioning based on the presence and requirements of the map component.

Another notable part of the code is the watchHash function, which is called at regular intervals (courtesy of the JavaScript setInterval function). The purpose of the function is to monitor the window.location.hash property and keep the application UI in sync. This means that the user will be able to use the back button on the browser, in addition to the Close button, which is placed in a child view to navigate back to the main screen.

Finally, we update the addMarker function to save the marker content into the markerContent object for each of the marker titles, and also call a new function (activateMarker) when a marker is clicked—rather than simply updating the title. At first glance, the activateMarker code may appear a little complicated, but it's reasonably simple once you break it down:

1. First, HTML elements with the marker-title class are updated with the title of the marker (retrieved using the marker.getTitle method). At the same time, the has-detail class is removed, and we unbind the click event handler, as the marker may not actually have any content and therefore no detail screen. The has-detail class was defined in the previous section's boilerplate CSS to simply show an underline under the text, thereby simulating a link.

2. Second, if the marker has content associated, then we add the has-detail class and bind a click handler to the marker title. Now, when the user clicks the marker title, they will be taken to the marker-detail screen and shown the HTML content that was specified for the marker.

With these modifications complete, we will be able to navigate to our placeholder child view by clicking the marker title that will be displayed underlined in the navigation bar. Figure 8–10 illustrates this.

NOTE: You might be wondering why we are reimplementing functionality that we have already covered in our previous to-do list application. This is because the navigation code we implemented as part of our to-do list application doesn't work well with the recommended Google Maps layout. Rather than attempt to retrofit the code to suit the Google Maps code, it was a simpler exercise to create a separate mapping application boilerplate.

As mentioned earlier in the book, the mobile web app space is crying out for a mature, mobile JavaScript framework that will take care of some of the grunt work that is involved with writing a mobile web app.

There are already some good contenders out there, but Android and other mobile device support isn't very extensive yet. My money is definitely on jQuery Mobile in the long run. This will hopefully be released shortly before this book, but not at the time of writing unfortunately.

Figure 8–10. *We are now able to navigate to a subscreen by clicking the marker title in the nav bar.*

Selecting Markers with the Navigation Bar

In this next section, we will populate the mapping display with a number of markers, and look at tweaking the boilerplate mapping app code to allow us to select between markers using the navigation bar in addition to tapping the map.

Setting Up the Markers and Showing Custom Icons

This will require us to add a few additional markers to the test boilerplate HTML code (mapapp.html) to ensure that the functionality works, so let's do that now. Replace the contents of the initialize function in the page with the following script:

```
function initialize() {
    var latlng = new google.maps.LatLng(-33.866, 151.209);

    MAPAPP.init(latlng, 13);
    MAPAPP.addMarker(latlng, 'Sydney', 'Sydney Australia');
    MAPAPP.addMarker(new google.maps.LatLng(-33.859, 151.209), 'The Rocks');
    MAPAPP.addMarker(new google.maps.LatLng(-33.857, 151.215), 'Sydney Opera House');
    MAPAPP.addMarker(new google.maps.LatLng(-33.861, 151.211), 'Circular Quay');
} // initialize
```

This will add a total of four markers to the display. Without adding any additional code, this will create a display similar to the one shown in Figure 8–11.

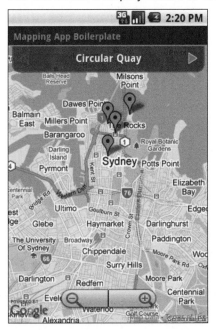

Figure 8–11. *Four markers are displayed, two of which are in close proximity.*

It's now time to implement some icons for the markers rather than using the default indicators. This will allow us to use two separate icons and indicate to the user which of the markers is the currently selected marker. The two marker image files are pin-active.png and pin-inactive.png, and these can be downloaded from the img directory of the prowebapps-code repository (http://github.com/sidelab/prowebapps-code) on GitHub.

The following code shows the modifications that are required to the addMarker and activateMarker functions to enable the use of a custom icon. When the first marker is added, this marker is automatically activated.

```
function activateMarker(marker, content) {
    // iterate through the markers and set to the inactive image
    for (var ii = 0; ii < markers.length; ii++) {
        markers[ii].setIcon('../../img/pin-inactive.png');
    } // for

    // update the specified marker's icon to the active image
    marker.setIcon('../../img/pin-active.png');

    ...
} // activateMarker

function addMarker(position, title, content) {
    // create a new marker to and display it on the map
    var marker = new google.maps.Marker({
        position: position,
        map: map,
        title: title,
        icon: '../../img/pin-inactive.png'
    });

    // add the marker to the array of markers
    markers.push(marker);

    // if the first marker, activate automatically
    if (markers.length === 1) {
        activateMarker(marker, content);
    } // if
    ...
} // addMarker
```

With the preceding code modifications in place, it is now possible to distinguish between the currently selected marker and inactive markers. We will now be able to implement navigating through the markers in the next section. The map display should appear as shown in Figure 8–12.

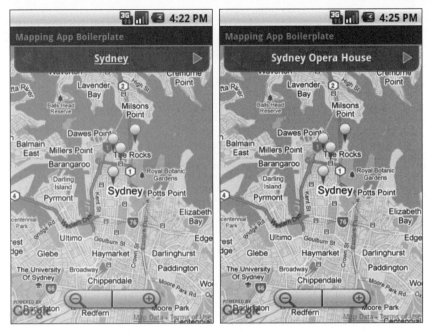

Figure 8–12. *When the map is first displayed, the Sydney marker is active, but others can be selected by tapping.*

Implementing the Tapless Marker Selection

Now that it is possible to distinguish between an active marker and an inactive one, it is time to implement the navigation controls to allow us to navigate through the markers without having to tap individual markers.

There isn't too much to this next section, as it is just a matter of keeping track of the activated marker's position in the marker array and updating the navigation controls accordingly. To do this, however, we will first need a utility function that will tell us a marker's position in the marker array. The following code defines a getMarkerIndex function that should be included in the mapapp.js code just before the initScreen function.

```
function getMarkerIndex(marker) {
    for (var ii = 0; ii < markers.length; ii++) {
        if (markers[ii] === marker) {
            return ii;
        } // if
    } // for

    return -1;
} // getMarkerIndex
```

We then implement an updateMarkerNav function that will update the navigation button state. The ideal location for this function in the mapapp.js is just above the existing watchHash function.

```
function updateMarkerNav(markerIndex) {
```

```
// find the marker nav element
var markerNav = $('#marker-nav');

// reset the disabled state for the images and unbind click events
markerNav.find('img')
    .addClass('disabled')
    .unbind('click');

// if we have more markers at the end of the array, then update
// the marker state
if (markerIndex < markers.length - 1) {
    markerNav.find('img.right')
        .removeClass('disabled')
        .click(function() {
            activateMarker(markers[markerIndex + 1]);
        });
} // if

if (markerIndex > 0) {
    markerNav.find('img.left')
        .removeClass('disabled')
        .click(function() {
            activateMarker(markers[markerIndex - 1]);
        });
} // if
} // updateMarkerNav
```

As per the earlier activateMarker function, the first thing the updateMarkerNav function does is reset the navigation buttons to the default state: disabled and with no click event handling.

Then, based on the value of markerIndex passed to the function, the navigation buttons are selectively enabled and click events bound. This will allow users of the application to navigate through markers without having to tap each one. We are not quite there yet, though, as our present logic is a little flawed in the addMarker function. Figure 8–13 shows the display after adding the four markers.

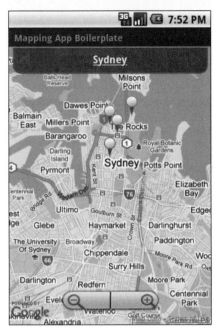

Figure 8–13. *Something isn't right here—we have our four pins but no navigation button. What gives?*

It turns out that navigation controls are displayed in response to the marker being activated, and previously this was triggered when our marker was detected as the only marker in the list. While this was fine before, we are now configuring UI elements based on the number of markers, so this will have to be dealt with slightly differently.

While there are a number of ways that we could solve this particular problem, erring on the side of simplicity is probably best. In this case, we can simply add another exported function (called updateDisplay) to the MAPAPP module:

```
MAPAPP = (function() {
    ...

    var module = {
        ...

        updateDisplay: function() {
            // if we have at least one marker in the list, then
            // initialize the first marker
            if (markers.length > 0) {
                activateMarker(markers[0]);
            } // if
        }
    };

    return module;
})();
```

With this new function in place, we can then remove the following lines from the addMarker function:

```
// if the first marker, activate automatically
if (markers.length === 1) {
    activateMarker(marker, content);
} // if
```

Finally, we add the MAPAPP.updateDisplay() call into the initialize function in mapapp.html:

```
function initialize() {
    var latlng = new google.maps.LatLng(-33.866, 151.209);

    MAPAPP.init(latlng, 13);
    MAPAPP.addMarker(latlng, 'Sydney', 'Sydney Australia');
    MAPAPP.addMarker(new google.maps.LatLng(-33.859, 151.209), 'The Rocks');
    MAPAPP.addMarker(new google.maps.LatLng(-33.857, 151.215), 'Sydney Opera House');
    MAPAPP.addMarker(new google.maps.LatLng(-33.861, 151.211), 'Circular Quay');

    // update the map display
    MAPAPP.updateDisplay();
} // initialize
```

Now we have quite a functional set of boilerplate files that we can use to build a mobile web-mapping application using Google Maps. However, before we move on to building our geosocial app in the next chapter, there is one final tweak that should be made to polish things up slightly.

Applying Sorting to Ensure Intuitive Marker Navigation

Presently, the order in which the markers are navigated is the order they were added to the list. To someone using the app, this would likely appear fairly random and not very intuitive. So, before we move on, let's get those markers in some kind of logical sort order—ideally top to bottom and left to right.

First of all, we will create a sortMarkers function that can take the markers and sort them in order of northwestern-most position to southeastern-most position. Ideally, this function should be just before the updateMarkerNav function, but this is not critical.

```
function sortMarkers() {
    // sort the markers from top to bottom, left to right
    // remembering that latitudes are less the further south we go
    markers.sort(function(markerA, markerB) {
        // get the position of marker A and the position of marker B
        var posA = markerA.getPosition(),
            posB = markerB.getPosition();

        var result = posB.lat() - posA.lat();
        if (result === 0) {
            result = posA.lng() - posB.lng();
        } // if

        return result;
    });
} // sortMarkers
```

The preceding code makes use of the built-in JavaScript sort function (see
(`https://developer.mozilla.org/en/JavaScript/Reference/Global_Objects/Array/sor`
`t`). When using the sort function, you simply provide a comparison callback to the `sort`
function that takes two parameters.

This callback will then be executed with members of the array until the array is sorted
according to the required order. To affect this sort order, simply return a value less than
0 if item A should occur earlier in the list than item B, and a value greater than 0 if the
reverse is true. If the items are equivalent, simply return 0.

With the `sort` function complete, we just need to modify the `MAPAPP.updateDisplay`
function to incorporate the sorting:

```
MAPAPP = (function() {
    ...

    var module = {
        ...

        updateDisplay: function() {
            // get the first marker
            var firstMarker = markers.length > 0 ? markers[0] : null;

            // sort the markers
            sortMarkers();

            // if we have at least one marker in the list, then
            // initialize the first marker
            if (firstMarker) {
                activateMarker(firstMarker);
            } // if
        }
    };

    return module;
})();
```

Essentially, the function is modified to first save the first marker in the array (as this is
assumed to be the most important marker and should probably be the first selected)
and then sort the markers. If an initial marker is saved, then this marker is activated.
Figure 8–14 shows the display after implementing the sort code and modified
`MAPAPP.updateDisplay` function.

Figure 8–14. *The mapping interface after sort logic has been applied. Sydney is still activated, but is now the last marker in the list based on its latitude and longitude.*

This brings us to the end of the boilerplate mapping application code. Essentially, the three files (mapapp.html, mapapp.css, and mapapp.js) can now be taken and used as a template for a mapping application that uses the Google Maps API.

Summary

This chapter covered a lot of material in the areas of mapping and location-based services. We looked at two different mapping APIs that are currently available, and looked in some depth at how to create a web-mapping application that uses the Google APIs and feels good in the Android browser.

Like most mobile web app development, this has involved being selective about the tools that we used and applying some different usability principles than might be used for building a desktop web application.

In the next chapter, we will take this boilerplate code and use it as the basis for our geosocial app. In addition to working through parts of the application, you will also get an introduction to PhoneGap as we wrap the web app in native code. By the end of the build, we'll have a product that can be deployed to the Android marketplace.

Chapter 9

Native Bridging with PhoneGap

In the previous chapter, we looked at working with mobile maps in preparation for writing our geosocial game. In this chapter, we will have a look at PhoneGap (http://phonegap.com) as a tool to assist us in deploying our web applications as native apps. This will give us the ability to deploy our applications to the Android marketplace, while letting us continue to build the core of the application using web technologies.

We will investigate some very good reasons that we might want to do this in the next section. First, it will allow our geosocial game to give native applications a run for their money, and it will make it difficult for consumers to distinguish between a native app and a web application deployed as native.

Essentially, we are going to be learning how to have our cake and eat it too—which in our opinion is always a good thing.

Introducing Bridging Frameworks

PhoneGap is a framework/tool for packaging a mobile web application for native distribution. Additionally, frameworks like PhoneGap provide capabilities for pure web applications to access functionality of the mobile device. This is achieved by the native wrapper application providing a *bridge* to the web application, and in the case of PhoneGap this is done using a JavaScript library (on the surface at least).

PhoneGap is just one of many bridging frameworks. While the term *bridging framework* isn't in wide usage at present, it does represent very well what they are designed to do. At its core, PhoneGap is the purest of these frameworks, offering just the bare bones required to access the native features, without making any suppositions about other parts of your application build.

Another bridging framework that is well worth a look is a product from Rhomobile called Rhodes (http://rhomobile.com/products/rhodes). Rhodes provides an application stack designed for building data-driven mobile web applications. If you are a user or fan of Rails (http://rubyonrails.org), then you are likely to find a comfortable fit with Rhodes.

One last framework that has gained quite a bit of attention (but wouldn't actually class as a bridging framework) is a product called Appcelerator Titanium (www.appcelerator.com). The Appcelerator approach is quite different from both PhoneGap and Rhodes. Rather than building an application that wraps a mobile web UI with a simple native wrapper application, Appcelerator builds a native app from JavaScript code. As more web-enabled mobile devices gain market share, this approach may show some limitations; however, it is worth a look all the same.

In terms of where to start with all of these different options, PhoneGap is an excellent choice—which is why we are using it in the book. There isn't much that you can't do with PhoneGap, and you always have the choice of what you will mix and match with it. Most other solutions won't give you the same scope to explore.

When to Use PhoneGap

There are two basic situations that would justify the use of a bridging framework such as PhoneGap:

- When a mobile web application that you are writing needs access to device functionality not currently exposed through an implemented web API. A good example is accessing either the accelerometer or the camera.

- When you want to package the application for native distribution in the Android marketplace (or equivalent device app store). With the various mobile application stores being common places for people to look for their applications, this is something always worth considering.

The second of these situations is probably the more common. One of the advantages of developing using PhoneGap (instead of another bridging framework) is that, even if this hasn't been considered when first writing a mobile web app, it is very simple to package an application with PhoneGap at a later stage.

Downloading PhoneGap

At the time of writing, the current stable release of PhoneGap is 0.9.3, which can be downloaded by going to the following URL and obtaining the release archive: www.phonegap.com/download.

Once you have downloaded the ZIP file, extract it and place it where you normally keep your developer tools. The distribution contains a number of folders with template projects designed to help you to build and deploy mobile applications for a variety of platforms using PhoneGap. The files for Android are sensibly located in the Android directory.

- `phonegap-0.9.3.jar`: This is a Java archive containing the compiled classes that are used to make PhoneGap function on Android. If you're interested in how pieces of PhoneGap work (and you're comfortable reading Java source code), then you can have a look at the `phonegap-android` project on GitHub (`http://github.com/phonegap/phonegap-android`). This is purely optional, though, as it is not required to build applications *using* PhoneGap.

- `phonegap-0.9.3.js`: This is the JavaScript file that provides the JavaScript stubs that manage the communication between the web application and the native wrapper. We'll take a look at some of the functionality offered by this JavaScript library later in the chapter.

- `Sample`: This is a sample project directory. We will use it as a base for creating our application using PhoneGap, and in the next section we'll look at the internals of the sample to gain an understanding of the capabilities of the PhoneGap framework.

A Sample PhoneGap Application

Now that we've downloaded PhoneGap, let's create a copy of the sample application and get an understanding of what can be done using PhoneGap. In the directory that you are using for the samples in this book, create a directory called `bridges`. Then copy the `Sample` directory from the `Android` directory located within the PhoneGap download to that new directory.

This will provide us with a skeleton PhoneGap native Android project in the `bridges/Sample` folder. The directory structure for this skeleton project is displayed in Figure 9–1.

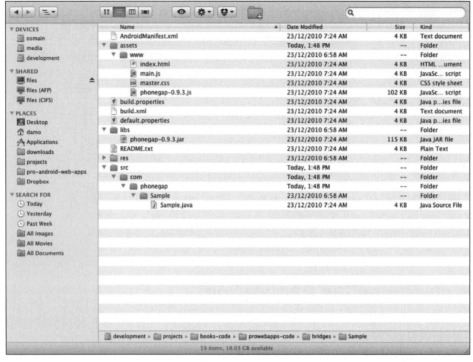

Figure 9–1. *The Sample PhoneGap application folder has everything you need to get started.*

While we won't go into detail on all the various files and folders in our Sample directory, as most pertain to the native wrapper application, there are some that deserve further explanation:

■   `AndroidManifest.xml`: This file is used by the native Android application in a number of ways, including specifying what kind of device permissions are required by the application and what classes are used to run the application.

■   `assets/www/`: This directory contains the HTML, CSS, and JavaScript files that are included in the WebView of the PhoneGap native wrapper (see `http://developer.android.com/reference/android/webkit/WebView.html` for more about WebViews). In particular, notice the `phonegap.js` file here. This file needs to be included in your web pages to properly access PhoneGap's bridging functionality. We will look at this in more detail soon.

■   `libs/phonegap-0.9.3.jar`: This is the Java library that is used to build the native application. Without it, your application won't work (or build).

- `res/`: This directory contains the various resources that are used by the native application. When it comes time to deploy your application, you will need to replace `icon.png` files in a few places under this directory so you aren't using the default PhoneGap icon.

- `src/*`: This directory contains the application source files that are used to create the native executable for the wrapper application.

- `build.xml`: For building the native wrapper application, the Android SDK uses a Java build system called Ant to build projects from the command line (see `http://ant.apache.org`). This `build.xml` file is essentially an instruction file that tells the Java SDK how to build an application.

That's pretty much it. While the other files are important and required to build the native wrapper, we really don't need to know what they do—our primary concern is with the web files that are embedded in the native app. Additionally, for the moment we will play with the sample application as is, but will work through which of the files in the sample application need to be changed when building an application of our own.

Building the Sample Application

Now that we have the sample application directory created, the next thing to do is work out how to build and run the native application in the Android emulator.

> **NOTE:** As mentioned previously, Ant is used by the Android SDK to build native applications. If you don't already have Ant installed on your system, then you will need to obtain and install it before you can go further in this chapter. Instructions for installing Ant on various systems are available at `http://ant.apache.org/manual/install.html`.

With Ant installed and available on your system path, in a terminal window or at command prompt, change directory to the newly created sample directory, and execute ant with no command-line parameters to see the list of valid build targets. Figure 9–2 shows output generated from running the command.

Figure 9–2. *Attempting to build the sample project fails, as the path to the Android SDK is not yet known.*

Hmmm, that can't be right—we should have seen a more meaningful message than that. While the sample project is quite complete in terms of everything required to create a PhoneGap project, it doesn't know the location of the Android SDK, and as a result the Ant build fails. This can be rectified by using the `android` command-line tool (one of the core tools in the Android SDK; it was introduced in Chapter 1) to generate a `local.properties` file for the build.

Simply run the following from the command line, with the copied sample directory as the current directory:

```
android update project -p ./
```

This creates a `local.properties` file for the project that contains a single property, `sdk.dir`. This tells Ant where it can find the Android SDK, and consequently the required build tools to build the sample application.

Attempting to run Ant again once the `local.properties` file has been created will generate output similar to that shown in Figure 9–3.

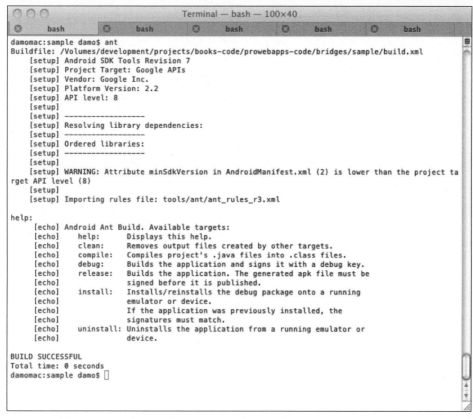

```
damomac:sample damo$ ant
Buildfile: /Volumes/development/projects/books-code/prowebapps-code/bridges/sample/build.xml
    [setup] Android SDK Tools Revision 7
    [setup] Project Target: Google APIs
    [setup] Vendor: Google Inc.
    [setup] Platform Version: 2.2
    [setup] API level: 8
    [setup]
    [setup] --------------------
    [setup] Resolving library dependencies:
    [setup] --------------------
    [setup] Ordered libraries:
    [setup] --------------------
    [setup]
    [setup] WARNING: Attribute minSdkVersion in AndroidManifest.xml (2) is lower than the project ta
rget API level (8)
    [setup]
    [setup] Importing rules file: tools/ant/ant_rules_r3.xml

help:
     [echo] Android Ant Build. Available targets:
     [echo]    help:      Displays this help.
     [echo]    clean:     Removes output files created by other targets.
     [echo]    compile:   Compiles project's .java files into .class files.
     [echo]    debug:     Builds the application and signs it with a debug key.
     [echo]    release:   Builds the application. The generated apk file must be
     [echo]               signed before it is published.
     [echo]    install:   Installs/reinstalls the debug package onto a running
     [echo]               emulator or device.
     [echo]               If the application was previously installed, the
     [echo]               signatures must match.
     [echo]    uninstall: Uninstalls the application from a running emulator or
     [echo]               device.

BUILD SUCCESSFUL
Total time: 0 seconds
damomac:sample damo$ []
```

Figure 9–3. *Running Ant with no command-line options provides information on how to build, and also validates that the build process is working correctly.*

Now that Ant is configured and working correctly, we can build our app. While a number of options are displayed, for the moment the following are of most interest:

- debug: The Ant debug target is used to build the application and sign it with a debug key. Once the application is built with the debug key, it can then be installed in the emulator (or a device configured for development) and therefore run.

- install: The install target is used to copy the compiled executable to the emulator or device.

- uninstall: Using the uninstall target in Ant will allow us to remove the application from either the emulator or the device. This can be very helpful, as removing an application from a device otherwise takes quite a bit of mucking around.

Now it's time to build the app. First, you will need an emulator or device connected for the install target to be able to run successfully. Run the following command from the command line to check that you have an emulator or device that the app can be installed to successfully:

```
adb devices
```

The adb command (which stands for *Android Debug Bridge*) is one of the tools installed with the Android SDK. This particular command provides information on the Android emulators and devices that are currently connected. Any Android device that is currently connected can then be interfaced with using a variety of developer tools. For more information regarding debugging Android web apps, see Appendix A.

If you have a valid emulator running, then you should see output similar to Figure 9–4. If not, then you will need to start an emulator instance or attach an Android device via USB.

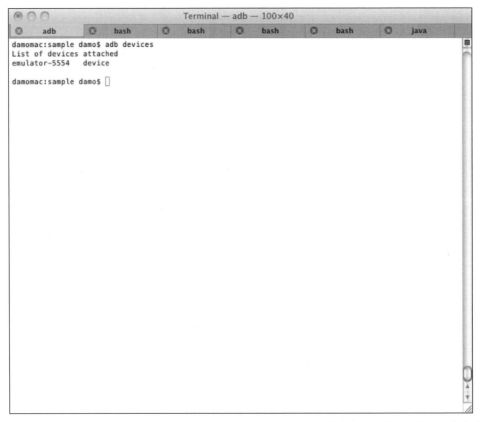

Figure 9–4. *If an emulator is running (or a device is attached), then it will be shown by running "adb devices."*

An emulator can be started by following the instructions outlined in Chapter 1. Alternatively, you can run the following command:

```
emulator @android_web_apps
```

The emulator executable is used to start the Android emulator directly from the command line. You specify which of the Android Virtual Device (AVD) images to use by providing a single parameter that has the ID of the AVD image with an @ symbol preceding it.

TIP: While it is not mandatory to include the `ANDROID_SDK/tools` directory in your system path, it's definitely worthwhile. Being able to access the `adb` and `emulator` commands without having to specify a full path will definitely save a lot of time. If you haven't already done so, then we'd recommend you do that now.

Given that you now (if you didn't already) have an Android emulator running or a device connected, you can run the build process to create a native Android application from the sample PhoneGap project and see how that looks.

Run the following from the command line, with the created `sample` directory as the current directory:

```
ant debug install
```

This will instruct Ant to execute both the debug and install targets in the `build.xml` file. If the build process completes successfully, you will see the magic words "BUILD SUCCESSFUL" (see Figure 9–5), and at this point you should be able to locate and run the sample PhoneGap application in your emulator.

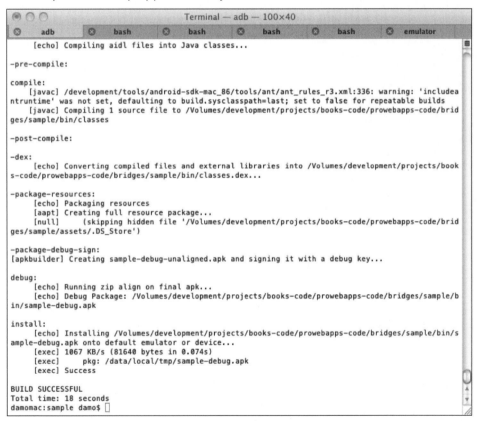

Figure 9–5. *Successful completion of the build and installation of the PhoneGap wrapper application*

If you see a message saying "BUILD FAILED," then unfortunately something has not gone to plan. In most cases, this will be related to the build process not being able to deploy the sample application to the emulator or device. Retrace your steps and recheck the output of the `adb devices` command; you need to see a device listed in the output of this command, and its status should be shown as "device." If the emulator is running but it is either not listed or is marked as "offline," then close and restart the emulator and try again.

Once the application is installed, you will be able to run the application. Note that this does not happen automatically; rather, you need to locate and launch the app as you would any other Android application. Figure 9–6 shows an example of the sample application successfully installed.

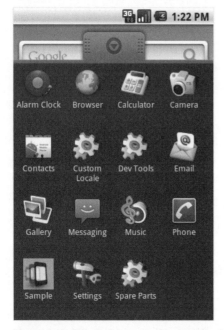

Figure 9–6. *If the build process has gone to plan, the sample application will be shown in the application menu.*

NOTE: With the release of the Android 2.3 SDK (Gingerbread) in early December 2010, a bug was introduced that prevents PhoneGap applications executing for this version of Android (previous versions are unaffected). At the time of writing, this bug is being monitored in the Android issue tracker at the following URL:

`http://code.google.com/p/android/issues/detail?id=12987`.

If you are looking to build and release an Android web application that ships natively using PhoneGap, then this is a very important issue to keep track of. Unfortunately, there is no way of working around this particular bug if deploying your web app with a native wrapper is a priority for you, so we would recommend starring the issue in the issue tracker if it is not resolved by the time you read this chapter.

Let's now have a look at the application. Figure 9–7 shows a screen capture of the sample PhoneGap application.

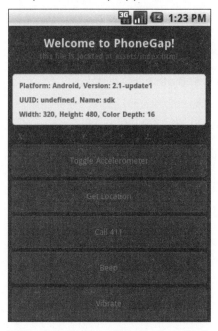

Figure 9–7. *The PhoneGap sample application is running. I wonder what those buttons do?*

With the application now running, we will dive in and have a look at some of the code behind the sample. This will give you an understanding of the kinds of things that you can do using PhoneGap that aren't possible in a standalone web application.

NOTE: Investigating and working with the PhoneGap sample application is best done if you actually have an Android device. This is because the sample works with device-level features (as you would expect) and the behavior of these is pretty limited in the emulator.

You will still be able to look at the code using the emulator, and we will look at alternative ways to monitor the device-level communication, but nothing beats holding your Android phone and having device-level features working from a web application.

Investigating the Sample Application

While dissecting the entire sample is probably overkill, it's worth having a look at the way PhoneGap does a few things. First, we will have a look at how PhoneGap communicates with the device's accelerometer.

Accelerometer Data Capture

As discussed in Chapter 1, PhoneGap provides support for bridging to a number of the device sensors. The accelerometer is one of the more interesting sensors, as it can be used to create some fairly novel interactions for games and other interactive applications.

The code generated in the PhoneGap sample application for monitoring the accelerometer is shown here:

```
var accelerationWatch = false;

var toggleAccel = function() {
    if (accelerationWatch) {
        navigator.accelerometer.clearWatch(accelerationWatch);
        updateAcceleration( {
            x : "",
            y : "",
            z : ""
        });
        accelerationWatch = false;
    } else {
        accelerationWatch = true;
        var options = new Object();
        options.frequency = 1000;
        accelerationWatch = navigator.accelerometer.watchAcceleration(
                updateAcceleration, function(ex) {
                    navigator.accelerometer.clearWatch(accel_watch_id);
                    alert("accel fail (" + ex.name + ": " + ex.message + ")");
                }, options);
    }
};

function updateAcceleration(a) {
    document.getElementById('x').innerHTML = roundNumber(a.x);
```

```
    document.getElementById('y').innerHTML = roundNumber(a.y);
    document.getElementById('z').innerHTML = roundNumber(a.z);
}
```

The preceding code defines a function called `toggleAccel`, which is called in the `onclick` event of the Toggle Accelerometer button (shown in Figure 9–7). As you can see, the code is reasonably trivial, and data is retrieved from the accelerometer by the JavaScript code making a call to the `accelerometer.watchAcceleration` method, which has been attached to the global `navigator` object.

The method takes three parameters:

- The first parameter is for a success callback; it is called when an accelerometer reading has been obtained from the device. When executed, the callback function is passed a single object parameter that has values in the x, y, and z attributes. In the sample application, these values are simply updated on the display via the `updateAcceleration` function.

- The second parameter is for a failure callback, and this is triggered if PhoneGap receives an error while attempting to obtain accelerometer data.

- The third and final parameter specifies options that can be used to influence the retrieval of the accelerometer data. In the sample application, we can see that the frequency of reporting data is set to 1000 milliseconds through the `frequency` option.

We can also see that, if we call the `toggleAccel` function a second time (when the accelerometer is being monitored), monitoring the accelerometer is cancelled via the `accelerometer.clearWatch` function.

Camera and Photo Library

Another useful bridging feature of PhoneGap is the ability to grab a photo from the device. Photos can be imported into the application either from the camera directly or from the user's photo library on the device. The code snippet in the PhoneGap sample is shown here:

```
function show_pic() {
  var viewport = document.getElementById('viewport');
  viewport.style.display = "";
  navigator.camera.getPicture(dump_pic, fail, { quality: 50 });
}

function dump_pic(data) {
  var viewport = document.getElementById('viewport');
  console.log(data);
  viewport.style.display = "";
  viewport.style.position = "absolute";
  viewport.style.top = "10px";
  viewport.style.left = "10px";
  document.getElementById("test_img").src = "data:image/jpeg;base64," + data;
```

```
}

function fail(fail) {
  alert(fail);
}
```

The `show_pic` function in the preceding code is called when the Get Picture button (shown in Figure 9–8) in the sample interface is clicked. To view this button in the emulator or standard DPI device, you will need to scroll down the page.

Figure 9–8. *Scroll down the sample interface to reveal the extra demo buttons.*

Using PhoneGap to retrieve a picture involves calling the `camera.getPicture` method, which is once again attached to the `navigator` object. As you can probably see, `getPicture` uses a method signature similar to `watchAcceleration`, which is used to monitor the accelerometer:

- The first parameter takes a success callback, and this will be called in the case that an image is back from the device.

- The second parameter takes a failure callback, which is called when no image is returned. This includes the situation where the user cancels taking the picture.

- The third and final parameter takes options that affect the behavior of the `getPicture` method. There are three different named options that can be specified for the options object:

- quality *(default:* 80*)*: A numeric value in the range of 1 to 100 that specifies the quality of the image that should be returned. While you may be thinking that you should just set the image quality to 100 so you get the very best image, images with quality values above 90 or so can get large very quickly. It is recommended that the default setting be used.

- destinationType *(default:* DATA_URL*)*: An enumerated value for how the image data should be returned. The two valid JavaScript values that can be specified for this option are Camera.DestinationType.DATA_URL and Camera.DestinationType.FILE_URI. (A comparison between data URLs and file URIs [uniform resource identifiers] can be found in the following note.)

- *sourceType (default:* CAMERA*)*: For Android, this can be specified as one of two values. One is Camera.Picturesourcetype.CAMERA, which specifies retrieving a new image from the camera, and the other is Camera.PictureSourceType.PHOTOLIBRARY, which specifies retrieving an image from the photo library on the device.

With that in mind, if we wanted to retrieve an image from our Android device's photo library rather than the camera, and then wanted to return the file URI for the selected image, the following code would do the trick:

```
navigator.camera.getPicture(successHandler, failureHandler, {
        quality: 50,
        destinationType: Camera.DestinationType.FILE_URI,
        sourceType: Camera.PictureSourceType.PHOTOLIBRARY
    });
```

The result of calling the preceding code would yield a display similar to that shown in Figure 9–9.

Figure 9–9. *PhoneGap can be used to retrieve photos from the photo library as well as the camera.*

NOTE: Previously, we made reference to the use of data and file URIs. Typically, images in HTML are loaded from either a file or an HTTP URI string—for example, `file://resources/test.jpg` and `http://test.com/test.jpg` are examples of a file and an HTTP URI, respectively. While these are the most common ways to load an image (or other resources) into an HTML document, they are not the only way to do so.

Data URIs offer an alternative to referencing an external resource, and are able to encapsulate the actual data that should be displayed. Data URIs can be particularly useful when developing mobile web apps, as resource data can be included within HTML or CSS, or even copied to local storage for caching purposes. This in turn reduces the number of remote requests that need to be made to display a page, which can go a long way toward speeding up a mobile web application.

For more information on the data URI format, the Mozilla Developer Center offers a nice explanation (see `https://developer.mozilla.org/en/The_data_URL_scheme`).

Notification Events

The last example from the PhoneGap sample project that we will work through involves how it exposes functions that allow you to make the phone beep or vibrate. It's reasonably trivial, and the code to make it work is and nice and simple too. Let's take a look:

```
var beep = function(){
    navigator.notification.beep(2);
}

var vibrate = function(){
  navigator.notification.vibrate(0);
}
```

Hooray for simplicity! In the preceding code, PhoneGap attaches a notification object to the global navigator object, and this provides a number of methods. The two that we are accessing here are beep and vibrate.

The beep method takes a single parameter that specifies the number of times that we would like the phone to beep. The vibrate method also takes a single parameter; however, in this instance we are specifying the length of time (in milliseconds) that we would like to phone to vibrate for. While this example is quite trivial, we should not discount the usefulness of being able to perform these kinds of operations using the device. When coupled with the ability to track a user's position and run applications in the background, there are some pretty useful things that we can implement in our applications—especially if we happen to be writing a geosocial game. We will start to look at our game in the next chapter.

A Simple PhoneGap Mapping App

In the last chapter, we worked through a number of examples involving mapping. Let's now look at how we take our final sample from the chapter and embed that in a PhoneGap native wrapper.

As we already have a sample project that has been configured to build correctly, let's copy that directory and create a new project called MapTest.

Tweaking the Sample PhoneGap Project

While the sample project does provide us all the basic building blocks that we need to build our application, there are some things we need to do if we want to actually build a production application on it.

Ideally, this would involve all references to "Sample" being replaced with something more meaningful. This is actually a little trickier than you might expect, but, if you have worked with native Android applications in the past, you should be comfortable with the process. If you haven't, don't worry—we'll walk you through what is required step by step.

First, we need to change the name of the native executable that is created during the build process. This is done using the `android` command-line tools—it's similar to what we did earlier when generating our `local.properties` file. Run the following command from the `maptest` directory:

```
android update project -n maptest -p ./
```

Running this command should produce output similar to that displayed in Figure 9–10.

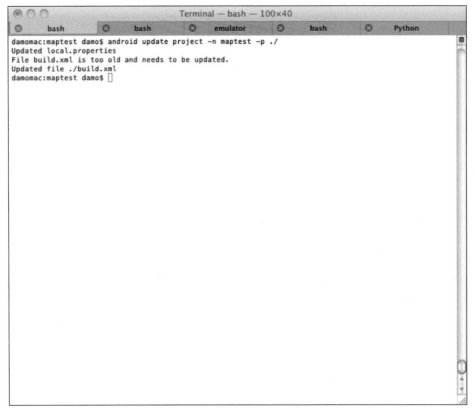

Figure 9–10. *Renaming the sample project to "maptest" is done using the android command-line tool.*

This will update `build.xml`, and means that our application will now be built as `maptest-debug.apk` instead of `sample-debug.apk` when built in debug mode (`ant debug`). All other references to "Sample" remain intact, though, so we need to continue on our mission.

Next up is updating the application title to "MapTest." Making this change means that our application will be shown on the device with the title of "MapTest" in the application menu, rather than "Sample."

To make this change, locate the `strings.xml` file in the `res/values` directory in your MapTest project, and then modify the reference of "Sample" to "MapTest."

The following is what the file should look like after you have made your changes, with the bold text highlighting the change:

```xml
<?xml version="1.0" encoding="utf-8"?>
<resources>
  <string name="app_name">MapTest</string>
  <string name="go">Snap</string>
</resources>
```

At this point, you should be able to build and install the application to the emulator and have it show up as "MapTest" rather than "Sample." So let's try that now. As we did earlier when we were working with the sample application, we'll use Ant to build and install the application to the emulator or device:

```
ant debug install
```

If you have completed the previous steps successfully, you should be able to see a MapTest application now installed in the emulator. An example screen capture is shown in Figure 9–11.

Figure 9–11. *After making some simple updates, our MapTest application is visible in the emulator—but we aren't finished yet.*

Tidying Up: Renaming Classes

We could now quite happily carry on and embed our mapping application into the PhoneGap application without making further changes. Given that we are going to be building applications that we want to deploy to the Android marketplace, it's probably worth looking at what is needed to remove additional references to "Sample" from the PhoneGap sample project.

There aren't too many places we have to do this, but it's worth pointing out that this is a little more complicated than what we did in our previous steps. So, if you would prefer to tackle this once you are actually building a production application instead, you are quite welcome to do so.

First, we need to change the class `com.phonegap.Sample.Sample` to something that makes sense for our application. Depending on the tools you are using, this process can be as simple as pressing a Refactor button and letting the IDE work it out. However, as we are building web apps and our primary tool is a text editor, we will need to make the change in a few more places. So let's begin:

1. Update the `com/phonegap/Sample` directory structure to match something more in line with what we are building. Something like `com/prowebapps/maptest` is a good choice.

2. Next, rename the `sample.java` file `MapTest.java`, as this better represents the application we are building.

3. Finally, you will need to update the contents of the Java file, and change the `com.phonegap.sample` and `sample` references to `com.prowebapps.maptest` and `MapTest`, respectively.

The following is a sample of what the `MapTest.java` file might look like after you have completed the necessary changes:

```
package com.prowebapps.maptest;

import android.app.Activity;
import android.os.Bundle;
import com.phonegap.*;

public class MapTest extends DroidGap
{
    @Override
    public void onCreate(Bundle savedInstanceState)
    {
        super.onCreate(savedInstanceState);
        super.loadUrl("file:///android_asset/www/index.html");
    }
}
```

Once the Java source file has been modified, we are halfway there. Now we just need to update the `AndroidManifest.xml` file in the project root directory to reflect the changes we have made. Once again, this involves modifying the `com.phonegap.Sample` reference to `com.prowebapps.maptest` and the `Sample` reference to `MapTest`.

The following is an example of what the `AndroidManifest.xml` file would look like after the changes. Once again, the modified sections are marked in bold.

```
<?xml version="1.0" encoding="utf-8"?>
<manifest xmlns:android="http://schemas.android.com/apk/res/android"
      package="com.prowebapps.maptest" android:versionName="1.1"
android:versionCode="1">
    <supports-screens
```

```
            android:largeScreens="true"
            android:normalScreens="true"
            android:smallScreens="true"
            android:resizeable="true"
            android:anyDensity="true"
            />
    <uses-permission android:name="android.permission.CAMERA" />
    <uses-permission android:name="android.permission.VIBRATE" />
    <uses-permission android:name="android.permission.ACCESS_COARSE_LOCATION" />
    <uses-permission android:name="android.permission.ACCESS_FINE_LOCATION" />
    <uses-permission android:name="android.permission.ACCESS_LOCATION_EXTRA_COMMANDS" />
    <uses-permission android:name="android.permission.READ_PHONE_STATE" />
    <uses-permission android:name="android.permission.INTERNET" />
    <uses-permission android:name="android.permission.RECEIVE_SMS" />
    <uses-permission android:name="android.permission.RECORD_AUDIO" />
    <uses-permission android:name="android.permission.MODIFY_AUDIO_SETTINGS" />
    <uses-permission android:name="android.permission.READ_CONTACTS" />
    <uses-permission android:name="android.permission.WRITE_CONTACTS" />
    <uses-permission android:name="android.permission.WRITE_EXTERNAL_STORAGE" />
    <uses-permission android:name="android.permission.ACCESS_NETWORK_STATE" />

    <application android:icon="@drawable/icon" android:label="@string/app_name"
        android:debuggable="true">
        <activity android:name=".MapTest"
                android:label="@string/app_name"
android:configChanges="orientation|keyboardHidden">
            <intent-filter>
                <action android:name="android.intent.action.MAIN" />
                <category android:name="android.intent.category.LAUNCHER" />
            </intent-filter>
        </activity>
    </application>
    <uses-sdk android:minSdkVersion="2" />
</manifest>
```

That should do it. To make sure you haven't made any typos, rebuild the application and attempt to run it in the emulator. If you made an error somewhere along the way, then a screen like Figure 9–12 will be displayed.

Figure 9–12. *Typos can occur while renaming classes in the sample project, resulting in application crashes.*

If you do see an error while trying to load your application, then double-check that the activity name in the AndroidManifest.xml file matches the name you gave to the main application class, bearing in mind case-sensitivity.

This brings us to the point where things are structured correctly for building our test mapping application. When deploying a production application, there are still a few additional things to cover (such as updating the application icon to something other than the default), but we will cover those in Chapter 11.

For now, let's continue to focus on getting some existing HTML code into our PhoneGap wrapper.

Transferring Existing Code into a PhoneGap App

In the last chapter, we put a fair bit of effort into our boilerplate mapping application, so we will use those files in the new MapTest project as well.

We will work through the process of embedding the application step by step here:

1. Copy the mapapp.html, mapapp.css, and mapapp.js files from the snippets directory into the assets/www folder of our new MapTest project.

2. Copy the entire img directory that accompanies the mapapp.html file to the assets/www folder also. This will result in the four images being stored in the assets/www/img directory.

3. Copy `jquery-1.4.2.min.js` from the shared `js` library of our sample code into the `assets/www` folder also.

4. Delete the existing `index.html` and `master.css` files from the `assets/www` folder, but leave `phonegap.js`, as it will be required to enable the bridging calls.

5. Rename the `mapapp.html` file to `index.html` so it becomes the file that is opened with the native application is launched. At this point, the folder structure of the `assets/www` folder should look like Figure 9–13. If your folder structure matches, then continue on and make the modifications to the `index.html` file to reference the updated file locations. These are outlined in the final two steps.

NOTE: While we have been very good at referencing and reusing libraries such as jQuery from a central location for the examples in the book so far, once we start working with a PhoneGap project, we aren't able to do that anymore.

We will instead have to copy these shared resources into the `assets/www` folder; otherwise, they will not be transferred as part of the native bundle. When working with larger projects, we would additionally recommend implementing some kind of build script to handle transferring the required resources into your bridge application. This will make it simpler to work on a central code base that is able to be deployed directly to the Web and also through native wrappers like PhoneGap.

For more information on build tools, we recommend looking at Apache Ant (`http://ant.apache.org`) given the Android platform is Java based; however, if you are looking for build alternatives, then Rake (`www.rubyrake.org`) is also worth a look.

Figure 9–13. *The structure of the assets/www folder in the MapTest PhoneGap project*

6. Make some tweaks to the new index.html and mapapp.js files so that they reference the files stored within the assets/www folder and nothing above that. The only modification that is required is changing the path of the jQuery library to reference the one stored in the assets/www folder instead of the shared location we have been using.

7. Include phonegap.js in the main HTML file so we can use the bridging functions provided by PhoneGap.

The modifications to the updated index.html file (previously mapapp.html) are shown here:

```
<!DOCTYPE html>
<html>
<head>
<meta name="viewport" content="initial-scale=1.0, user-scalable=no" />
<link rel="stylesheet" media="screen" href="mapapp.css" />
<script type="text/javascript" src="jquery-1.4.2.min.js"></script>
<script type="text/javascript" src="mapapp.js"></script>
<script type="text/javascript" src="phonegap.js"></script>
<script type="text/javascript" src="http://maps.google.com/maps/api/js?sensor=false">
</script>
<script type="text/javascript">
function initialize() {
```

```
        var latlng = new google.maps.LatLng(-33.866, 151.209);

        MAPAPP.init(latlng, 13);
        MAPAPP.addMarker(latlng, 'Sydney', 'Sydney Australia');
        MAPAPP.addMarker(new google.maps.LatLng(-33.859, 151.209), 'The Rocks');
        MAPAPP.addMarker(new google.maps.LatLng(-33.857, 151.215), 'Sydney Opera House');
        MAPAPP.addMarker(new google.maps.LatLng(-33.861, 151.211), 'Circular Quay');

        // update the map display
        MAPAPP.updateDisplay();
    } // initialize
    </script>
    </head>
    <body onload="initialize()">
    <h1 class="simple floating">Mapping App Boilerplate</h1>
    <div id="map_canvas" style="width:100%; height:100%"></div>
    <div id="marker-nav">
        <img src="img/navigation-arrow.png" class="left disabled" />
        <span class='marker-title'>Test Text</span>
        <img src="img/navigation-arrow.png" class="right" />
    </div>
    <div id="marker-detail" class="child-screen">
        <div class='content'>Some Test Content</div>
        <button class='close'>Close</button>
    </div>
    </body>
    </html>
```

As you can see, although we went through a number of steps to copy the files across, only very simple changes are required to the HTML. Our web application is now all wrapped up in PhoneGap and can be deployed as a native application. This is done by once again building the application (using Ant) to redeploy the application to the emulator.

A screen capture from the emulator running our native MapTest application is shown in Figure 9–14.

Figure 9–14. *Our boilerplate mapping application wrapped up as a PhoneGap native application*

If you get a different result and the map does not display as expected, then try running the following command and look for possible JavaScript errors:

```
adb logcat
```

For instance, Figure 9–15 shows some example output when the jQuery JavaScript included in the index.html file isn't updated correctly.

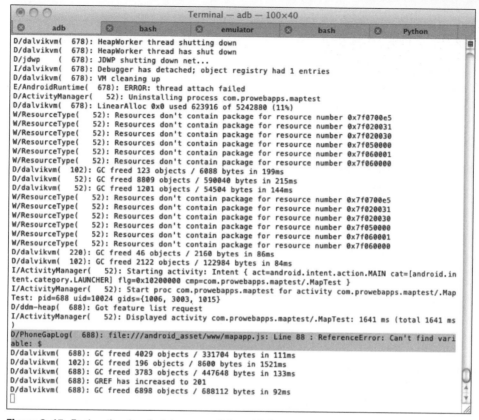

```
D/dalvikvm( 678): HeapWorker thread shutting down
D/dalvikvm( 678): HeapWorker thread has shut down
D/jdwp   ( 678): JDWP shutting down net...
I/dalvikvm( 678): Debugger has detached; object registry had 1 entries
D/dalvikvm( 678): VM cleaning up
E/AndroidRuntime( 678): ERROR: thread attach failed
D/ActivityManager( 52): Uninstalling process com.prowebapps.maptest
D/dalvikvm( 678): LinearAlloc 0x0 used 623916 of 5242880 (11%)
W/ResourceType( 52): Resources don't contain package for resource number 0x7f0700e5
W/ResourceType( 52): Resources don't contain package for resource number 0x7f020031
W/ResourceType( 52): Resources don't contain package for resource number 0x7f020030
W/ResourceType( 52): Resources don't contain package for resource number 0x7f050000
W/ResourceType( 52): Resources don't contain package for resource number 0x7f060001
W/ResourceType( 52): Resources don't contain package for resource number 0x7f060000
D/dalvikvm( 102): GC freed 123 objects / 6088 bytes in 199ms
D/dalvikvm( 52): GC freed 8809 objects / 590040 bytes in 215ms
D/dalvikvm( 52): GC freed 1201 objects / 54504 bytes in 144ms
W/ResourceType( 52): Resources don't contain package for resource number 0x7f0700e5
W/ResourceType( 52): Resources don't contain package for resource number 0x7f020031
W/ResourceType( 52): Resources don't contain package for resource number 0x7f020030
W/ResourceType( 52): Resources don't contain package for resource number 0x7f050000
W/ResourceType( 52): Resources don't contain package for resource number 0x7f060001
W/ResourceType( 52): Resources don't contain package for resource number 0x7f060000
D/dalvikvm( 220): GC freed 46 objects / 2160 bytes in 86ms
D/dalvikvm( 102): GC freed 2122 objects / 122984 bytes in 84ms
I/ActivityManager( 52): Starting activity: Intent { act=android.intent.action.MAIN cat=[android.in
tent.category.LAUNCHER] flg=0x10200000 cmp=com.prowebapps.maptest/.MapTest }
I/ActivityManager( 52): Start proc com.prowebapps.maptest for activity com.prowebapps.maptest/.Map
Test: pid=688 uid=10024 gids={1006, 3003, 1015}
D/ddm-heap( 688): Got feature list request
I/ActivityManager( 52): Displayed activity com.prowebapps.maptest/.MapTest: 1641 ms (total 1641 ms
)
D/PhoneGapLog( 688): file:///android_asset/www/mapapp.js: Line 88 : ReferenceError: Can't find vari
able: $
D/dalvikvm( 688): GC freed 4029 objects / 331704 bytes in 111ms
D/dalvikvm( 102): GC freed 196 objects / 8600 bytes in 1521ms
D/dalvikvm( 688): GC freed 3783 objects / 447648 bytes in 133ms
D/dalvikvm( 688): GREF has increased to 201
D/dalvikvm( 688): GC freed 6898 objects / 688112 bytes in 92ms
```

Figure 9–15. *For locating JavaScript errors, adb logcat is invaluable.*

As mentioned earlier, Appendix A contains more information on debugging Android web apps (and JavaScript) in general, so, if things aren't going to plan, it's well worth a look.

Summary

In this chapter, we looked at PhoneGap and explored the capabilities it offers. Additionally, we walked you through the changes that need to be made to correctly structure the sample application provided with a PhoneGap release for distribution at a later stage.

Finally, we took the boilerplate mapping application that we built in the previous chapter and examined what was required to package that code in a PhoneGap wrapper.

In the next chapter, we will start putting together the building blocks that we have worked through in the previous two chapters, and actually get into putting some code together for our geosocial game, Moundz.

Chapter 10

Integrating with Social APIs

Now that we've put many of the foundations in place, we can start putting together our geosocial game application. In this chapter, we'll build a game called Moundz. Moundz is a geosocial game that piggybacks off existing geosocial networks such as Foursquare and Gowalla. The general concept is that geosocial check-ins of people around the world become resources. These resources are then collected and redeployed in a quest for virtual world domination. In Moundz, players help to build ant mounds that become their strongholds, from which they can launch an assault on enemy territory. Only the strong and diligent will survive.

Interested? Well, let's get started.

Connecting to Web APIs

One of the best things you can do as an application developer is consider what other existing web applications you can hook into to service some of the needs of your app. This will not only save a significant amount of development required to build your application, but will likely provide you access to an established group of users that are actively using another application.

For instance, in Moundz we are going to need some kind of geographically located resources that people playing the game can "mine" to build their "bases." Rather than building our own database of locations, we are much better served by tapping into an existing application that provides that kind of data already.

As it turns out, geosocial networks like Gowalla and Foursquare have exactly the kind of information we need, and they both provide an API that exposes their data. Like most things in life, though, it's not quite that easy. The majority of APIs that have been built usually offer integration via XML and sometimes JSON, but, when you are building an application that is going to be "mashed up" at the client, you often need something called JSONP support. The next section gives an overview as to why.

What Is JSONP?

Essentially, JSONP is a workaround to a problem we will look at throughout this section. It involves a clever technique that web developers started using to get around what is known as the *same-origin policy* (http://en.wikipedia.org/wiki/Same_origin_policy), which is enforced in web browsers. With the same-origin policy in place, JavaScript code running in a browser is prevented from making an XMLHttpRequest (http://en.wikipedia.org/wiki/XMLHttpRequest) to a URL that is different from the domain the script is running from. Therefore, if you attempt to access an application's API from a client-side script running on a separate domain, the browser will step in and prevent it from happening.

To illustrate the problem, we will work through a small example. For example, consider the following code, which accesses the public Twitter API (see http://dev.twitter.com for more information) and displays the tweets on the page.

```html
<html>
<script src="../../js/jquery-1.4.2.min.js"></script>
<script>
function showData(data) {
    var tweetItems = '';

    if (! data) {
        tweetItems = '<li><strong>Could not retrieve tweets.</strong></li>';
    }
    else {
        for (var ii = 0; ii < data.length; ii++) {
            tweetItems += '<li>' + data[ii].text + '</li>';
        } // for
    }

    $('#tweets').html(tweetItems);
} // showData

$(document).ready(function() {
    // make the request to the geonames server
    $.ajax({
        url: 'http://api.twitter.com/1/statuses/public_timeline.json',
        dataType: 'json',
        success: showData
    });
});
</script>
<body>
    <ul id="tweets">
    </ul>
</body>
</html>
```

The sample itself is simple enough—we make a request to the endpoint for the Twitter public timeline and then parse the response, filling the #tweets element with the tweets retrieved.

Let's run that now. So that you can easily look at what's going on in the background, we recommend working through this sample in your desktop browser. (We will be using Chrome.) Figure 10–1 shows the output generated from attempting to access the Twitter API using JSON from our local web server.

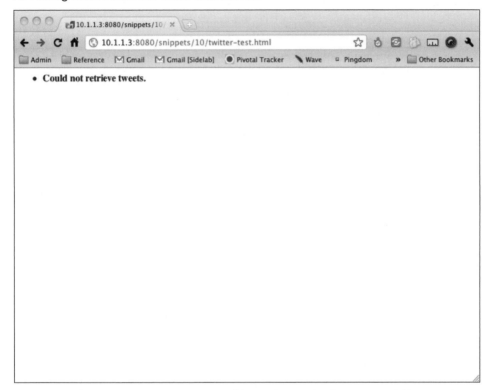

Figure 10–1. *Attempting to access the Twitter JSON API from our local web server yields no results.*

Unfortunately, Figure 10–1 really doesn't give us much idea as to what is going on— except for the fact that our error-handling code is working correctly. So it's time to dig in a little. For this sample, we will be using the WebKit Inspector (see Appendix A for more details on debugging tools) to have a look behind the scenes. If you are using Chrome, try looking in the View ➤ Developer menu for the developer tools. Other browsers offer similar tools, so feel free to use your preferred toolset here.

Figure 10–2 shows the network view from the Chrome developer tools.

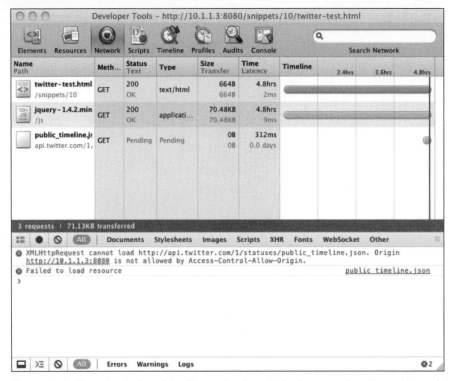

Figure 10–2. *The network view of the Chrome developer tools shows us where the problem exists.*

The network view in the developer tools confirms that the browser has indeed blocked the cross-domain request in accordance with the same-origin policy.

This is where a JSONP workaround comes into play. JSONP works within the bounds of the same-origin policy, using rules that permit `script` includes from other domains. So, whereas a standard JSON request occurs via the XMLHttpRequest mechanism, a JSONP request is inserted and run as a `script` tag. This may sound a little confusing and take some time to get your head around if you haven't come across JSONP before.

Well, let's update our Twitter sample to use JSONP and see if we can gain an understanding of what's going on.

```
<html>
<script src="../../js/jquery-1.4.2.min.js"></script>
<script>
function showData(data) {
    var tweetItems = '';

    if (! data) {
        tweetItems = '<li><strong>Count not retrieve tweets.</strong></li>';
    }
    else {
        for (var ii = 0; ii < data.length; ii++) {
            tweetItems += '<li>' + data[ii].text + '</li>';
        } // for
```

```
    }

    $('#tweets').html(tweetItems);
} // showData

$(document).ready(function() {
    // make the request to the geonames server
    $.ajax({
        url: 'http://api.twitter.com/1/statuses/public_timeline.json',
        dataType: 'jsonp',
        success: showData
    });
});
</script>
<body>
    <ul id="tweets">
    </ul>
</body>
</html>
```

The preceding code shows the modification required to have our test application communicate via JSONP rather than JSON. You can see here that jQuery does an excellent job of abstracting the complexity of JSONP away from us behind its $.ajax function. Figure 10–3 shows an example of the output generated by the modified sample.

Figure 10–3. *Using JSONP, we can now retrieve the tweets of the world via the Twitter public timeline.*

Now that we have looked at how simple it is to have jQuery issue a JSONP request for us, let's take a quick look at what is going on behind the scenes. To achieve this, we will make a copy of our `twitter-test.html` file and replace the previous `showData` function with the following code:

```
function showData(data) {
    var tweetItems = '';

    for (var ii = 0; ii < document.scripts.length; ii++) {
        var script = document.scripts[ii];

        if (script.src) {
            tweetItems += '<li>' + script.src + '</li>';
        } // if
    } // for

    $('#tweets').html(tweetItems);
} // showData
```

So, rather than outputting the text of the tweets to the HTML, we are now writing out the source file location of any scripts that are currently included in the page. Figure 10–4 shows an example of what is displayed.

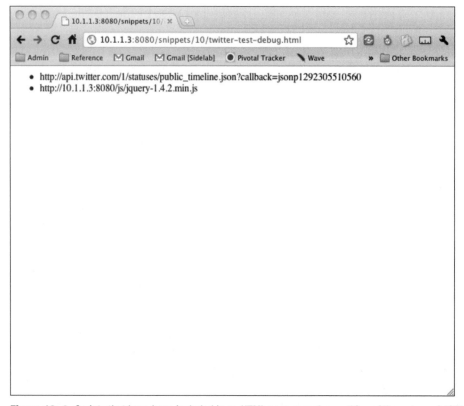

Figure 10–4. *Scripts that have been included in an HTML page reveal something of the nature of JSONP.*

Ah, there we go—our call to Twitter has been included as a separate script in our page, but this doesn't explain how we get the data back into our application. For that, we need to dig a little further. Figure 10–5 shows an example of the output that Twitter is generating when we call the script shown on this page.

Figure 10–5. *Example output of the Twitter API when called using JSONP*

Things are starting to make sense now—the included script passes data back through a function call. However, this is not a function that we have defined, but rather a function that has been created by jQuery with the specific purpose of receiving the data from the JSONP call. Once the jQuery function has received the data, it simply passes that information along to the callback that we provided when we made our `$.ajax` call.

> **NOTE:** In general, you are probably better off using a JavaScript library such as jQuery to handle your JSONP calls, given the steps that are involved in getting it working. While we have covered some of what goes on behind the scenes here, it is far from an exhaustive list of the work that needs to be done. For further information, the following blog post provides a lightweight script that shows how JSONP works, and also provides an alternative to some of the more heavyweight implementations in jQuery and the like:
>
> `www.nonobtrusive.com/2010/05/20/lightweight-jsonp-without-any-3rd-party-`
> `libraries`.

Dealing with APIs That Lack JSONP Support

In the instances where an API does not provide JSONP access, what are the options? This is a pretty important question in our case, as at the time of writing neither Gowalla nor Foursquare supports JSONP-style calls in its API.

We will briefly look at three different options that will provide us access to web services that do not provide JSONP-style access.

Writing a Server-Side Proxy

Before JSONP became a popular option for writing client-side "mashups," developers would traditionally write their own set of web services that would proxy the remote services. These web services would be deployed to the same domain that would serve the application, and this would mean no calls violated the same-origin policy. The implementation of such a solution will vary depending on the language you are working with, and the implementation details are beyond the scope of this book, but there is a lot of good information out there if this is something that you require.

Another alternative to writing your own server-side proxy, given that JSONP is now available to you, is to use a third-party service to wrap web services that provide only a JSON implementation with JSONP. A couple of good examples of this are the following:

- `http://jsonpify.heroku.com`
- `http://jsonproxy.appspot.com`

Both services have source code available and are hosted in cloud-hosting services, so you can modify them to suit your own specific requirements.

Yahoo Query Language

Yahoo Query Language (YQL) is fantastic; there really aren't enough nice things that can be said about it. It is essentially a very robust and generic proxy that can be used to request data from varying sources and return it in a standardized XML or JSON (with JSONP support) format.

Interacting with YQL is done through the use of an SQL-like syntax, which is where the QL part of the name comes from. Figure 10–6 shows a screenshot of the developer console, which is one of the core tools of the YQL suite. The console can be found at `http://developer.yahoo.com/yql/console`.

Figure 10–6. *The developer console is a great place to begin to understand the possibilities of YQL.*

One of the really nice things about YQL is its use of *data tables*. These data tables provide YQL information on how to interact and obtain information from various services around the Web. When you first load the YQL console, you will probably see around 160 data tables initially available, and these relate mostly to tables that interface with other Yahoo! services. By accessing the community tables (which you can do by selecting the Show Community Tables link on the right), you gain access to almost 1,000 different tables that you can interact with, and both Foursquare and Gowalla tables are included in this set.

In Foursquare's case, the following is a YQL query that is designed to interact with its venues API endpoint:

```
select *
from foursquare.venues
where geolat="33.7772869"
and geolong="-84.3976068"
```

In addition to running requests through the console, you can execute YQL through a set of published web services. In each case, a REST query for the information is displayed at the bottom of the console interface. This REST query can then be copied and pasted into your own client-side JavaScript—for instance, directly into a jQuery `ajax` function call. We won't include a sample URL here, as these are fairly unreadable, since they contain the escaped SQL statement as part of the query. It is fairly simple to recognize an application using YQL though (using the developer tools of course), as it will be routing requests through `http://query.yahooapis.com/v1/public/`.

While it would be great to go into more depth on YQL, we won't be using it to solve our current issue for accessing Foursquare or Gowalla (the reasons for this will be outlined very soon), so that would be counterproductive. However, it is definitely worth a look when you have the time, as it can definitely be extremely useful.

PhoneGap Native App

As strange as it may seem, using PhoneGap as a native wrapper actually provides you some additional advantages beyond what we have been talking about so far. PhoneGap accesses the HTML, CSS, and JS files for the mobile application using the *file* URI scheme (`http://en.wikipedia.org/wiki/File_URI_scheme`) rather than HTTP (or HTTPS). In doing this, PhoneGap actually circumvents most of the security restrictions that are placed on web applications and pages that are loaded from a web server.

This is more of a side effect than a design feature, and it is not something that will be available in all bridging frameworks. As such, it is recommended that you only use this workaround when you are sure that you will be deploying your mobile web application only via PhoneGap.

Introducing the Geominer API

In the previous section, we looked at a number of different strategies for dealing with an API that doesn't support JSONP requests. We now have to decide which one we want to use. Before we do that, let's consider our available tools and design goals for the project:

- While the YQL solution is elegant, the preferred geosocial API is Gowalla (given some excellent API features), and the current YQL community datatables (`www.datatables.org`) for Gowalla don't support all of the Gowalla API features.

- In Moundz, we will be using Twitter for authenticating users rather than writing our own login system. We will go into this process in more detail soon, but for now let's just say that, at the time of writing, Twitter does a better job of offering mobile-friendly experiences through its more established APIs. While it recently released a JavaScript toolset called Twitter Anywhere (`http://dev.twitter.com/anywhere`), login features are still very desktop oriented.

- Our primary focus in this book is building Android web apps, which means that, while using PhoneGap would be a suitable workaround, the deployment of the app as a standalone web application would not be an option. This is less than ideal.

Based on these factors, it is probably best for us to implement our own server-side API that will handle the interaction with other application APIs for us, and provide a single JSONP-enabled API that both our mobile web application and others could deal with. Figure 10–7 shows how this API provides some "middleware" for building our geosocial game.

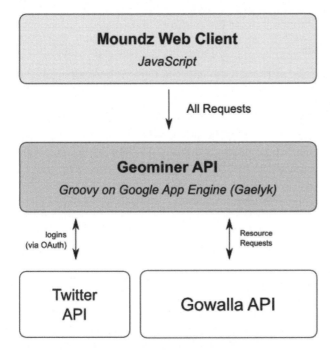

Figure 10–7. *The Moundz API aggregates our multiple external APIs into a single interface.*

Given that the title of this book is not *Building API Mashups with Google App Engine*, we won't be going into great depth about the work required on the server side. We will instead be focusing on how to use the API to build our mobile application on the client side.

Additionally, rather than build an API that is suited only to the needs of the Moundz sample application, we will build the Geominer API as generically as possible. This way, if you feel inspired to write an application similar to Moundz, you should be able to use the information in these last few chapters of the book and the Geominer API to create your own masterpiece.

For more information on the Geominer API and an inside look at the source code showing how it was built, check out the source code on GitHub, at `http://github.com/sidelab/geominer`.

Well, that's enough talk—let's write some code.

Locating Resources in Moundz

The first step to world domination in Moundz is collecting resources with which to start to build your ant mound. Your mound is essentially your base, which you will build over time, and you will need to mine resources from locations around your area and bring them back to your base. This is where the geosocial network data comes in—it supplies the base data that the Geominer API uses to feed the game data.

Essentially, the process is as follows:

1. Moundz requests resource data for resources near the current position from the Geominer API.

2. Geominer passes the request to the Gowalla API and receives a list of Gowalla "spots" back for the specified position. This includes the total number of check-ins that have been made for each spot. If you are interested, have a look at the Gowalla API Explorer (http://gowalla.com/api/explorer)—we are using the list method of the spots endpoint.

3. Geominer then returns a subset of the information received from Gowalla, with a value for resources available. This value is equal to the total number of check-ins for the spot, less any resources already mined from that location since the game started.

4. Moundz displays the information received.

With that in mind, let's start putting the skeleton of the Moundz application together and implement a Nearby Resources screen. We will base the general structure for the Moundz application on our mapping application boilerplate, so let's create a new directory for Moundz and copy the boilerplate files there.

The simplest place to take a copy of the files from will be the directory that we were working in when implementing our PhoneGap wrapper in the previous chapter. So, copy the files from /bridges/maptest/assets/www to /moundz. Once you have done this, you should have a directory structure that looks similar to Figure 10–8.

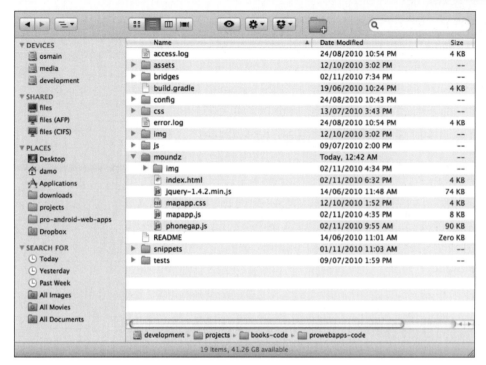

Figure 10–8. *We will use our work from Chapter 9 for the starting point of the Moundz app.*

Then just a few tidy-ups are required before we can get into coding our game. First, rename `mapapp.js` and `mapapp.css` to `moundz.js` and `moundz.css`, respectively.

Next, change the name of the `MAPAPP` module to `MOUNDZ`, as shown in the following code sample:

```
MOUNDZ = (function() {
    ...

    var module = {
        ...
    };

    return module;
})();
```

And finally, make the following updates to the `index.html` file:

- Remove (or comment out) the script include for `phonegap.js`, but leave the actual script there, as we will use it later when we bundle Moundz as a native app for marketplace distribution.

- Replace references to `mapapp.js` and `mapapp.css` with the Moundz equivalents.

- Replace references to `MAPAPP` with `MOUNDZ`.

Once those changes have been completed, your index.html file should appear similar to the following sample. The lines that have been modified are shown in bold.

```
<!DOCTYPE html>
<html>
<head>
<meta name="viewport" content="initial-scale=1.0, user-scalable=no" />
<link rel="stylesheet" media="screen" href="moundz.css" />
<script type="text/javascript" src="jquery-1.4.2.min.js"></script>
<script type="text/javascript" src="moundz.js"></script>
<!-- <script type="text/javascript" src="phonegap.js"></script> -->
<script type="text/javascript" src="http://maps.google.com/maps/api/js?sensor=false">
</script>
<script type="text/javascript">
function initialize() {
    var latlng = new google.maps.LatLng(-33.866, 151.209);

    MOUNDZ.init(latlng, 13);
    MOUNDZ.updateDisplay();
} // initialize
</script>
</head>
<body onload="initialize()">
<h1 class="simple floating">Moundz</h1>
<div id="map_canvas" style="width:100%; height:100%"></div>
<div id="marker-nav">
    <img src="img/navigation-arrow.png" class="left disabled" />
    <span class='marker-title'>Test Text</span>
    <img src="img/navigation-arrow.png" class="right" />
</div>
<div id="marker-detail" class="child-screen">
    <div class='content'>Some Test Content</div>
    <button class='close'>Close</button>
</div>
</body>
</html>
```

With the application template complete, we are ready to start putting the elements of our game together.

Finding Nearby Resources with the Geominer API

Again, the first step is gathering resources with which to build your base. As stated previously, resources are actually geosocial network check-ins that have been collected from either Foursquare or Gowalla (depending on the game).

To find nearby resources, we will use the Geominer API resources search in combination with the Geolocation API that we looked at in Chapter 6. The Geominer resources search follows the naming convention for all web services in the Geominer suite. The following is the URL that we will be using for Moundz:
http://api.geominer.net/v1/moundz/resources.

Each web service in Geominer follows the basic format of
`http://api.geominer.net/`*api-version*`/`*appid*`/`*webservice*`/`*method*. The following list
describes the details:

- *api-version* relates to the version of the Geominer API that we are
  using. We are using version 1, so this becomes v1.

- *appid* refers to the application that is currently accessing the Geominer
  services. The Moundz application has been configured to use the
  Moundz application ID, so this becomes moundz.

- *webservice* refers to the particular group of tools that we are using in
  the Geominer toolbox. In this case, we are using the resources tools.

- *method* is used to indicate the particular operation that we are
  executing with the tools that we are using. This particular section of
  the call can be omitted if we want to access the default operation for
  the webservice. In the case of the resources tools, this is a search
  operation, which is what we wish to use, so this section can be
  omitted.

We will now add some functionality to our MOUNDZ module to enable us to retrieve those
resources through the Geominer API:

```
MOUNDZ = (function() {
    // initialize constants
    var DEFAULT_ZOOM = 8,
        GEOMINER_MOUNDZ_URL = 'http://api.geominer.net/v1/moundz';

    ...

    function findResources(callback) {
        // get the map center position
        var center = map.getCenter();

        $.ajax({
            url: GEOMINER_MOUNDZ_URL + '/resources',
            dataType: 'jsonp',
            data: {
                lat: center.lat(),
                lng: center.lng()
            },
            success: function(data) {
                processResourceSearch(data);
                if (callback) {
                    callback();
                } // if
            }
        });
    } // findResources

    ...

    var module = {
```

```
            addMarker: addMarker,
            clearMarkers: clearMarkers,

            findResources: findResources,

            ...
        };

        return module;
    })();
```

The preceding code shows the modifications required. We are adding a findResources
function to our MOUNDZ module that will find resources based on the current map center
position. The majority of this function is a jQuery Ajax call using JSONP, as we used
earlier to access the Geonames data when first getting an understanding of JSONP.
When we receive successful results from Geominer, these are passed to the
processResourceSearch function. Let's have a look at this function and its associated
code now.

```
function markResources(resourceType, deposits) {
    for (var ii = 0; ii < deposits.length; ii++) {
        // add the marker for the resource deposit
        addMarker(
            new google.maps.LatLng(deposits[ii].lat, deposits[ii].lng),
            deposits[ii].name,
            '<div class="resinfo">' + deposits[ii].total +
            ' resources at this location</div>');
    } // for
} // markResources

function processResourceSearch(data) {
    // clear any existing markers
    clearMarkers();

    // iterate through the resource types and pin
    for (var ii = 0; ii < data.resourceTypes.length; ii++) {
        var resType = data.resourceTypes[ii];

        // mark the resources
        markResources(resType.typeName, resType.deposits);
    } // for
} // processResourceSearch
```

The two functions in this code are included in the MOUNDZ module as internal functions.
As you saw in the findResources function, processResourceSearch is called when we
have received a successful response from the Geominer API. When this happens,
existing markers are first removed, and then new markers are added for each of the
different resource types that have been retrieved from the API.

In the case of Moundz, we have only one type of resource for the sake of simplicity, but
we have implemented a for loop here to enable us to support additional resource types
with relative ease if that is something that is desired at a later stage.

For each of the resource types, the markResources function is called to display markers
on the map as per the boilerplate mapping application that we explored in Chapter 8.

All we need to do now is to adjust the index.html file to make the call to the findResources function of the MOUNDZ module when the page is loaded:

```
<script type="text/javascript">
function initialize() {
    var latlng = new google.maps.LatLng(-33.866, 151.209);

    MOUNDZ.init(latlng, 17);
    MOUNDZ.findResources(function() {
        MOUNDZ.updateDisplay();
    });
} // initialize
</script>
```

For the moment, we will leave out the location-detection part just to check that everything operates correctly. This leaves us having to make only a very simple change to our initialize function (shown in bold). Additionally, we increase the zoom level to 17 from 13, which is more appropriate given the results we will get back from Geominer (courtesy of Gowalla in this initial case). Figure 10–9 shows an example of what we should see if everything has gone according to plan.

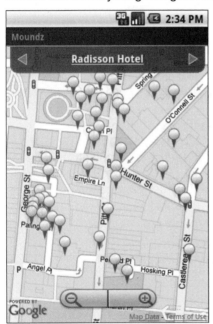

Figure 10–9. *For Moundz, the Geominer API returns a list of Gowalla spots near the center of the map.*

As with our earlier work with the boilerplate mapping application, the resource locations can be selected either by tapping a marker or by navigating using the left and right navigation arrows. Additionally, more detail for that location can be displayed by tapping the title of the location as before. At this stage, we have included some simple debug information about the number of resources available. Figure 10–10 shows the example debug information that we have included for the moment.

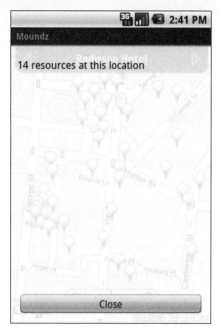

Figure 10–10. *We will expand the resource information screen to include actions relating to the resource.*

Using Geolocation to Track Your Position

Before we move on to including those extra features in the application, let's make the modifications required to have the application use our current location instead of the static testing location that we have been using so far. Chapter 6 gave an introduction to the Geolocation API and the getCurrentPosition method. However, for Moundz it would be great if we could *track* the user's location rather than just get the location in a single-shot request.

This is actually very simple, and will involve replacing all of the code that we were using in the index.html initialize function with a run function in the moundz.js file as per the following code:

```
MOUNDZ = (function() {
    ...

    // initialize variables
    var map = null,
        ...
        posWatchId = 0;

    ...

    function run(zoomLevel) {
        // check that the watch hasn't already been set up
        // if it has, then exit, as we don't want two watches...
        if (posWatchId !== 0) {
            return;
```

```
    } // if

    // create the watch
    posWatchId = navigator.geolocation.watchPosition(
        function(position) {
            var pos = new google.maps.LatLng(
                position.coords.latitude,
                position.coords.longitude);

            if (map) {
                map.panTo(pos);
            }
            else {
                module.init(pos, zoomLevel ? zoomLevel : 15);
            } // if..else

            findResources(function() {
                module.updateDisplay();
            });
        },
        null,
        {
            enableHighAccuracy: true
        });
} // run
...

var module = {
    ...
    run: run,
    ...
};

    return module;
})();
```

The `run` function defined in the preceding code is exposed through the `MOUNDZ` module and provides a simple interface for setting up the Geolocation `watchPosition` method.

The `watchPosition` method provides a mechanism for us to access the user's position, and then to continue to monitor the position for changes. By monitoring the user's position, we will be able to update the display as they move around, which is ideal when building games and other such interactive applications.

> **NOTE:** As mentioned in Chapter 1, there is overhead involved when regularly accessing a device's current position. So, while the preceding code is effective at monitoring the user's position accurately, it's important that we provide the ability to turn it off to allow people to conserve battery life on their mobile device.
>
> Notice that in the preceding code we obtain an ID that relates to the position watch that has been created, and we will be able to use this later to stop monitoring the location.

While the `watchPosition` method differs in the number of times that the callback passed to it will be executed, the data returned in the callback is identical to the `getCurrentPosition` method, which we investigated previously. Basically, the `watchPosition` method will be called until the `clearWatch` method is called, whereas `getCurrentPosition` will execute once and once only. For instance, in the preceding code, the value that we assign to the `posWatchId` variable could be passed to the `clearWatch` function, and we would stop receiving location updates.

Additionally, the error callback and options parameters are the same. In this particular case, we supply the `enableHighAccuracy` option as `true` to indicate to the device that we would like to use the GPS in the device, rather than just using network triangulation.

In the callback within our `run` function, we simply map the returned latitude and longitude into a `google.maps.LatLng` object, and then pass that to our map as the position that we wish to use. As our `findResources` function works with the current center position of the map, all we have to do is call it once the position changes (and we have updated the map position to match), and relevant resources will be returned for our current location.

> **NOTE:** While building location-based services and applications is interesting, testing them can be a challenge. Often it is a case of writing some code, and then taking a device out into the field to ensure that the code is behaving as expected. If you find a problem, then it's back to the desk to tweak the code. Then you rinse and repeat until everything works as expected.
>
> Android actually offers some better-than-average tool support for building and testing geolocation-based applications. For more information on how to use the Android debug tools to simplify your development experience, including how to simulate GPS information and paths, have a look at the following article:
>
> http://xpmobi.org/tutorials/android-emulator-geolocation-testing.html
>
> The downside, though, is that, without using these tools, the emulator will not return any useful position information, and you will see a blank screen. So, if you don't have experience using the tools, or you don't have an Android device that you can test with instead, we would recommend working through the article and then carry on after that.

If you have a working Android device or have simulated geolocation events in the emulator when running the application, you should now see screens similar to the ones shown in Figure 10–11. The first of the screen captures shows the permission dialog that is displayed when the application requests the user's position, and the second shows the screen once permission has been granted.

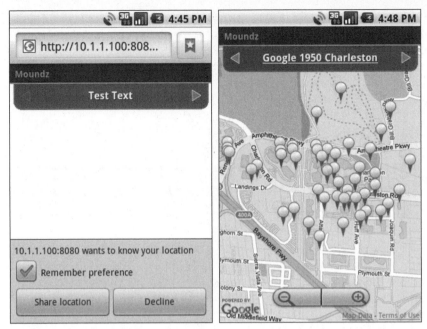

Figure 10–11. *With geolocation data simulated in the emulator, you should see results similar to the images above.*

With the application now tracking our position and providing information on resources around us, it's time to implement some more of the game functionality.

Implementing a User Login

Up until now, nothing in the game has required any knowledge of the user, but we are getting to the point where the user will probably want to mine some resources to start building their base.

Additionally, it's unlikely that we'll want to allow a user to walk around with a limitless amount of resources, so we are going to need to implement some limits. While the Geominer API will take care of most of the work for us, we are going to need to maintain a session key on the client, which we will include with any requests that need information on who the current user is.

While the Geominer suite of tools could implement its own username and password management to meet this need, it's definitely not the optimal solution. A much better solution is to integrate with an existing API that many users find themselves using on a day-to-day basis. As shown previously in Figure 10–7, the Twitter API (http://dev.twitter.com) has been chosen to meet this need in version 1 of Geominer.

In the future, additional authentication options will most likely be added, including other social networks such as Facebook and the geosocial networks that actually provide the check-in data. For the moment, though, Twitter provides a good middle ground in terms of an easy-to-implement solution with a reasonably strong existing user base.

> **NOTE:** You may be wondering why Twitter was chosen as the authentication provider when the Geominer API presumably already talks to geosocial networks such as Gowalla and Foursquare. This is a fair question, given that both of those networks offer authentication support through their APIs. Primarily, this is because those geosocial networks still do not have as large a user base as Twitter.
>
> Geosocial games like Moundz may interest users outside of the current geosocial networking users, so it is desirable for people to be able to access the game without needing a user account on a specific geosocial network. In many respects, Twitter is neutral ground.

We now have a design decision to make: do we ask someone to log in at the point that authentication is required (i.e., when they start to collect resources), or do we create a welcome page and ask them to log in right from the start? There are definite merits to both solutions, and, while many would argue that from a usability perspective it would be better to leave logging in only until required, for the sake of simplicity we will build a simple application splash screen with a very clear "Sign in with Twitter" button.

Constructing the Welcome and Login Screen

Creating a welcome screen for our application is a reasonably trivial exercise (as far as the appearance goes, anyway). First, let's modify the HTML of the index.html file:

```
<!DOCTYPE html>
<html>
<head>
...
</head>
<body onload="initialize()">
<div id="splash">
    <strong>Welcome to</strong>
    <img src="img/moundz_logo.png" />
    <p class="hint">
        Press the 'Sign in with Twitter' button below to get started playing.
    </p>
    <span id="login"></login>
</div>
<div id="app">
...
</div>
</body>
</html>
```

The modifications to the HTML are simple, with the only real point of note being that the #splash div has been added as another top-level container alongside the #app div. The Moundz logo image used on this page can be downloaded from prowebapps GitHub repository at the following URL: https://github.com/sidelab/prowebapps-code/tree/master/moundz/img.

As usual, without any CSS styling applied, the screen is pretty ugly. Figure 10–12 shows an example of the screen layout without any CSS applied.

Figure 10–12. *The welcome screen without any CSS*

Let's sort that situation now by adding the following CSS to the moundz.css file:

```
/* application window styles */

#app {
    height: 100%;
    width: 100%;
    display: none;
}

/* splash screen styles */

#splash {
    height: 100%;
    width: 80%;
    background: -webkit-gradient(linear, left top, left bottom, from(#c4c8b7),
to(#cddd87));
    padding: 0 10%;
}

#splash > * {
    display: block;
    margin: 0 auto;
    text-align: center;
```

```
}

#splash strong {
    color: hsla(0, 10%, 30%, 0.6);
    font-size: 2.0em;
    text-shadow: hsla(0, 10%, 90%, 0.8) 0 1px 0px;
    padding: 20px 0 0 0;
}

#splash p.hint {
    -webkit-border-radius: 4px;
    background: hsla(0, 10%, 30%, 0.5);
    margin: 5px;
    padding: 10px 15px;
    color: white;
    font-size: 0.80em;
}

#login {
    position: fixed;
    width: 80%;
    bottom: 20px;
}
```

With this CSS active, the welcome screen is displayed in a much more presentable fashion, as shown in Figure 10–13.

Figure 10–13. *With the CSS applied, we have a more presentable welcome screen.*

OK, the welcome page is done. Don't worry that the actual "Sign in with Twitter" button is absent—we'll take care of that soon.

For the most part, the CSS implemented here has been discussed before, so we won't go into any great detail on what has been done to lay out the welcome screen. One aspect that we haven't looked at, however, is the use of the hsla color function to specify coloring for various elements on the page.

The hsla function takes values for hue, saturation, lightness, and alpha, and offers an alternative to specifying colors using the more common rgba (for red, green, blue, alpha) function. While we won't go into great depth about how to use the hsla scheme, there definitely are some great benefits to using it, so it's well worth investigating if you have the time. For more information on the topic, the article at the following URL provides a great introduction: http://css-tricks.com/yay-for-hsla.

Twitter Anywhere and the Login Process

The process for adding a third-party authentication service to your application is easy in some respects, but can also be pretty painful in other ways. With mobile web apps being very much a minority group at the moment, we don't exactly have solutions that are tailor-made for our requirements.

The current mechanism for providing authentication services to an API such as Twitter centers around a standard called OAuth (http://oauth.net). OAuth provides a robust authentication mechanism that prevents users from having to supply their username and password to the application using the service. It does, however, come with some complexity. The process of authenticating via OAuth involves directing your users to the third-party service, which then asks the user to grant permission to your application.

In the case of Moundz, we will not ask users to provide Moundz with a username and password, but rather direct them to Twitter. If they are already logged into Twitter, then they will be asked permission for Moundz to use their Twitter account. If they accept, then they'll be logged into Moundz successfully.

Let's look at implementing that using the *Twitter Anywhere* JavaScript libraries (http://dev.twitter.com/anywhere). Following the instructions in the Twitter Anywhere Getting Started documentation (http://dev.twitter.com/anywhere/begin), the first thing to do is to create an application. This can be done by visiting the following URL: http://dev.twitter.com/anywhere/apps/new.

The registration screen is shown in Figure 10–14, and you can see that most of the details asked for are pretty obvious, with the exception of the callback URL. For this field, supply the domain that you think you will deploy the application to eventually. The information is used as part of the authentication process.

> **NOTE:** If you like, you can avoid creating a new application for now, and instead use the existing Moundz key that has been created to work through the sample code. Then you can create your own application later.

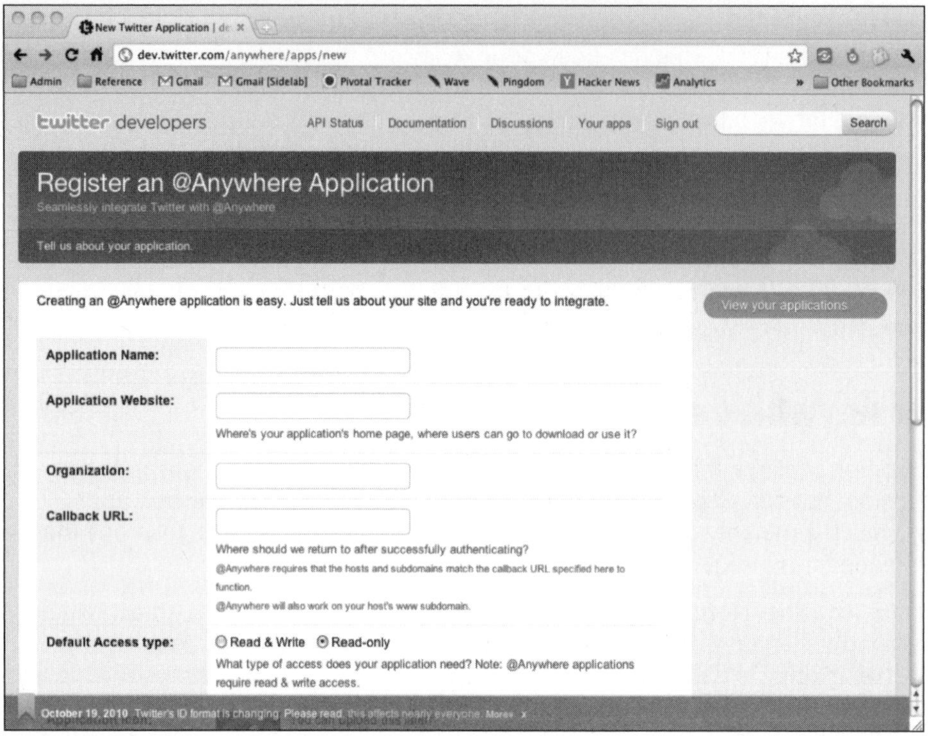

Figure 10–14. *Registering a new application with Twitter is relatively simple, but feel free to use the sample key and complete the process later.*

We now move on to prepping our application for Twitter Anywhere integration. The next steps are including the required JavaScript library in our index.html page and instructing the Twitter Anywhere library to create a login button in our designated #login area.

```
<!DOCTYPE html>
<html>
<head>
...
<script type="text/javascript" src="http://maps.google.com/maps/api/js?sensor=true">
</script>
<script type="text/javascript"
src="http://platform.twitter.com/anywhere.js?id=K7BhAacKov8QoFwEHYRU7Q&v=1">
</script>
<script type="text/javascript">

  twttr.anywhere(function (T) {
    T("#login").connectButton();
  });


</script>
<script type="text/javascript">
function initialize() {
    MOUNDZ.run();
```

```
} // initialize
</script>
</head>
<body onload="initialize()">
...
</body>
</html>
```

The inclusion of the script is shown in bold in the preceding code, using the Moundz application sample key. This should create a nice login button at the base of the screen (after a little browser activity). The result is displayed in Figure 10–15.

Figure 10–15. *A Connect with Twitter button should appear on the Moundz welcome screen.*

To log into your application, click the Connect with Twitter button. At this point, the user experience of the Twitter Anywhere solution starts to go downhill for mobile devices. Figure 10–16 shows the resulting login screen at Twitter.

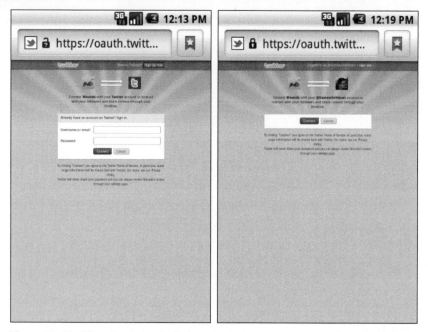

Figure 10–16. *When directed to the Twitter site for login, we receive a desktop login/permission screen.*

We'll want to avoid presenting the user a non-mobile-optimized screen and, while there is little we can do about it here, we will investigate an alternative approach later in the chapter.

Once a user has completed the login process (or the permission-granting process, if they're already logged in), they will be returned to the application screen. As Twitter Anywhere opens a new window for the authentication process, this new window will simply be closed. The Moundz welcome screen should now appear similar to Figure 10–17.

Figure 10–17. *Once you complete the authentication process with Twitter, the login button is replaced with a "Connected with Twitter" image.*

From here, all that is left to do is to bind to event handlers provided in the Twitter Anywhere API so our web page can respond to the authentication process completing successfully. Handling these events is covered in detail in the Twitter Anywhere documentation (http://dev.twitter.com/anywhere/begin#login-signup). While implementing this would probably be the simplest way to provide the login functionality for our application, unfortunately it has some drawbacks:

- As demonstrated, the login screen provided by Twitter for our users is not optimized for mobile, and this provides a poor user experience.

- The generic Twitter Anywhere authentication process requires a callback URL to complete successfully. While this works well for mobile web applications that are deployed to a web server, it doesn't work for PhoneGap-wrapped mobile applications. These applications are run from a file-based URL (as discussed earlier in the chapter), which prevents the Anywhere API from completing its signin process.

While the first issue is cosmetic, the second is a bit of a deal breaker. Not having the option to wrap an application for native deployment cuts you off from a large portion of your potential application market. We need an alternative.

NOTE: You will likely encounter an additional issue if you have a server-side component to your application that is attempting to manage some application state, which is the case in Moundz. While transmitting your users' Twitter IDs to the server to assist with managing that state won't expose them to any great risk, this isn't the most robust solution. Thankfully, the Twitter API team is already on the case, and has provided a mechanism called *Bridge Code* for bridging between the client and server. More information can be found on implementing this in presentation at the following URL: http://slideshare.net/thematthharris/twitterapi-at-socialapp-workshop-4829646.

Alternative Twitter Authentication via Geominer

It would have been wonderful if we could have used the Twitter Anywhere API for our application, but, as we want to package the application for marketplace distribution using PhoneGap, that is off the table—at least for the moment. In this section, we will investigate implementing some alternative authentication using some helpful parts of the Geominer API.

Let's start by including the Geominer JavaScript library into index.html, replacing the previous Twitter Anywhere references:

```html
<!DOCTYPE html>
<html>
<head>
...
<script type="text/javascript" src="http://maps.google.com/maps/api/js?sensor=true">
</script>
<script type="text/javascript" src="http://api.geominer.net/jsapi/v1/geominer.js">
</script>
<script type="text/javascript">
function initialize() {
    MOUNDZ.init();
} // initialize
</script>
</head>
<body onload="initialize()">
...
</body>
</html>
```

Next, let's wire the Geominer initialization the MOUNDZ.init function:

```javascript
MOUNDZ = (function() {
    ...

    // initialize variables
    var geominer = null,
        ...
        posWatchId = 0;
```

```
...

    function gotoPosition(position, zoomLevel) {
        // define the required options
        var myOptions = {
            zoom: zoomLevel ? zoomLevel : DEFAULT_ZOOM,
            center: position,
            mapTypeControl: false,
            streetViewControl: false,
            mapTypeId: google.maps.MapTypeId.ROADMAP
        };

        // initialize the map
        map = new google.maps.Map(
            document.getElementById("map_canvas"),
            myOptions);
    } // gotoPosition

    ...

    var module = {
        ...
        init: function(zoomLevel) {
            // initialize the geominer bridge
            geominer = new GEOMINER.Bridge({
                app: 'moundz',
                login: '#login'
            });

            $(geominer).bind('authenticated', function(evt) {
                $('#splash').hide();
                $('#app').show();

                run(zoomLevel);
            });

            // initialize the screen
            initScreen();
        },

        ...
    };

    return module;
})();
```

We have made a few changes to the MOUNDZ module here, which in addition to wiring in
the Geominer JavaScript API helps to reorganize things a little:

1. The previous contents of the MOUNDZ.init function have been moved to a new
   internal function called gotoPosition.

2. A new module variable, geominer, is defined at the beginning of the module.

3. The geominer variable is initialized with a new GEOMINER.Bridge object as part of the refined init function. At this stage, the bridge is created and two parameters are specified—the name of the app that we are running now (the Geominer API has been built to support multiple apps) and the login container that will receive the login button (as per the Twitter Anywhere initialization).

4. Finally, we use the jQuery bind function to listen for "authenticated" events, which flag to us that a user has completed the login process. In response to this event, we will close the welcome screen and display the main application view.

Very little code is actually required to implement the connectivity within the MOUNDZ module, and this is due to the behind-the-scenes work that the Geominer API is doing for us. If you are interested, we encourage you to check out the source code for the Geominer JavaScript API, at http://api.geominer.net/jsapi/v1/geominer.js.

If everything has gone according to plan, we should have a slightly different login experience now. Figure 10–18 shows the updated login screen, which is quite similar in appearance to the Twitter Anywhere version.

Figure 10–18. *The welcome screen using the Geominer API*

While the initial welcome screen looks similar, the process will differ from this point forward. Figure 10–19 shows the mobile-optimized permissions screen that we receive while using the established server-side APIs (via Geominer) rather than Twitter Anywhere.

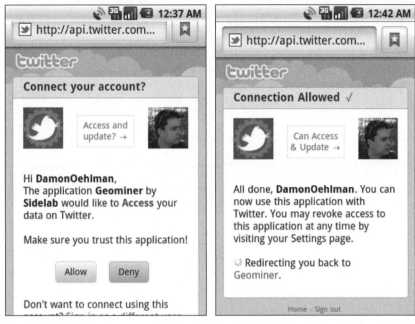

Figure 10–19. *Using the more established Twitter RESTful API provides a better mobile experience.*

Given that we accept the connection to Twitter, we will be returned to our application via the Geominer API. While this is going on, the client-side Geominer API script that we included is monitoring the login process, and, once it has determined that the process has completed successfully, the welcome screen is hidden and the user is taken to the main application screen as per earlier in the application.

> **NOTE:** One aspect of this solution that is not as elegant as using Twitter Anywhere is that the application is shown as "Geominer" rather than "Moundz" when we are going through the authentication process. While future versions of Geominer may use different OAuth parameters to show the request as coming from an application rather than itself, the current version doesn't.

If you are looking to build an application that is not a geosocial game, but you are interested in how we implemented the alternative login mechanism using Geominer, then it is probably worthwhile to fork the Geominer project on GitHub, which can be found at the following URL: https://github.com/sidelab/geominer.

Summary

In this chapter, we have looked at some of the challenges around integrating with third-party APIs that are currently available. Using these APIs is still very important given the benefits that they bring to applications that work with them; however, at this stage, most are geared toward server-side integration or native desktop and mobile development. As such, we looked at ways to work around the limitations in the current APIs while giving mobile web apps the opportunity to access those APIs.

We then moved on to looking at how to add authentication into a mobile web application using Twitter as an authentication service. Once again, while this appears simple, particular use cases required in mobile web apps can make the standard integration path less effective. We investigated alternative solutions to counter current limitations in this regard as well.

In the next chapter, we will use the work we have done in this chapter to allow the players to interact with the game, now that we have the ability to manage our game state via some user information. Additionally, we will polish up Moundz and get it ready for distribution to the Android marketplace by once again making use of PhoneGap.

Chapter 11

Mobile UI Frameworks Compared

Before we get into the final stages of preparing our application for packaging for the Android marketplace, it's worth taking some time to practically compare the various mobile frameworks that are available right now. During the time it has taken to write this book, about three new frameworks have come onto the scene, and without doubt there will be others still.

While it has been important to understand the fundamental building blocks for building mobile web applications, it is also important to consider what tools and frameworks are available that make our lives easier.

In this chapter, we will look at some of the mobile UI frameworks that are becoming popular. We will do this by taking the current Moundz UI and converting it to each of the frameworks, which should provide a feel for how the various UI frameworks operate and also how they differ from working with a bare-bones HTML UI.

Mobile UI Frameworks Overview

Getting started with mobile frameworks can be a little overwhelming, and choosing the right one can feel like a mammoth task. This is definitely compounded by the fact that, when building an app for the mobile Web, you may focus on building your application for one device without really knowing what other devices might end up using it eventually. So, when you choose a framework, you want one that is going to work well on as many of those devices as possible.

The world of mobile UI web frameworks is moving pretty fast at the moment. When we started writing this book, only one of the four frameworks that we are covering here (jQTouch) was even released. Additionally, at the time of writing, Sencha Touch was the only framework to have reached a stable 1.0 release.

NOTE: The list of frameworks that we looked at in this book is not exhaustive, and there are some excellent frameworks in addition to these. If you are interested in other frameworks that are available, or don't find a framework to fit your needs in this chapter, then the following URL may be worth a look: `www.xpmobi.org/mobile-ui-frameworks`.

Similarities and Differences Between Frameworks

In this chapter, we will be taking a look at Jo, jQTouch, jQuery Mobile, and Sencha Touch. For each of these frameworks, we will take a simplified version of our Moundz application and modify it to suit the framework. As mentioned in the chapter introduction, this will give you a good feel for the differences between each of the frameworks, and should assist you in choosing a framework that suits you in your future Android web app projects.

At a conceptual level, each of the frameworks is fairly similar:

- Each provides a mechanism for supporting multiple mobile application "pages" without the need for reloading these pages from the server. Given the limited screen real estate on a mobile device, it is normal for mobile applications to contain twice as many application pages as a desktop equivalent.

- When you consider the preceding point combined with the higher latency of mobile broadband, one of the most important things that a mobile UI framework can provide is an effective way to assist you in managing high-latency situations.

- Each provides a level of UI customization to help mobile web apps feel more like native apps. The challenge here is making a web application feel consistent with the native feel of a multitude of devices.

When it comes to how each of the frameworks is implemented, however, things start to differ. The biggest difference is around whether a framework uses a markup-based approach or is more declarative in the way the UI is created. We'll briefly explore these two concepts before looking at each of the frameworks individually.

Markup-Based UI Frameworks

In a markup-based UI framework, you commonly define the UI layout using pure HTML with CSS classes (or alternative attributes in the HTML) that influence the behavior of the frameworks.

In the cases where CSS is used to control this behavior (jQTouch, for example), the CSS classes serve to influence the look and feel of the application through stylesheets, and additionally to provide guidance to the accompanying JavaScript on how to handle those elements programmatically.

When an alternative attribute is used (jQuery Mobile adopts a suite of data attributes—see www.w3.org/TR/html5/elements.html for more information), these attributes are postprocessed by the JavaScript, and the appropriate CSS classes are applied (where required).

Declarative UI Frameworks

Using a declarative UI framework is quite different from the markup-based experience. Whereas in the markup-based approach you would start first with your HTML (and possibly CSS), in a declarative framework it's all about the code. The UI elements are declared and defined, and programmatically added to the UI.

Finding Your Own Best Fit

The choice between a markup-based or declarative UI framework very much comes down to personal preference. For this reason, we really will try to avoid making strong recommendations for one framework over another. If you haven't done a lot of work with JavaScript before, then it is likely you will be open to different approaches; in this case, we would recommend trying a few and seeing what is a better fit for you.

If, however, you have worked with HTML and JavaScript previously, then you might have a preference one way or another already. In this case, you can focus first on the two frameworks that match your currently preferred style, and, if you don't find a good fit there, you can take a look at the other two.

Given our extensive use of jQuery throughout the book already, it will probably come as no surprise that beyond this chapter we will continue to work with jQuery Mobile. This should not be taken as a rubber-stamping of jQuery Mobile as the best framework looked at here—rather, it is simply the best fit for the exercises in this book. This chapter is provided primarily to assist you in finding your own best fit.

Setting Up for the Framework Comparison

Before we get started on the challenge, let's simplify some of the Moundz source code so we don't have to go through the Twitter authentication step or location detection (which can be pretty frustrating in the emulator).

To do this, we will need to make some modifications to the Moundz source files. Comment out (or remove) the splash screen div element in the index.html file:

```
<!DOCTYPE html>
<html>
<head>
...
</head>
<body onload="initialize()">
<!--
<div id="splash">
    <strong>Welcome to</strong>
```

```
    <img src="img/moundz_logo.png" />
    <p class="hint">
        Press the 'Sign in with Twitter' button below to get started playing.
    </p>
    <span id="login"></span>
</div>
-->
<div id="app">
    ...
</div>
</body>
</html>
```

Next, we need to make some modifications to the moundz.js file that will make the process of testing the various mobile frameworks less painful.

Firstly, locate the run function and provide an ability to specify a *mock location*. This comes in the form of a second, optional parameter that we can pass to the run function. When the second parameter is supplied, location detection will be bypassed and that location will be used instead.

```
function run(zoomLevel, mockPosition) {
    // check that the watch hasn't already been set up
    // if it has, then exit, as we don't want two watches...
    if (posWatchId !== 0) {
        return;
    } // if

    // if mock position, then use that instead
    if (mockPosition) {
        gotoPosition(mockPosition, zoomLevel ? zoomLevel : 15);
        findResources(function() {
            module.updateDisplay();
        });
    }
    else {
        // create the watch (original non-mock code)
        posWatchId = navigator.geolocation.watchPosition(
            function(position) {
                var pos = new google.maps.LatLng(
                    position.coords.latitude,
                    position.coords.longitude);

                if (map) {
                    map.panTo(pos);
                }
                else {
                    gotoPosition(pos, zoomLevel ? zoomLevel : 15);
                } // if..else

                findResources(function() {
                    module.updateDisplay();
                });
            },
            null,
            {
                enableHighAccuracy: true
```

```
            });
        } // if..else
    } // run
```

Next, modify the `MOUNDZ.init` function and comment out the authenticated event handler. Additionally, place a call to the `run` function in the main body of the `init` function so the application initializes properly.

```
MOUNDZ = (function() {
    ...

    var module = {
        ...

        init: function(zoomLevel) {
            // initialize the geominer bridge
            geominer = new GEOMINER.Bridge({
                app: 'moundz',
                login: '#login'
            });

            /*
            $(geominer).bind('authenticated', function(evt) {
                $('#splash').hide();
                $('#app').show();

                run(zoomLevel);
            });
            */

            // initialize the screen
            initScreen();

            // run the application
            run(zoomLevel, new google.maps.LatLng(-33.86, 151.21));
        },

        ...
    };

    return module;
})();
```

All right, we're almost there. Finally, make one simple change to the `moundz.css` file to have the #app div display on application start by default.

```
/* application window styles */

#app {
    height: 100%;
    width: 100%;
    /* display: none; */
}
```

While we may need to modify this CSS later when integrating the various frameworks, it would be nice to know that the code for our starting point works correctly. If everything is going to plan, your Moundz application should start up and resemble Figure 11–1.

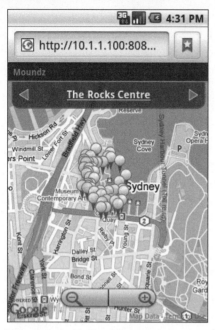

Figure 11–1. *The baseline Moundz app, ready for UI framework testing*

We now have Moundz at a suitable baseline ready for our framework comparison. Now make copies of the modified source into four directories—one for each of the frameworks that we are going to compare. Figure 11–2 shows an example structure.

Figure 11–2. *The folder structure for the UI framework comparison—one base directory and one directory for each of the frameworks*

This structure will serve you well if you wish to make comparisons against the frameworks. The completed code for each of the frameworks is available from the following URL: `https://github.com/sidelab/prowebapps-code/tree/master/frameworks/challenge`.

> **NOTE:** If you would prefer to have a quick look at any one of the frameworks rather than work through each separately, then accessing the code from the GitHub repository can be very useful. Additionally, it might give you a feel for which of the frameworks you have a preference for, and you can then have a look at that particular framework in more depth.

Jo

The first framework that we will be having a look at is Jo. Jo follows a declarative style and offers a lightweight but rich framework for developing mobile applications. The following list gives some important information about Jo:

- *Framework*: Jo
- *Style*: Declarative
- *Web site*: `http://joapp.com`
- *License*: Open source (OpenBSD)
- *Source code*: `https://github.com/davebalmer/jo`
- *Requirements*: None

The following list describes some of Jo's strengths:

- Jo comes with excellent documentation. In fact, the author of Jo (Dave Balmer; `http://twitter.com/balmer`) created a specialized documentation tool (JoDoc) for creating higher-quality JavaScript API documentation.
- Jo is built for a multidevice environment. It has been built for and tested on a wide variety of devices that support HTML5 and CSS3 (iOS, Android, webOS, and Symbian).
- Jo is extremely lightweight with regard to size, and, since Jo has no dependencies on other JavaScript libraries, your application will probably be smaller using Jo than any other mobile UI framework.
- Jo plays nicely with other JavaScript libraries (including jQuery).

The following are some of its weaknesses:

■ Its library is not as feature complete as some of the other mobile UI frameworks (on the other hand, it's a great open source project to get involved with if you're interested in contributing).

■ Its UI look and feel is not quite as polished as other frameworks.

Getting Started with Jo

First, we will download a distribution of Jo from the web site (http://joapp.com). At the time of writing, the latest stable version is 0.3.0, but there may well be a later version by the time you read this. If that is the case, you should be able to access version 0.3.0 from the downloads area on GitHub (https://github.com/davebalmer/jo/downloads).

Alternatively, you can download a more recent version and just adapt the code to cater for any changes (usually changes are pretty minor, and Jo has great documentation so it should be very simple).

Once you have downloaded a distribution of Jo, unzip the archive. You should see a directory structure similar to that displayed in Figure 11–3.

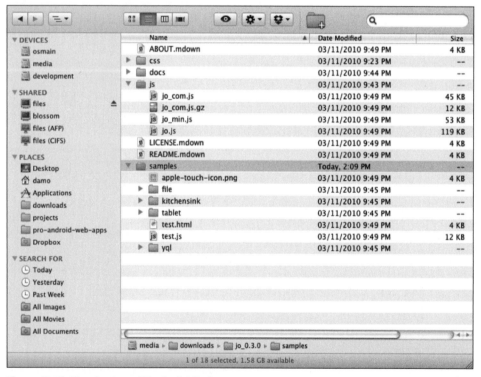

Figure 11–3. *The structure of the Jo distribution*

If you would like to see the kind of things that Jo can do, then feel free to open the test.html file in the samples directory and play with the Kitchen Sink demo.

Moving back to Moundz, we need to copy the `css` and `js` directories from the Jo distribution into the Moundz directory we have set up for the framework comparison. As per earlier instructions, copy these files into the directory created for the Moundz Jo sample. Figure 11–4 shows a sample of how that directory structure will look.

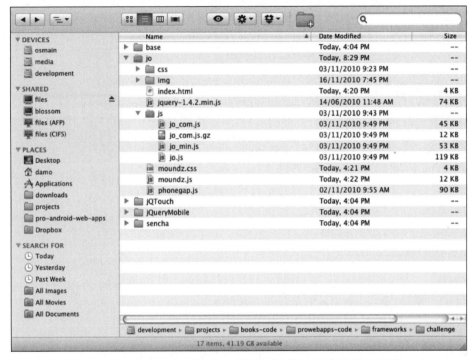

Figure 11–4. *The required Jo resource files are added to the Moundz UI challenge folder.*

Finally, before we get stuck into the detail, let's add the required includes into the index.html file for Moundz:

```
<!DOCTYPE html>
<html>
<head>
<meta name="viewport" content="initial-scale=1.0, user-scalable=no" />
<!-- <link rel="stylesheet" media="screen" href="moundz.css" /> -->
<link rel="stylesheet" media="screen" href="css/jo.css" />
<script type="text/javascript" src="jquery-1.4.2.min.js"></script>
<script type="text/javascript" src="js/jo.js"></script>
<script type="text/javascript" src="moundz.js"></script>
<!-- <script type="text/javascript" src="phonegap.js"></script> -->
<script type="text/javascript" src="http://api.geominer.net/jsapi/v1/geominer.js">
</script>
<script type="text/javascript" src="http://maps.google.com/maps/api/js?sensor=true">
</script>
<script type="text/javascript">
function initialize() {
    MOUNDZ.init();
} // initialize
</script>
```

```
</head>
<body onload="initialize()">
...
</body>
</html>
```

Essentially, include css/jo.css and js/jo.js using suitable HTML and Jo will be available for you to use in moundz.js (this is covered in the next section). Additionally, to prevent any CSS conflicts, comment out the moundz.css file.

Moundz, Meet Jo

As Jo is a declarative UI framework, most of the existing HTML that we have needs to be removed. By making appropriate Jo calls (a surprisingly succinct amount), suitable HTML will be generated. So, first things first, remove the HTML that is shown in bold and italicized in the following code sample:

```
<!DOCTYPE html>
<html>
<head>
...
</head>
<body onload="initialize()">
<!-- DELETE FROM HERE
<div id="app">
    <h1 class="simple floating">Moundz</h1>
    <div id="map_canvas" style="width:100%; height:100%"></div>
    <div id="marker-nav">
        <img src="img/navigation-arrow.png" class="left disabled" />
        <span class='marker-title'>Test Text</span>
        <img src="img/navigation-arrow.png" class="right" />
    </div>
    <div id="marker-detail" class="child-screen">
        <div class='content'>Some Test Content</div>
        <button class='close'>Close</button>
    </div>
</div>
TO HERE (or just leave commented out) -->
</body>
</html>
```

After the code has been removed (you can also remove the earlier splash page HTML as well) or commented out, we are left with an HTML document that contains an empty body tag. This is the ideal blank canvas with which Jo likes to work. We will now hand it over to Jo to create the required elements. We do this by replacing the code in the initScreen function with the following code (and defining a few extra variables):

```
MOUNDZ = (function() {
    // initialize constants
    var DEFAULT_ZOOM = 8,
        GEOMINER_MOUNDZ_URL = 'http://api.geominer.net/v1/moundz';

    // initialize variables
    var geominer = null,
```

```
        // new jo variables
        container = null,
        mapCard = null,
        detailCard = null,
        resourceButton = null,
        navbar = null,
        stack = null,
        toolbar = null,
        map = null,
        ...
        posWatchId = 0;

...

function initScreen() {
    var stackHeight;

    jo.load();

    // create a stack that we will use for paging
    stack = new joStack();

    // create the navbar for the app
    navbar = new joNavbar('Jo Moundz');
    navbar.setStack(stack);

    // define the resource details button
    resourceButton = new joButton("Resource");

    // attach the select event handler
    resourceButton.selectEvent.subscribe(function() {
        // when the button is pushed, then show the detail page
        stack.push(detailCard);
    });

    // create the toolbar
    toolbar = new joToolbar([
        new joFlexrow([
            new joButton("Previous").selectEvent.subscribe(function() {
                activateMarker(markers[markerIndex - 1]);
            }),
            resourceButton,
            new joButton("Next").selectEvent.subscribe(function() {
                activateMarker(markers[markerIndex + 1]);
            })
        ])
    ]);

    // create the wrapper to the body
    container = new joScreen([
        navbar,
        toolbar,
        stack
    ]);

    // now that the screen is created, calculate the available height
    stackHeight = stack.container.getBoundingClientRect().height -
```

```
        toolbar.container.getBoundingClientRect().height -
        navbar.container.getBoundingClientRect().height;

    // create the map card
    mapCard = new joCard([
        joDOM.create('div', {
            id: 'map_canvas',
            height: stackHeight + 'px'
        })
    ]);

    // create the detail card
    detailCard = new joCard();

    // add the map to the view
    stack.push(mapCard);
} // initScreen

    ...
})();
```

Let's now walk through what's happening step by step:

1. Firstly, we tell Jo that we are ready for it to initialize with a call to `jo.load()`.

2. Then we create a new `joStack` that is used to handle paging in the application. A stack is typically made up of multiple `joCard` objects, but this isn't a hard-and-fast rule.

3. Next, we create a `joNavBar`, which will provide our application a title bar and handle displaying a back button at the appropriate time (for example, when more than a single card has been added to the stack). We then also create a `joToolbar`, which will contain our buttons for navigating through the markers.

4. With our top-level controls defined, we then move on to telling Jo where to put these controls. This is done by creating a `joScreen` object and passing it our two controls in an array. At this point, we have an interface that we can work with, but we don't have our map.

5. To add our map, we create a new `joCard` to hold our map. We're working at a lower level here than we usually would for a Jo application, by accessing the `joDOM` utility to manually create the `div` within which Google Maps will generate the map.

6. After creating the card for the map, we create one more `joCard`, which will be used to show the detail for a search result.

7. Finally, we push the map card that we created (in step 5) to the stack (created in step 2).

The process is quite logical, and having built mobile UIs from scratch you should have a pretty good understanding of what is going on. In addition to the preceding steps, it is worth noting the following also:

- As the map does not display well using the previous instructions of 100 percent height and width, we need to calculate the height that we should specify the map to. We do this by calculating the available height in the stack, and then subtracting the height of the navbar and toolbar from the total.

- Additionally, note that, when we create our button, we use Jo's `subscribe` method to attach to the `selectEvent` of each of the buttons. The `subscribe` method in Jo is quite similar to the `bind` function in jQuery.

Once all of that is completed, we have a screen that resembles the image shown in Figure 11–5.

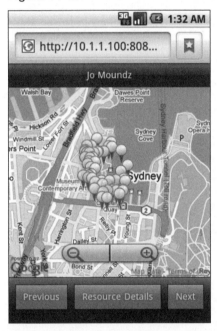

Figure 11–5. *The Moundz application interface created in a Jo web app*

We are now almost finished with our Jo sample. All that is required to make the application behave as it should are some changes to the `activateMarker` function, as shown in bold in the following code:

```
MOUNDZ = (function() {
    // initialize constants
    var DEFAULT_ZOOM = 8,
        GEOMINER_MOUNDZ_URL = 'http://api.geominer.net/v1/moundz';

    // initialize variables
    var geominer = null,
        ...
        markerIndex = 0,
        posWatchId = 0;
```

```
/* private functions */

function activateMarker(marker) {
    // iterate through the markers and set to the inactive image
    for (var ii = 0; ii < markers.length; ii++) {
        markers[ii].setIcon('img/pin-inactive.png');
    } // for

    // update the specified marker's icon to the active image
    marker.setIcon('img/pin-active.png');

    // update the text of the resource button
    resourceButton.setData(marker.getTitle());

    // update the contents of the detail card
    detailCard.setData(markerContent[marker.getTitle()]);

    // get the updated active marker index
    markerIndex = getMarkerIndex(marker);
} // activateMarker

    ...
})();
```

While we leave the marker updating in the activateMarker function, we remove all of the other existing content and replace it with three simple calls:

1. We update the text of the resource button using Jo's setData method.

2. We update the contents of the detailCard once again using the setData method, which gives us some nice consistency.

3. We then save the value of the current marker index to the markerIndex variable (also note the variable definition in the module scope). This final step allows our Next and Previous button handlers to operate correctly.

At this point, we should have a sample Jo web app that functions as per our previous hand-constructed Moundz UI. Figure 11–6 shows an example of the expected display.

Figure 11–6. *Our Moundz application converted to a Jo web app*

Well, that's one down and three to go. Our next framework is jQTouch, which is a markup-based UI framework. It will be interesting to compare the two approaches.

jQTouch

As mentioned previously, when writing first began on this book, jQTouch was the only framework of the four investigated here that was actually released. In many ways, jQTouch demonstrated what could be achieved using web technologies to create native-like interfaces for mobile devices. This included using WebKit animations to produce very fluid interfaces.

- *Framework*: jQTouch
- *Style*: Markup based
- *Web site*: http://jqtouch.com
- *License*: Open source (MIT)
- *Source code*: https://github.com/senchalabs/jQTouch
- *Requirements*: jQuery

The following are some of jQTouch's strengths:

- It is the most established of the frameworks looked at in this chapter, and has good community resources.

- It contains a large variety of well-implemented page transition effects.

- Its familiar jQuery experience is a plus for those experienced with jQuery.

The following are some of its weaknesses:

- Updates to the stable releases of the library are very infrequent; however, the GitHub repository is updated regularly.

- With change of library maintainer under the Sencha Labs transition, and with jQuery Mobile on the horizon, jQTouch has one of the more uncertain futures of the libraries looked at in this chapter.

Getting Started with jQTouch

At the time of writing, the current stable release of jQTouch that is available for download from the jQTouch web site is version 1, beta 2. Due to some changes that are going to be coming in a future release of the library, however, it is recommended that a more recent release be obtained from GitHub. The latest source snapshot can be downloaded from the following URL:

```
https://github.com/senchalabs/jQTouch/zipball/master
```

> **NOTE:** If you encounter any problems using the latest version of jQTouch from GitHub, then it is probably worth checking the jQTouch web site to see if a new release has been published since the publication of this book. Alternatively, the version of jQTouch files used in the samples are available through the Apress source code repository for the book (at www.apress.com), so you can always take a look there also.

Once you have a copy of the jQTouch files, you should have a folder structure similar to the one displayed in Figure 11–7.

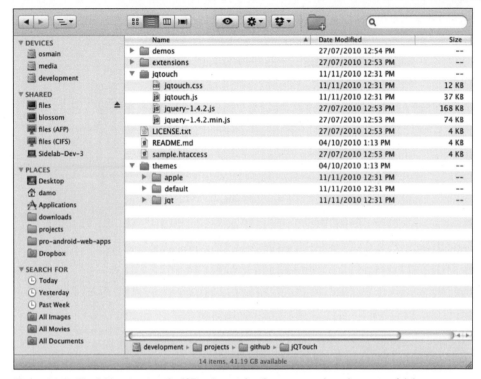

Figure 11–7. *The folder structure for jQTouch contains the source code and some useful demos.*

Within the jQTouch files there are two main directories of interest. The first is jqtouch, which contains the core JavaScript and CSS files required when using jQTouch, and the second is themes directory, which contains CSS and image resources that are used to customize the look and feel of a jQTouch application.

jQTouch also provides samples in its demos directory—these are well worth a look if you are interested in seeing what jQTouch can do.

For our Moundz jQTouch app, we will need to copy both the jqtouch and themes directories into our jQTouch challenge directory. Figure 11–8 shows how the structure of that folder should look after copying the files.

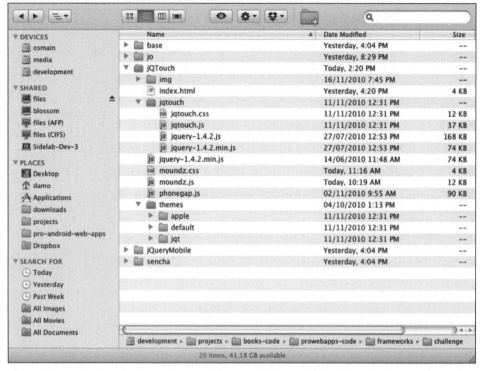

Figure 11–8. *Copy the jqtouch and themes folders from the jQTouch distribution into the Moundz challenge folder.*

There are only a few modifications we need to make to our code to make it usable for jQTouch.

```
<!DOCTYPE html>
<html>
<head>
<meta name="viewport" content="initial-scale=1.0, user-scalable=no" />
<link rel="stylesheet" media="screen" href="jqtouch/jqtouch.css" />
<link rel="stylesheet" media="screen" href="themes/default/theme.css" />
<link rel="stylesheet" media="screen" href="moundz.css" />
<script type="text/javascript" src="jquery-1.4.2.min.js"></script>
<script type="text/javascript" src="jqtouch/jqtouch.js"></script>
<script type="text/javascript" src="moundz.js"></script>
<!-- <script type="text/javascript" src="phonegap.js"></script> -->
<script type="text/javascript" src="http://api.geominer.net/jsapi/v1/geominer.js">
</script>
<script type="text/javascript" src="http://maps.google.com/maps/api/js?sensor=true">
</script>
<script type="text/javascript">
function initialize() {
    MOUNDZ.init();
} // initialize
</script>
</head>
<body onload="initialize()">
```

```
...
</body>
</html>
```

Essentially, to get jQTouch in a position where it is ready to be used, we need to include jqtouch.js, jqtouch.css, and an appropriate theme file. In this particular case, we're using the default theme, but both apple and jqt are also available.

In the next section, we will need to make changes to our HTML, CSS, and JavaScript files so that the application will behave as it should.

Applying Some jQTouch-Ups to Moundz

Now that we have jQTouch available to us in the Moundz application, let's go about making the changes to have it display effectively. First, let's start with the changes required in the HTML. Here we will change the code for the layout of the HTML body to the following:

```
<body onload="initialize()">
<div id="jqt">
    <div id="mapper">
        <div class="toolbar">
            <h1>Moundz</h1>
        </div>
        <div id="map_canvas" style="width:100%; height: 100%;"></div>
        <div id="marker-nav">
            <img src="img/navigation-arrow.png" class="left disabled" />
            <span class='marker-title'>Test Text</span>
            <img src="img/navigation-arrow.png" class="right" />
        </div>
    </div>
    <div id="marker-detail">
        <div class="toolbar">
            <a href="#mapper" class="back">Back</a>
            <h1>Test Location</h1>
        </div>
        <div class='content'>
        </div>
    </div>
</div>
</body>
```

In the preceding code, we make some relatively major changes to the HTML to structure things appropriately for jQTouch. jQTouch requires that a top-level #jqt div element be the container for the jQTouch components of your application. CSS rules are crafted around this principle, and without it your application won't display as it should. This is one of the primary differences between the older release that is available on the jQTouch web site and the new version—the older version does not have the #jqt container requirement, and, while it makes things simpler, it also makes it more difficult to include non-jQTouch parts of your application.

In our case, we made the following changes:

1. We replaced our top-level #app div with a top-level #jqt div.

2. We created "page" divs within the #jqt div to house our application pages. We have one for the map (#mapper) and one for the detail display (#marker-detail). This is somewhat similar to the layout we had prior to adding jQTouch.

3. Next, we added div elements with the class of toolbar to the pages that we want a toolbar for (which is all of them). In the case of the #marker-detail page, we also added a Back button, as, when the detail view is displayed, we want to be able to return to the main map view.

4. We moved our #marker-nav bar to within the #mapper div so that we can navigate around our markers.

If you have applied the changes successfully, your jQTouch version of Moundz will simply display an empty page (due to CSS rules). We now need to activate jQTouch within the moundz.js file to get things displaying correctly. We will do this by modifying the initScreen function inside moundz.js.

```
function initScreen() {
    jQT = new $.jQTouch();

    $('#map_canvas').height(
        $('#mapper').height() -
        $('#mapper .toolbar').outerHeight() -
        $('#marker-nav').outerHeight()
    );
} // initScreen
```

In addition to activating jQTouch, we set the height of the map canvas to fill the available space in the #mapper div. Once this is done, you should see a screen similar to the one displayed in Figure 11–9.

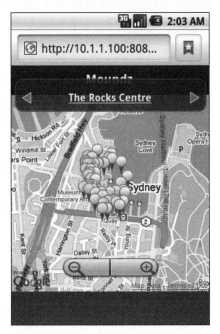

Figure 11–9. *Once both the HTML and JavaScript changes have been completed, things start to come together.*

With those modifications made, all of the basic elements are there. However, we have a rather unappealing marker navigation bar displayed. Let's make some modifications to the moundz.css file to improve the look and feel of the marker navigation bar. Locate the rule for the #marker-nav element and strip it back to a very basic look and feel:

```
#marker-nav {
    /* set general color and style */
    color: white;
    font-weight: bold;
    text-align: center;
    padding: 10px;
}
```

With that simple modification, we should have a more appealing display. Figure 11–10 shows an example of what you should expect to see.

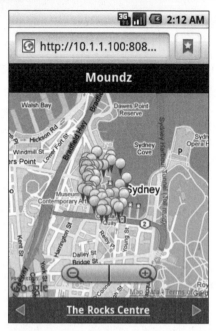

Figure 11–10. *With some CSS simplification, the display looks much improved.*

As we have kept our structure from the original application with regard to the #marker-nav bar, the application code all works as it did before. Clicking the left and right arrows will toggle between resources and the title updates, as it should. All that remains now is to update the functionality within the MOUNDZ module to properly handle showing the resource details when the resource title is clicked.

Because we have kept many of the UI elements the same for the jQTouch sample, the changes required here are very simple. All we need to do is update the code in our showScreen function to call the correct method in jQTouch to update the screen:

```
function showScreen(screenId) {
    jQT.goTo('#' + screenId, 'slide');
} // showScreen
```

Essentially, we remove all of our custom code and pass the request on to the goTo method of our jQTouch object. This takes care of the screen navigation, but we also need to very slightly tweak the activateMarker function to update the title of the detail page:

```
function activateMarker(marker) {
    // iterate through the markers and set to the inactive image
    for (var ii = 0; ii < markers.length; ii++) {
        markers[ii].setIcon('img/pin-inactive.png');
    } // for

    // update the specified marker's icon to the active image
    marker.setIcon('img/pin-active.png');

    // update the navbar title using jQuery
```

```
$('#marker-nav .marker-title')
    .html(marker.getTitle())
    .removeClass('has-detail')
    .unbind('click');

$('#marker-detail h1').html(marker.getTitle());

// if content has been provided, then add the has-detail
// class to adjust the display to be "link-like" and
// attach the click event handler
var content = markerContent[marker.getTitle()];
if (content) {
    $('#marker-nav .marker-title')
        .addClass('has-detail')
        .click(function() {
            $('#marker-detail .content').html(content);
            showScreen('marker-detail');
        });
} // if

// update the marker navigation controls
updateMarkerNav(getMarkerIndex(marker));
} // activateMarker
```

Once we have done this, we have successfully integrated jQTouch into Moundz. Figure
11–11 shows the screen you should see once you are able to navigate from a marker to
the detail page.

Figure 11–11. *We are now able to navigate to the details for a resource in our jQTouch Moundz app.*

This concludes our sample integrating with jQTouch. Next up is jQuery Mobile.

jQuery Mobile

While third on our list of mobile frameworks, jQuery Mobile is one of the frameworks that has probably attracted the most attention. This is due in part to the popularity of the jQuery library, and also in part to the amount of planning that has gone into the library.

- *Framework*: jQuery Mobile

- *Style*: Markup based

- *Web site*: http://jquerymobile.com

- *License*: Open source (MIT or GPL)

- *Source code*: https://github.com/jquery/jquery-mobile

- *Requirements*: jQuery (1.4.4)

The following are some of jQuery Mobile's strengths:

- A great deal of research went into the state of mobile device browsers before any work commenced on the library. An excellent resource created as part of this research is the Mobile Graded Browser Support chart, available at http://jquerymobile.com/gbs.

- There are sponsors and a very strong team behind this library.

- jQuery Mobile is based on and well integrated with jQuery.

- jQuery Mobile provides great documentation.

- It's likely to be considered a quality solution by tech-savvy clients when building mobile applications, given that it is an official jQuery Foundation product. Thus, there's little need to justify its use when building a mobile web application.

The following are some of its weaknesses:

- At the time of writing, it's still only in an alpha release state.

- For some, the tight integration with jQuery will be considered a weakness.

> **NOTE:** While the Mobile Graded Browser Support data was primarily developed as a tool to assist with the development of the jQuery Mobile library, this is an excellent resource when building mobile web applications in general. This chart is invaluable for making quick determinations of where particular mobile applications may or may not run. Theoretically, the code that we have worked on throughout the course of the book should work on any WebKit-powered device that is rated with A-class support.

Getting Started with jQuery Mobile

At the time of writing, jQuery Mobile is in its 1.0 alpha 2 release. While there are likely to be some changes between this version and the eventual stable release of 1.0, things should work in more or less the same way. As such, it's probably best to download the latest stable release, which can be obtained from `http://jquerymobile.com/download`.

While that page includes information on how to include jQuery from a CDN (content delivery network—see `http://en.wikipedia.org/wiki/Content_delivery_network` for more information), it is recommended that you download the ZIP file so that wrapping the application with PhoneGap is still an option.

> **NOTE:** While a CDN offers an efficient way for web sites to optimize load times for scripts by making use of a distributed network of servers, this does prevent applications from being wrapped effectively for offline distribution. Carefully consider the type of application distribution before using a CDN in mobile web application code.

Once you have downloaded the jQuery Mobile distribution, you should have a set of files similar to that shown in Figure 11–12.

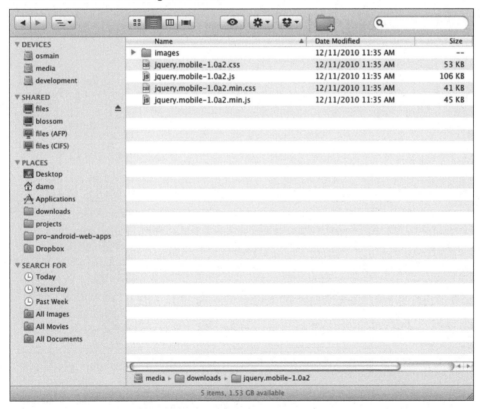

Figure 11–12. *Currently, the jQuery Mobile distribution is very simple and light.*

While the distribution does not contain any samples, these can be viewed online. For instance, the 1.0 alpha 2 demos are available at `http://jquerymobile.com/demos/1.0a2`.

In addition to the jQuery Mobile library files, we will also need to obtain jQuery 1.4.4, as this is a prerequisite for the jQuery Mobile framework. One of the simplest ways to get jQuery 1.4.4 is to download it from the CDN location, at `http://code.jquery.com/jquery-1.4.4.min.js`.

Now that we have the files that we need, let's copy them into our jQuery Mobile Moundz project. From the jQuery Mobile distribution, copy all the files into the main Moundz directory, and copy the `jquery-1.4.4.min.js` file there also. After you have done this, the Moundz application directory should resemble Figure 11–13.

Figure 11–13. *Moundz application folder structure after adding required jQuery Mobile files*

Once we have added the required jQuery Mobile (and jQuery) files, there will be a little duplication. If we were building a production application, we would probably clean that up, but for the sake of our challenge we'll let it slide. We'll now make the required modifications to the HTML:

```
<!DOCTYPE html>
<html>
<head>
<meta name="viewport" content="initial-scale=1.0, user-scalable=no" />
<link rel="stylesheet" media="screen" href="jquery.mobile-1.0a2.min.css" />
```

```
<!-- <link rel="stylesheet" media="screen" href="moundz.css" /> -->
<script type="text/javascript" src="jquery-1.4.4.min.js"></script>
<script type="text/javascript" src="jquery.mobile-1.0a2.min.js"></script>
<script type="text/javascript" src="moundz.js"></script>
<!-- <script type="text/javascript" src="phonegap.js"></script> -->
<script type="text/javascript" src="http://api.geominer.net/jsapi/v1/geominer.js">
</script>
<script type="text/javascript" src="http://maps.google.com/maps/api/js?sensor=true">
</script>
<script type="text/javascript">
function initialize() {
    MOUNDZ.init();
} // initialize
</script>
</head>
<body onload="initialize()">
...
</body>
</html>
```

In the preceding code, we added the required jQuery Mobile files to the index.html file and also changed the version of jQuery that is included in the sample (from jQuery-1.4.2.min.js to jQuery-1.4.4.min.js). Additionally, we commented out the moundz.css file to prevent any CSS conflicts.

We are now ready to get Moundz working with jQuery Mobile.

Moundz and jQuery Mobile

Like jQTouch, jQuery Mobile uses a markup-based approach to a UI framework. This means that we need to construct our HTML so that jQuery Mobile can interpret it correctly and apply necessary styling and JavaScript processing. A good starting point for our jQuery Mobile Moundz application's index.html file follows.

```
<!DOCTYPE html>
<html>
<head>
...
</head>
<body onload="initialize()">
<div id="main" data-role="page">
    <div data-role="header">
        <h1>Moundz</h1>
    </div>
    <div id="map_canvas" data-role="content"></div>
    <div data-role="footer" class="ui-bar" data-id="moundz_footer">
        <div id="marker-nav" data-role="controlgroup" data-type="horizontal">
            <a href="#" data-role="button" data-icon="arrow-l" class="left">Previous</a>
            <a href="#marker-detail" data-role="button">** Place Name **</a>
            <a href="#" data-role="button" data-icon="arrow-r" class="right">Next</a>
        </div>
    </div>
</div>
<div id="marker-detail" data-role="page">
    <div data-role="header">
```

```
        <h1>Location Detail</h1>
    </div>
    <div data-role='content'>
    </div>
</div>
</body>
</html>
```

In the preceding code, we created two separate pages for our application display. First, we have our main application page, which will contain the map, and, second, we have the page that will display the detail from the selected location (as per our non-framework version).

In jQuery Mobile, the `data-role` attribute in an HTML element is used to provide jQuery Mobile with information regarding its purpose. Our pages have a data role of `page`, and inside each page we have more `div`s with different values for the `data-role` attribute. jQuery Mobile makes extensive use of `data-*` attributes to specify how UI elements should behave; while not exhaustive, Table 11–1 lists a few that we will encounter in this sample.

Table 11–1. *Some of the Common jQuery Mobile Data Attributes*

Attribute	Description
data-role	The value of the `data-role` attribute defines the type of UI element that will be created once the HTML has been processed by jQuery Mobile. Primarily, UI elements are transformed by the jQuery Mobile library at runtime by simply adding relevant CSS classes which influence the look and feel of the original HTML. In some cases, jQuery Mobile will also add additional HTML elements to the DOM to create the relevant mobile web page.
data-id	The `data-id` element is used to specify a unique identifier for the UI control. This ID can be used to tell jQuery Mobile that a particular element should remain consistent between different pages in the UI.
data-icon	Some UI elements (such as the `button` control) can contain icons to help represent the purpose of the control. Icons are specified using a name that relates to a particular icon. There are a number of built-in icons that can be used, such as the one in our sample. Additionally, you can use custom icons by specifying a unique identifier and then defining some custom CSS for that icon. More information can be found at the following URL: http://jquerymobile.com/demos/1.0a2/#docs/buttons/buttons-icons.html

With our modified HTML with the `data-role` attributes in place, jQuery Mobile can begin to work with our application layout. Figure 11–14 shows an example of the UI generated from the preceding `index.html` file.

Figure 11–14. *The initial effort with jQuery Mobile yields a header and footer, but not much of a map.*

As with our work with the other frameworks so far, the default instructions for including a Google map don't yield a very positive result. As such, some special treatment is going to be required to display the map correctly.

> **NOTE:** When writing this book, we got to framework three and the integration of a Google map still consistently failed, so it was time to do some further investigation. Was it just one version of Android that had this issue? It would appear not—testing with Android 1.6, 2.1, and 2.2 all revealed the same problem across the board.
>
> While not conclusive, this seems tied to the fact that each of the frameworks makes use of absolute positioning to some degree with regard to controlling their layouts. This in turn makes correctly sizing child `div` elements difficult, and yields an incorrect map display. It's something that can be worked around, but it is nonetheless frustrating.

As with our work with jQTouch, the fix is to manually size the map container to fit the containing page. We will make our adjustments to `moundz.js` to do that, and perform some other initialization to prepare the Moundz UI. As with earlier examples, we make our adjustments to the screen layout in the `initScreen` function:

```
function initScreen() {
    // size the canvas to the height of the page minus the header
    $('#map_canvas').height(
        $('#main').height() -
        $('#main div[data-role="header"]').outerHeight() -
        $('#main div[data-role="footer"]').outerHeight() - 30
```

```
    );
} // initScreen
```

In this case, the changes required are relatively minor, but hardly scientific. We essentially size the height of the map to the height of the page (the #main div) minus the height of the header and footer within the page (plus a fudge factor of 30 pixels to have everything display accurately). With that change complete, our Moundz main screen is starting to look the part. Figure 11–15 shows an example.

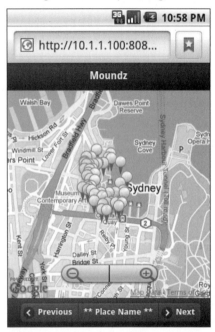

Figure 11–15. *The jQuery Mobile Moundz interface is starting to come together.*

With the interface starting to come together, we just need to make some further modifications to moundz.js to get things working with our modified HTML.

First, we will update the activateMarker function to update the middle button on the page footer:

```
function activateMarker(marker) {
    // iterate through the markers and set to the inactive image
    for (var ii = 0; ii < markers.length; ii++) {
        markers[ii].setIcon('img/pin-inactive.png');
    } // for

    // update the specified marker's icon to the active image
    marker.setIcon('img/pin-active.png');

    // update the navbar title using jQuery
    $('#marker-nav a[href="#marker-detail"]')
        .unbind('tap')
        .find('.ui-btn-text')
            .html(marker.getTitle());
```

```
        // if content has been provided, then add the has-detail
        // class to adjust the display to be "link-like" and
        // attach the click event handler
        var content = markerContent[marker.getTitle()];
        if (content) {
            $('#marker-nav a[href="#marker-detail"]')
                .tap(function() {
                    $('#marker-detail div[data-role="content"]').html(content);
                });
        } // if

        // update the marker navigation controls
        updateMarkerNav(getMarkerIndex(marker));
} // activateMarker
```

While the start of the code here is exactly the same as we had in the non-framework version, there are some differences after that:

1. Rather than target the anchor using a class selector, we are now using an attribute selector to find the link that takes us to the #marker-detail page.

2. Once that link is found, we unbind from the tap event rather than the click event, as jQuery Mobile uses these tap events to communicate that the user has tapped a particular control on the screen.

3. Next, we locate a span with the ui-btn-text class within the anchor tag and replace its content with the title of the marker. As mentioned previously, for some of the data-role types, jQuery Mobile will generate additional HTML elements to properly create the look and feel needed for the UI. This is the case with buttons. As such, we need to update the text within the ui-btn-text span within the anchor rather than the text of the anchor itself.

4. We then move on to binding to the tap event of the button when a marker has content. As before, we locate the link that will take us to the #marker-detail page and add a handler to the tap event that will occur. The handler for this tap event simply updates the HTML content in the content area of the #marker-detail page, in a similar way to what our non-framework UI did previously.

Once these changes have been made, you should be able to navigate to a detail screen in the application by clicking the middle button in the footer. Figure 11–16 shows how the two pages should look in an Android emulator.

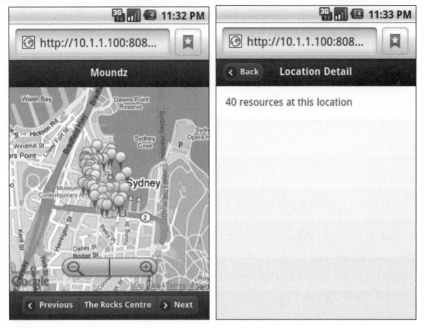

Figure 11–16. *We now have the basis of a working multipage jQuery Mobile application.*

Now that we have simple paging working in the application, we just need to attach appropriate event handlers to allow our user to navigate between all the resource locations that are displayed. We do this by making some fairly subtle changes to the updateMarkerNav function:

```
function updateMarkerNav(markerIndex) {
    // find the marker nav element
    var markerNav = $('#marker-nav');

    // reset the disabled state for the images and unbind click events
    markerNav.find('a')
        .addClass('disabled')
        .unbind('tap');

    // if we have more markers at the end of the array, then update
    // the marker state
    if (markerIndex < markers.length - 1) {
        markerNav.find('a.right')
            .removeClass('disabled')
            .tap(function() {
                activateMarker(markers[markerIndex + 1]);
            });
    } // if

    if (markerIndex > 0) {
        markerNav.find('a.left')
            .removeClass('disabled')
            .tap(function() {
                activateMarker(markers[markerIndex - 1]);
```

```
        });
    } // if
} // updateMarkerNav
```

Here, we're essentially just replacing our search for `img` tags within the `#marker-nav` div with a search for anchor elements instead. Additionally, as before, we replace references to `click` events with appropriate `tap` handlers.

That's it. Our Moundz application as it existed before has been converted to a jQuery Mobile application with relative ease.

Sencha Touch

Sencha Touch is the last of the frameworks that we will look at in this chapter with our Moundz conversion challenge. In some respects, Sencha Touch could be considered the next evolution of jQTouch, considering that jQTouch's creator (David Kaneda) joined Sencha and became part of the team that eventually released Sencha Touch. Like Jo, Sencha Touch follows a declarative style.

- *Framework*: Sencha Touch

- *Style*: Declarative

- *Web site*: www.sencha.com/products/touch

- *License*: Dual-licensed (GPL and commercial—currently free)

- *Source code*: Available in download

- *Requirements*: None

The following are some of Sencha Touch's strengths:

- Sencha Touch has an extremely robust and well-tested framework, so, when building a mobile web UI for Android, it will also work well on iOS devices.

- The framework also has user interface elements that cater for larger mobile device screen sizes (such as tablet devices)..

- It has excellent touch event support, so it's a great choice for building touch- and canvas-oriented applications.

- It has the most complete suite of UI widgets of any of the frameworks covered in this chapter.

- It has very solid documentation.

The following are some of its weaknesses:

- Sencha Touch is the most heavyweight of the frameworks we've looked at (by quite a bit). Its large library size is mitigated by the ability to customize the build of the library, but it is inconvenient.

■ There is some uncertainty about its commercial licensing. It's free for open source projects, but the commercial license applies for closed-source projects. Currently, the library is provided at no charge, but this could always change.

Getting Started with Sencha Touch

As with the other frameworks we have worked with so far, we first need to download Sencha Touch. As Sencha Touch is the only framework in this chapter that is covered by a commercial license (when used for commercial development), you will need to register your details before downloading. You can, however, download the GPL version if you intend to release an application built with Sencha Touch under a GPL license.

Either way, head to the Sencha Touch product page and follow the instructions to download the library. Once you have the library, extract the archive, and you should see a folder structure similar to what is displayed in Figure 11–17.

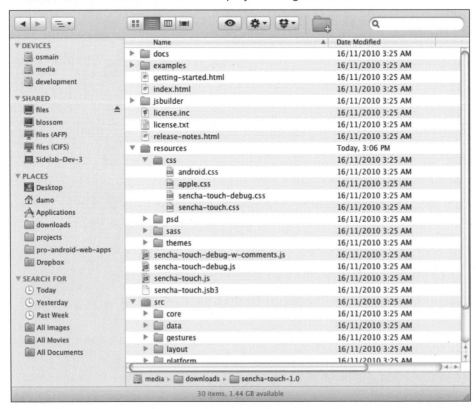

Figure 11–17. *The Sencha Touch 1.0 release folder structure*

The Sencha Touch distribution contains quite a large number of files, including the source files for the library and some pretty useful tools for working with the library. We won't go into detail on these here, but if you have the time they are definitely worth investigating.

For the purposes of the challenge, let's take the files that we need and copy them into the Moundz challenge directory. For this exercise, we will take the JavaScript files from the main directory, and the css directory from the resources folder. Once we have done this, the Sencha Moundz directory should look something like Figure 11–18.

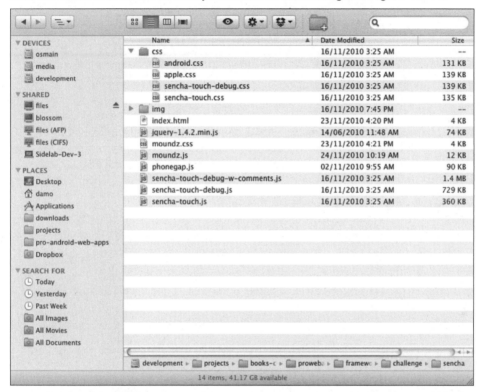

Figure 11–18. *After adding the required Sencha Touch files to the Moundz directory, we will have a css directory and a few extra JavaScript files.*

With the required files in places, let's now modify our HTML to include the required files. As with our earlier example with Jo, we will remove the HTML elements from the body tag, as Sencha uses a declarative style to create the required HTML elements.

```
<!DOCTYPE html>
<html>
<head>
<meta name="viewport" content="initial-scale=1.0, user-scalable=no" />
<link rel="stylesheet" media="screen" href="css/android.css" />
<!-- <link rel="stylesheet" media="screen" href="moundz.css" /> -->
<script type="text/javascript" src="jquery-1.4.2.min.js"></script>
<script type="text/javascript" src="sencha-touch-debug.js"></script>
<script type="text/javascript" src="moundz.js"></script>
<!-- <script type="text/javascript" src="phonegap.js"></script> -->
<script type="text/javascript" src="http://api.geominer.net/jsapi/v1/geominer.js">
```

```
</script>
<script type="text/javascript" src="http://maps.google.com/maps/api/js?sensor=true">
</script>
<script type="text/javascript">
function initialize() {
    // MOUNDZ.init();
} // initialize
</script>
</head>
<body onload="initialize()">
</body>
</html>
```

In the preceding code, we included the `android.css` stylesheet, which is part of the Sencha Touch distribution, and commented out `moundz.css` to prevent any CSS conflicts. We then included the `sencha-touch-debug.js` file so we can work through any problems that might arise during the integration effort (this file would be replaced with `sencha-touch.js` before being released). Finally, we commented out the call to `MOUNDZ.init()` from the `initialize` function. We did this because Sencha Touch has its own "ready" event that we will need to hook into to properly initialize the application.

Moundz and Sencha Touch

By now, you should be feeling pretty comfortable integrating frameworks into Moundz. Integrating Sencha will be a little different from our previous experiences due to the way Sencha libraries function.

The first part of this process is to call `Ext.setup` within our `MOUNDZ` module to properly initialize our Sencha Touch application:

```
MOUNDZ = (function() {
    ...

    Ext.setup({
        onReady: function() {
            module.init();
        }
    });

    return module;
})();
```

In this case, we are simply telling Sencha Touch that, when it is properly initialized, we want to execute the `init` function of our `MOUNDZ` module. In addition to the `onReady` handler defined in the preceding code, the `Ext.setup` function can take parameters that can be used to configure the look and feel of the application and device integration for various platforms. More details on the `setup` function can be found in the Sencha Touch documentation, at `http://dev.sencha.com/deploy/touch/docs/?class=Ext`.

From this point, we then proceed to update our `initScreen` function to create the main `Ext.Panel` that will be used to drive our application.

```
MOUNDZ = (function() {
    // initialize variables
```

```
    var mainPanel = null,
        ...
        posWatchId = 0;

...

    function initScreen() {
        mainPanel = new Ext.Panel({
            id: 'mainPanel',
            layout: 'card',
            dockedItems: [
                createHeader(),
                createFooter()
            ],
            fullscreen: true,
            ui: 'light',
            defaults: {
                scroll: false
            },
            items: [{
                    xtype: 'map',
                    id: 'main_map'
                }, {
                    xtype: 'sheet',
                    id: 'details_panel',
                    style: 'color: white'
                }
            ],
            listeners: {
                cardswitch: function(container, newCard, oldCard, index, animated) {
                    var backButton = Ext.getCmp('goback');
                    if (backButton) {
                        backButton[index === 0 ? 'disable' :
'enable'].apply(backButton);
                    } // if
                }
            }
        });
    } // initScreen    ...

    var module = {
        ...
    };

    Ext.setup({
        onReady: function() {
            module.init();
        }
    });

    return module;
})();
```

In this code, we update the `initScreen` function to create the main panel for the application. We are creating an `Ext.Panel` that will be used to hold the two pages for our application. The first of these pages is the map control, and the second is a details panel that we will show the resource information on—you can see the pages defined in the items array of the panel definition.

At this point, it is worth noting that Sencha Touch actually provides a map control for embedding a Google map into our UI. This is definitely going to come in handy, as the map integration has been problematic in most of the previous frameworks.

Additionally, note the two function calls that are embedded within the dockedItems array. This is where we will create our top and bottom toolbars for our application layout.

Let's now take a look at the createHeader function that is used to create the application header:

```
function createHeader() {
    return new Ext.Toolbar({
        dock: 'top',
        ui: 'light',
        defaults: {
            iconMask: true
        },
        layout: {
            pack: 'justify'
        },
        items : [{
            xtype: 'button',
            text: 'Back',
            ui: 'back',
            id: 'goback',
            disabled: true,
            handler: function(button, event) {
                Ext.getCmp('mainPanel').setCard(0);
            }
        }, {
            xtype: 'spacer'
        }, {
            xtype: 'panel',
            html: '<h1>Moundz</h1>'
        }, {
            xtype: 'spacer'
        }]
    });
} // createHeader
```

You can probably see in this code that the process of creating a header in Sencha is not as easy as in some other frameworks. The payoff is some extra robustness when it comes to rendering the display, but for some people the cost is too high. Additionally, the learning curve with Sencha is probably a little steeper than with other frameworks, purely due to the amount of functionality it offers.

NOTE: Due to the complexity of the Sencha Touch framework, we won't be able to explain all of the components in detail. We will, however, endeavor to provide a feel for how the framework operates and put you on the path to finding out more and being able to explore the framework on your own.

One of the most important things to be aware of is the use of `xtype` to define UI elements. This is similar in many respects to the way jQuery Mobile uses the `data-role` attribute in the HTML to specify the kind of UI element that should be created.

UNDERSTANDING OBJECT INITIALIZATION IN SENCHA TOUCH

The main thing to get your head around when using the `xtype` attribute (as we did in the previous code sample) is that it is essentially interchangeable with manually creating its relevant class and referencing that variable. This is one of the quite clever aspects of the Sencha Touch approach, and it does create some interesting possibilities.

While it may take a while to digest and understand, there is a very fluid mapping between the object definitions using object literals and `xtype`s and their more formal definitions. For an example, take a moment to review the `Ext.Toolbar` reference at the following URL:

http://dev.sencha.com/deploy/touch/docs/?class=Ext.Toolbar

You should start to see the relationship between the preceding definition and the attributes in the `Ext.Toolbar` class. Try another one—this time `Ext.Button`:

http://dev.sencha.com/deploy/touch/docs/?class=Ext.Button

Notice that, if we were to create a new `Ext.Button` object, it would accept a number of configuration options, and this would include items such as `text` and `disabled`. These are defined in the preceding object literal definition.

To demonstrate the point, let's quickly refactor the `createHeader` function to first define an `Ext.Button` class and then include the object in our definition of the `Ext.Toolbar`:

```
function createHeader() {
    var backButton = new Ext.Button({
        text: 'Back',
        ui: 'back',
        id: 'goback',
        disabled: true,
        handler: function(button, event) {
            Ext.getCmp('mainPanel').setCard(0);
        }
    });

    return new Ext.Toolbar({
        dock: 'top',
        ui: 'light',
        defaults: {
            iconMask: true
        },
```

```
            layout: {
                pack: 'justify'
            },
            items : [backButton, {
                xtype: 'spacer'
            }, {
                xtype: 'panel',
                html: '<h1>Moundz</h1>'
            }, {
                xtype: 'spacer'
            }]
        });
} // createHeader
```

What we have done in this code is equivalent to the earlier code. Hopefully, this gives a bit of insight as to the different ways in which UI elements can be defined in Sencha Touch.

With the createHeader function complete, we now just need to implement the createFooter function to finish off the basic layout of our application.

```
function createFooter() {
    return new Ext.Toolbar({
        dock: 'bottom',
        ui: 'light',
        layout: {
            pack: 'justify'
        },
        items: [{
            xtype: 'button',
            text: 'Previous',
            handler: function(button, evt) {
                activateMarker(markers[markerIndex - 1]);
            }
        }, {
            xtype: 'button',
            id: 'btnResource',
            text: 'Resource Title',
            handler: function(button, evt) {
                mainPanel.setActiveItem(1);
            }
        }, {
            xtype: 'button',
            text: 'Next',
            handler: function(button, evt) {
                activateMarker(markers[markerIndex + 1]);
            }
        }]
    });
} // createFooter
```

In this code, we create another Ext.Toolbar that is set to dock at the bottom of the screen. For the toolbar items, we specify three buttons, one each for moving forward and back, and another to take us to the resource details page.

Each of the buttons is assigned appropriate event handlers, the Next and Previous buttons activate the appropriate markers in the marker list, and the button that will display the resource title takes the user to the details screen when it is clicked.

All being well, a screen similar to the one in Figure 11–19 should be displayed.

Figure 11–19. *The initial display of our UI in Sencha Touch actually displays a map—impressive.*

As you can see, we have an application laid out with a mapping control appropriately sized to the screen. So, while we had to do some extra work to get the UI set up, the inclusion of the mapping control into Sencha Touch has made life easy here. We now need to move on to initializing the map with the appropriate location and get some markers displayed on the map.

To have the map display integrate with our existing Moundz application code, we need to make some modifications to the gotoPosition function.

```
function gotoPosition(position, zoomLevel) {
    // define the required options
    var myOptions = {
        zoom: zoomLevel ? zoomLevel : DEFAULT_ZOOM,
        center: position,
        mapTypeControl: false,
        streetViewControl: false,
        mapTypeId: google.maps.MapTypeId.ROADMAP
    };

    /*
    // initialize the map
    map = new google.maps.Map(
        document.getElementById("map_canvas"),
```

```
        myOptions);
    */

    // save a reference to the map control
    map = Ext.getCmp('main_map').map;

    // set the options of the map
    map.setOptions(myOptions);
} // gotoPosition
```

In the preceding code, we do three things:

1. We comment out the previous code that created a Google map control for us; this is no longer required, since Sencha Touch has created one for us.

2. We get a reference to the map that Sencha Touch has created, and we save that to the map variable that is part of the MOUNDZ module. As we use this variable in other function calls, our existing functionality should just work.

3. We update the options of the map to match the options we would have provided if we had created the map ourselves.

Once this is done, you should get a display similar to the one shown in Figure 11–20.

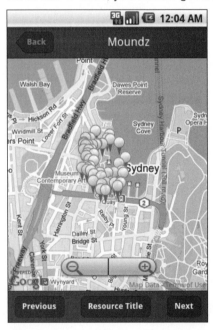

Figure 11–20. *Our Sencha Touch version of Moundz now displays markers.*

We now just need to make some changes to functions within the MOUNDZ module to synchronize our application state with the UI controls. We will start with the activateMarker function:

```
MOUNDZ = (function() {
```

```
    // initialize constants
    var DEFAULT_ZOOM = 8,
        GEOMINER_MOUNDZ_URL = 'http://api.geominer.net/v1/moundz';

    // initialize variables
    var geominer = null,
        ...
        markerIndex = 0,
        posWatchId = 0;

    /* private functions */

    function activateMarker(marker) {
        // iterate through the markers and set to the inactive image
        for (var ii = 0; ii < markers.length; ii++) {
            markers[ii].setIcon('img/pin-inactive.png');
        } // for

        // update the specified marker's icon to the active image
        marker.setIcon('img/pin-active.png');

        Ext.getCmp('btnResource').setText(marker.getTitle());
        Ext.getCmp('details_panel').update(markerContent[marker.getTitle()]);

        // update the marker navigation controls
        markerIndex = getMarkerIndex(marker);
    } // activateMarker

        ...
})();
```

Interestingly, the `activateMarker` function has actually been simplified using Sencha Touch here. We simply set the text of the middle button using the `setText` method of the button, and call the `update` method of the `details_panel` to supply the appropriate content to the details page.

Additionally, we assign the current marker index to the new module variable `markerIndex`, which will allow the buttons that we defined in the `createFooter` function to switch between the various resource locations.

Once this is done, we can navigate through the markers using the navigation buttons, and display the details for a resource by clicking the resource information button in the footer.

There we have it—a Sencha Touch version of our Moundz application, as shown in Figure 11–21.

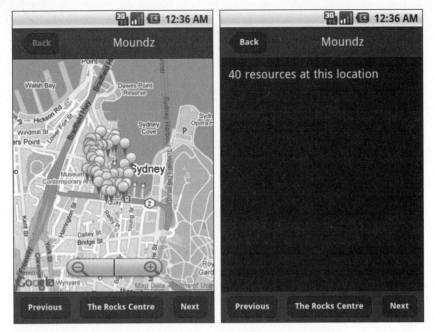

Figure 11–21. *The final Sencha Touch version of our Moundz application*

Summary

This brings us to the end of our look at four different mobile UI frameworks. As we have seen, each of the four frameworks discussed in this chapter is quite different in its approach, and each has strengths and weaknesses in different areas.

As mentioned, there really is no best framework. jQuery Mobile and Sencha Touch are definitely both going to be heavy hitters over the next couple of years, and it's likely that fans of one framework will dislike the other due to the different approaches. Additionally, Jo is gaining popularity and jQTouch has a loyal community behind it (how it competes with jQuery Mobile in the long run, though, will be interesting).

Hopefully, this chapter has assisted you in identifying a mobile UI framework that sits well with your own particular style. Or perhaps you'd prefer to construct your own application interface due to particular requirements that you have.

For our sample game application, we will take the jQuery Mobile interface that we worked through and polish it up in the next chapter. We're using jQuery Mobile primarily because we have worked extensively with jQuery throughout the book.

Chapter 12

Polishing and Packaging an App for Release

One of the great things about developing mobile application using web technologies is that you have a choice about how you package and deploy your application. If you build with native tools, then you have only one option. Admittedly, it's a very good option, but still you don't have a choice.

By using web technologies coupled with tools like PhoneGap, you can choose to deploy you application for consumption via a web browser, or wrap your web application for native marketplace distribution.

In this chapter, we will finish writing our sample geosocial game app, Moundz, using the jQuery Mobile sample that we compiled in the previous chapter. Once coding is complete (we still have a bit to do), we will package that for marketplace distribution.

Continuing on with jQuery Mobile

In the last chapter, we looked at four different mobile UI frameworks, one of which was jQuery Mobile. Given that throughout the book we have used jQuery extensively, it makes sense that we carry the jQuery Mobile sample forward to completion.

> **NOTE:** At the time of writing, jQuery Mobile is still in an alpha release status, so minor tweaks may be required to make the samples work on the latest stable version that is presently available.

Reinstating the Login Screen

When we first put together the Moundz application without using a mobile UI framework, we included a splash and login screen for the application. We'll put that back in for our jQuery Mobile version of the application. But first, let's copy the jQuery Mobile challenge code from the previous chapter to a place where we can finish it off. Rather than overwriting our previous `moundz` directory, copy the files from `frameworks/challenge/jQueryMobile` to a `moundz-jqm` directory. Once you have done this, you should have a directory structure that resembles Figure 12–1.

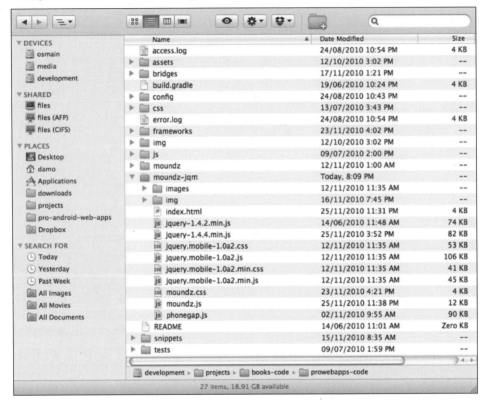

Figure 12–1. *The directory structure for the jQuery Mobile version of Moundz*

We will now go about making the required modifications to the code. Let's start with the `index.html` file:

```html
<!DOCTYPE html>
<html>
<head>
<title>jQueryMobile Moundz</title>
<meta name="viewport" content="initial-scale=1.0, user-scalable=no" />
<link rel="stylesheet" media="screen" href="jquery.mobile-1.0a2.min.css" />
<link rel="stylesheet" media="screen" href="moundz.css" />
<script type="text/javascript" src="jquery-1.4.4.min.js"></script>
<script type="text/javascript" src="jquery.mobile-1.0a2.min.js"></script>
<script type="text/javascript" src="moundz.js"></script>
<!-- <script type="text/javascript" src="phonegap.js"></script> -->
<script type="text/javascript" src="http://api.geominer.net/jsapi/v1/geominer.js">
</script>
<script type="text/javascript" src="http://maps.google.com/maps/api/js?sensor=true">
```

```
    </script>
    <script type="text/javascript">
    function initialize() {
        MOUNDZ.init();
    } // initialize
    </script>
    </head>
    <body onload="initialize()">
    <div id="splash">
        <strong>Welcome to</strong>
        <img src="img/moundz_logo.png" />
        <p class="hint">
            Press the 'Sign in with Twitter' button below to get started playing.
        </p>
        <span id="login"></login>
    </div>
    <div id="main" class="noauth" data-role="page">
        <div data-role="header">
            <h1>Moundz</h1>
        </div>
        <div id="map_canvas" data-role="content"></div>
        <div data-role="footer" class="ui-bar" data-id="moundz_footer">
            <div id="marker-nav" data-role="controlgroup" data-type="horizontal">
                <a href="#" data-role="button" data-icon="arrow-l" class="left">Previous</a>
                <a href="#marker-detail" data-role="button">** Place Name **</a>
                <a href="#" data-role="button" data-icon="arrow-r" class="right">Next</a>
            </div>
        </div>
    </div>
    <div id="marker-detail" class="noauth" data-role="page">
        <div data-role="header">
            <h1>Location Detail</h1>
        </div>
        <div data-role='content'>
        </div>
    </div>
    </body>
    </html>
```

In the preceding code, we make only a few changes, and these mainly involve reinstating code that we had earlier.

First, we once again include the `moundz.css` stylesheet, as it includes styles that are needed to properly style the splash screen. Next, we reinstate the `#splash` div to have the splash screen properly displayed, and finally we add the class `noauth` to both of the jQuery Mobile pages that we created in the previous chapter.

We now need to make some changes to `moundz.css` to bring the old and the new together nicely. The first change that is required to the CSS file is updating the rule that previously specified the style for the `#app` div with the following:

```
/* application window styles */

div.noauth {
    visibility: hidden;
}
```

Very simply, this means that any div elements with the class of noauth will not be displayed at application start. The next step in tweaking the moundz.css file involves completely removing any CSS rules that relate to the #marker-nav element. The segment of CSS that you need to remove is shown (summarized) here:

```
/* marker navigation bar */
#marker-nav {
    /* set general color and style */
    background: rgba(33, 69, 123, 0.8);
    color: white;
    font-weight: bold;
    text-shadow: 1px 1px 1px rgba(50, 50, 50, 0.85);
    text-align: center;

    /* initialize positioning and layout */
    position: absolute;
    top: 20px;
    z-index: 90;
    width: 90%;
    margin: 0 2%;
    padding: 18px 3% 10px;

    /* add the 'mandatory' border radius */
    border: 2px solid rgba(255, 255, 255, 0.2);
    -webkit-border-radius: 12px;
}

...

#marker-nav span.has-detail {
    text-decoration: underline;
}
```

Once these changes are complete, running Moundz in the emulator should display as it did before. Figure 12–2 shows an example of what you should see.

Figure 12–2. *The login screen for Moundz has been restored in our jQuery Mobile version.*

While the screen displays correctly, things will not work as they should yet. An attempt to authenticate will simply return you to the splash screen again, as in the previous chapter we just disabled handling of the `authenticated` event on our `GEOMINER.Bridge` instance. It is quite trivial to reinstate, however, as shown in the following code:

```
MOUNDZ = (function() {
    ...

    var module = {
        addMarker: addMarker,
        clearMarkers: clearMarkers,

        findResources: findResources,

        init: function(zoomLevel) {
            // initialize the geominer bridge
            geominer = new GEOMINER.Bridge({
                app: 'moundz',
                login: '#login'
            });

            $(geominer).bind('authenticated', function(evt) {
                $('#splash').hide();
                $('.noauth').removeClass('noauth');

                // run the app
                run(zoomLevel, new google.maps.LatLng(-33.86, 151.21));
            });
```

```
            // initialize the screen
            initScreen();
        },

        ...

    };

    return module;
})();
```

Although we were simply able to uncomment the actual authenticated event handler, we also need to tweak the display logic a little. While we do still want to hide the #splash div once we have successfully authenticated, we no longer want to display the #app div when completed. Instead, we want to remove any instances of the noauth class from divs that have been initialized with that in the HTML.

Additionally, to help keep the chapter flowing, we have left the mock location in for the time being (as specified in the second parameter of the run function), but we will remove it before the end of the chapter so we can go back to using the location detection routines.

Once these modifications have been completed successfully, it should be possible to log into Moundz as we were doing in Chapter 10. Figure 12–3 shows an example of how this appears with the updated jQuery Mobile interface.

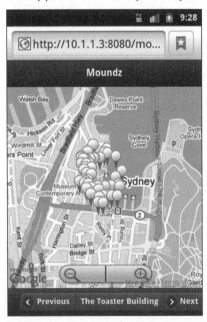

Figure 12–3. *Moundz displaying markers in the jQuery Mobile interface—some polishing is still required, though.*

With that complete, we are on the road to being able to polish up our application and add some of those outstanding features. On the to-do list we have:

- Cleaning up the alignment of the bottom buttons to achieve a nice, centered alignment and prevent wrapping

- Adding the ability for a user to collect resources

Improving Navigation Layout

While we won't spend too much time on it, it is worth having a quick look at ways that we can improve how those navigation controls format. As shown in Figure 12–3, the alignment of the controls is not optimal; also, it is possible for the Next button to wrap over to the next line when a long place name is found.

The good news is that half the work is already taken care of for us thanks to the CSS that is packaged with jQuery Mobile—any text that cannot fit into a button of a particular fixed width (or maximum width) will be shortened with an ellipsis (a series of three dots; see http://en.wikipedia.org/wiki/Ellipsis). All we have to do is appropriately limit the button sizes.

To achieve this, we will use another new CSS3 feature—the flexible box layout (see www.w3.org/TR/css3-flexbox)—combined with some standard CSS rules to control HTML element width.

No changes are required to our HTML, so simply add the following CSS to the end of the moundz.css file:

```
/* navigation control visual treatment */

#marker-nav a {
    max-width: 32%;
}

#marker-nav a.left, #marker-nav a.right {
    width: 90px;
}

#marker-nav {
    display: -webkit-box;
    -webkit-box-pack: center;
}
```

Now, there is nothing overly complicated here. We have a CSS class that tells anchor tags within the #marker-nav element to have a width no greater than 32 percent (of the parent element). We then override that style for any anchors with left or right classes to set their width manually to 90px.

Finally, we specify a rule that implements some CSS3 flexbox magic for the #marker-nav element. First, we modify the display to -webkit-box (as per the previous CSS3, we prepend the proprietary webkit prefix) and then tell the element that we want to display any child elements in the center of the control. This is done using the -webkit-box-pack rule, and it is set to the value of center.

> **NOTE:** Using the CSS3 flexible box layout is a good option here, but you might be looking at the code and HTML elements involved and wondering why a simple `text-align` rule wasn't used. In truth, it could have been in this particular case; however, it doesn't yield as visually pleasing results given some of the other CSS rules put in place by jQuery Mobile.
>
> As such, we have gone with the CSS3 flexible box layout approach. Here's some further reading on the topic: `www.html5rocks.com/tutorials/flexbox/quick`.

Once we have made our changes to the CSS, the button alignment should be much more visually pleasing—as is displayed in Figure 12–4.

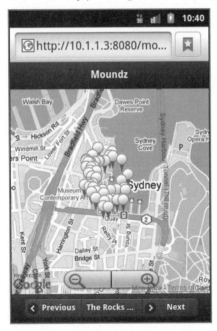

Figure 12–4. *With some CSS we can constrain our button sizes, replacing overflow text with an ellipsis.*

With the navigation buttons more attractively displayed, having that Next arrow left-aligned on the button is standing out more than it did before. Time to do something about that. Thankfully, this is made super simple by jQuery Mobile.

Locate the anchor tag for the Next button in the HTML and simply add a `data-iconpos` attribute with the value of `right` to the HTML.

```
<div id="marker-nav" data-role="controlgroup" data-type="horizontal">
    <a href="#" data-role="button" data-icon="arrow-l" class="left">Previous</a>
    <a href="#marker-detail" data-role="button">Info</a>
    <a href="#" data-role="button" data-icon="arrow-r" data-iconpos="right"
class="right">Next</a>
</div>
```

With this trivial change in place, our navigation button now displays with the icon to the right of the button, as shown in Figure 12–5.

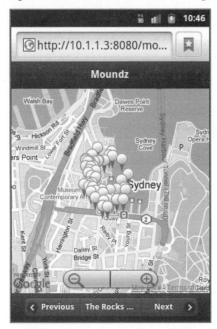

Figure 12–5. *Our navigation bar is starting to look pretty polished—time to work on the rest of the app.*

Gathering Resources

With the front screen of the application starting to come together, it's time to work on some of those features that we left out of the build so far. One of the most important is the ability to gather our resources for the game. These resources could be whatever you need them to be for your geosocial game. If you are building a classic strategy game, then the resources could be things like wood, coal, or gold. But they could just as easily be something completely different—it really is up to you. For the purposes of our sample here, however, we will just keep the term generic.

Building the Resource Details Screen

Before we implement functionality for gathering the resources, though, there are a few things that we need to do in the main moundz.js file that will assist us with managing the state of the application. Until now, we have simply been displaying some debug-level information when a marker has been selected, and that really is no longer appropriate for what we need to do. The following code shows the modifications required to the moundz.js file to assist with keeping track of resource data in the application.

```
MOUNDZ = (function() {
    // initialize constants
    var DEFAULT_ZOOM = 8,
```

```
        GEOMINER_MOUNDZ_URL = 'http://api.geominer.net/v1/moundz';

// initialize variables
var geominer = null,
    ...
    markerData = {},
    currentResource = '',
    posWatchId = 0;

/* private functions */

function activateMarker(marker) {
    // iterate through the markers and set to the inactive image
    for (var ii = 0; ii < markers.length; ii++) {
        markers[ii].setIcon('img/pin-inactive.png');
    } // for

    // update the specified marker's icon to the active image
    marker.setIcon('img/pin-active.png');

    // update the navbar title using jQuery
    $('#marker-nav a[href="#marker-detail"]')
        .find('.ui-btn-text')
            .html(marker.getTitle());

    // update the active marker title
    currentResource = marker.getTitle();

    // update the marker navigation controls
    updateMarkerNav(getMarkerIndex(marker));
} // activateMarker

function markResources(resourceType, deposits) {
    for (var ii = 0; ii < deposits.length; ii++) {
        // add the marker for the resource deposit
        addMarker(
            new google.maps.LatLng(deposits[ii].lat, deposits[ii].lng),
            deposits[ii].name,
            deposits[ii]);
    } // for
} // markResources

...

/* exported functions */

function addMarker(position, title, data) {
    // create a new marker and display it on the map
    var marker = new google.maps.Marker({
        position: position,
        map: map,
        title: title,
        icon: 'img/pin-inactive.png'
    });

    markerPosition = position;
```

```
    // save the marker data
    markerData[title] = data;

    // add the marker to the array of markers
    markers.push(marker);

    // capture touch click events for the created marker
    google.maps.event.addListener(marker, 'click', function() {
        // activate the clicked marker
        activateMarker(marker);
    });
} // addMarker

...

var module = {
    ...
};

return module;
})();
```

These changes to the code have been put in place to facilitate storing the data received from the Geominer API. While storing some arbitrary content was useful back when we were putting together our boilerplate mapping application, we have outgrown it here.

The changes to the addMarker and markResources functions are simple inline changes, in which we change references of content to data (e.g., markerContent becomes markerData).

The changes to the activateMarker function do a little more. Previously, the activateMarker function set the active marker (and the inactive markers) to have the correct icon, updated the marker title in the nav button, and also updated the marker detail content and attached relevant events. Now that we are working with data instead of the marker content, it makes sense for us to handle things slightly differently. The code for updating the #marker-detail div content and binding and unbinding to the events of the appropriate links has been removed, and has been replaced with a simple call to set the currentResource variable to the title of the selected marker.

With the currentResource variable in place, we can move on to updating the details for that resource in the #marker-detail display. Let's begin by making some changes to our index.html file:

```
<div id="marker-detail" class="noauth" data-role="page">
    <div data-role="header">
        <h1>Resource Details</h1>
    </div>
    <div data-role='content'>
        <h2></h2>
        <div id="resavail"></div>
        <div data-role="fieldcontain">
            <label for="slider">Amount to Gather:</label>
            <input type="range" name="slider" id="slider" value="1" min="1" max="5"  />
        </div>
        <a id="btnGather" href="#" data-role="button">Gather</a>
```

```
    </div>
</div>
```

Here we see some more jQuery Mobile code coming into play. For instance, notice the div marked with the `data-role="fieldcontain"` attribute. This tells jQuery Mobile that we are dropping in a section of form controls. Additionally, note the use of the new HTML5 range input type (www.w3.org/TR/html-markup/input.range.html), which jQuery Mobile replaces with its own interpretation of the range control by way of an attractive graphical slider. With this HTML in place, our Resource Details screen will look similar to Figure 12–6.

Figure 12–6. *jQuery Mobile does a very nice job of providing a simple, clean mobile UI.*

OK, it's time to actually show some useful information on this screen. We will do this by detecting the user navigating to the Resource Details screen by capturing tap events on relevant links. The following modifications to `moundz.js` demonstrate how we do this:

```
MOUNDZ = (function() {
    ...

    // initialize variables
    var geominer = null,
        ...
        supportsTouch = 'ontouchstart' in window;

    /* private functions */

    ...

    function updateResourceDetails() {
        var currentData = markerData[currentResource];
```

```
        if (currentData) {
            $('#marker-detail h2').html(currentData.name);
        } // if
    } // updateResourceDetails

    /* exported functions */

    ...

    function initScreen() {
        // size the canvas to the height of the page minus the header
        $('#map_canvas').height(
            $('#main').height() -
            $('#main div[data-role="header"]').outerHeight() -
            $('#main div[data-role="footer"]').outerHeight() - 30
        );

        // bind to the marker detail tap event
        $('a[href="#marker-detail"]').live(supportsTouch ? 'tap' : 'click',
updateResourceDetails);
    } // initScreen

    ...

    var module = {
        ...
    };

    return module;
})();
```

This code performs a couple of functions:

1. It defines a new function, updateResourceDetails, which uses the currentResource variable that we defined earlier to retrieve the data on the resource. This data is then used to update the app display; in this case, we are simply updating the header within the display, but we will add more functionality very soon.

2. The initScreen function is modified to attach an event handler to any links that direct the user to the #marker-detail screen. This is done using the jQuery live function (http://api.jquery.com/live), which means that the event handler is put in place for any elements (including ones that might be dynamically created later) matching the selector.

Also worth noting in this code is the use of the ternary (or elvis) operator with the supportsTouch variable. This, combined with the initialization of the supportsTouch variable at the start of the module, provides us with a useful mechanism that will allow us to test our application both on mobile and desktop browsers. It does this by appropriately attaching to either the tap or the click event handler, depending on whether the current device supports touch interaction.

This is very useful during the development of mobile web applications, as debugging with a desktop browser is generally a more pleasant experience than working with the Android debugging console—see Appendix A for more information on the topic.

With the code in place, tapping the Resource Details button in the navigation bar will show us a Resource Details screen similar to that shown in Figure 12–7.

Figure 12–7. *Our Resource Details screen is now dynamically updated.*

Now that we have the groundwork in place to update the display of the Resource Details screen, it's time to make it pretty—we are definitely overdue for some more CSS3 gradients.

The following CSS (added to the end of moundz.css) gets us partway there:

```
/* resource details screen styles */

#marker-detail h2 {
    text-align: center;
    margin: 0 0 10px;
    color: #777;
}

#resavail {
    background: #333 -webkit-gradient(linear, left top, right top, from(#099), to(#0A0))
no-repeat;
    border: 2px #333 solid;
    -webkit-border-radius: 8px;
    -webkit-box-shadow: #555 0 1px 2px;
    height: 20px;
    font: bold 0.9em Arial;
    letter-spacing: 3px;
```

```
        text-align: center;
        color: white;
        padding: 5px 0 2px;
        text-shadow: none;
}
```

With the CSS applied, the Resource Details screen should appear similar to Figure 12–8.

Figure 12–8. *Our Resource Details screen is starting to look good, but what is that under the resource name?*

While the CSS makes things look a little prettier, that bar beneath the resource name is a bit of a mystery. What is it for? Well, we are going to turn that into a bar that displays the current resource availability for the resource by adding some additional code to the updateResourceDetails function that we recently created.

```
function updateResourceDetails() {
    var currentData = markerData[currentResource];
    if (currentData) {
        var percAvail = 0;

        // determine the resource available percentage
        if (currentData.total !== 0) {
            percAvail = Math.round((currentData.avail / currentData.total) * 100);
        } // if

        $('#marker-detail h2').html(currentData.name);
        $('#resavail')
            .html(currentData.avail + ' / ' + currentData.total)
            .css('-webkit-background-size', percAvail + '% 100%');
    } // if
} // updateResourceDetails
```

In the preceding code you should be able to see where we are tapping into some of the extra data that is returned from the Geominer API. With that data we do two things:

1. Calculate the percentage of resources available using some trivial math. That percentage value is then used to dynamically apply a -webkit-background-size style to the #resavail div. Our particular definition for the style instructs the div to size the background image (note that gradients are treated as images) to a calculated percentage of the width and 100 percent of the height. Essentially, we have created a simple progress bar with very little code at all.

2. Update the content of the #resavail div to display a textual description of the quantity of resource available at the particular location.

After implementing this JavaScript code, our Resource Details screen will be similar to Figure 12–9.

Figure 12–9. *The Resource Details screen showing that this location already has many resources gathered*

This brings us to the point where our Resource Details screen is showing us some sensible, reasonably well-presented information. It's now time to look at gathering some resources.

Using Geominer for Resource Tracking

Once again, we will make use of the Geominer API to perform the actual gathering of resources. Behind the scenes Geominer will track the amount of resources that have been gathered from a particular location and subtract that amount from the total amount of resources (remember that these are in fact Gowalla check-ins) to report available quantities. For Geominer to be able to track these quantities, we will need to tell it we are gathering resources—and that is the purpose of this section.

The following code shows the modifications required to moundz.js to hook into the Geominer API functionality and start gathering resources:

```
MOUNDZ = (function() {
    ...

    /* private functions */

    ...

    function gatherResource() {
        var currentData = markerData[currentResource];
        if (currentData && geominer) {
            var qty = $('#slider').val();
            geominer.gather(currentData.id, qty, function(totalGathered) {
                // update the quantity available
                currentData.avail = Math.max(currentData.total - totalGathered, 0);

                // if the resource is still the same, then update the display
                if (currentData.name === currentResource) {
                    updateResourceDetails();
                } // if
            });
        } // if
    } // gatherResource

    ...

    /* exported functions */

    ...

    function initScreen() {
        ...

        $('#btnGather').live(supportsTouch ? 'tap' : 'click', gatherResource);
    } // initScreen

    ...

    var module = {
        ...
    };

    return module;
})();
```

In this code we once again attach a tap handler to the Gather button on the Resource Details screen. When the user taps this button, the gatherResource function will then be called, which simply makes use of the bundled Geominer API via the exported gather function call. We pass the ID of the resource the quantity of resources that we wish to gather and a callback that will receive the total quantity (from all users and previous gather operations) of resources that has been gathered for that particular resource.

With the information that we receive back, we can then update our own local data for the resource in an attempt to keep the two in sync. Should we receive a response from the server fast enough (which we should), the current resource screen will be updated to reflect the revised quantity of resources available.

As mentioned in previous chapters, if you are interested in what Geominer does behind the scenes, you can look at the source on GitHub, at the following URL: `https://github.com/sidelab/geominer`.

Remember, though, that Geominer is a bit of a work-in-progress, and has been built to support the samples in this book, so it would require a good deal of work before it could be considered a truly useful API.

While there is still so much that we could potentially do, and so much that needs to be done to make Moundz a useful playable game, this book would never have been published if we didn't draw the sample to a close somewhere. We still have work to do in the chapter, but, as far as implementing functionality in the Moundz application, this is where we will draw things to a close.

> **NOTE:** If you are interested in how to take Moundz further or have questions about how Geominer works under the hood, feel free to join the Pro Android Web Apps group and ask questions there (`http://groups.google.com/group/pro-android-web-apps`). We will try to find time to answer any questions posted.

Packaging Moundz As a Native Application

Now that Moundz has all the features that we are going to implement in the context of the book, it's time to package it up as a native application using PhoneGap. We won't go through the entire process again here, as we covered it pretty thoroughly in Chapter 9.

Bundling for PhoneGap

First, we need to create a directory for our Moundz application. As in Chapter 9, this is done most simply by copying an existing project to a new moundz directory. Figure 12–10 shows an example of what you should see after the copy operation.

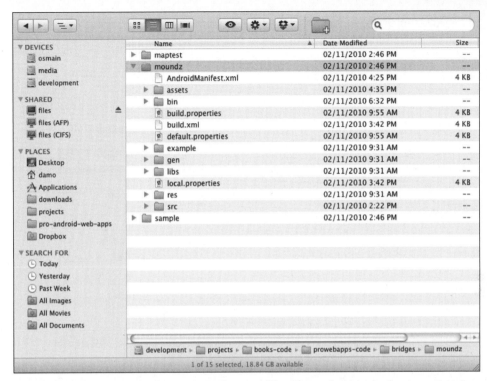

Figure 12–10. *As discussed in Chapter 9, starting a new PhoneGap project is a simple copy-and-paste operation.*

In keeping with our theme of copy-and-paste deployment, taking our Moundz source code and integrating that into our Moundz project is also simple. If you recall from Chapter 9, all that is required is to take the HTML files that we have in our moundz-jqm folder and copy them to the assets/www folder within our new Moundz PhoneGap project. After completing the process, you should have a folder structure that resembles Figure 12–11.

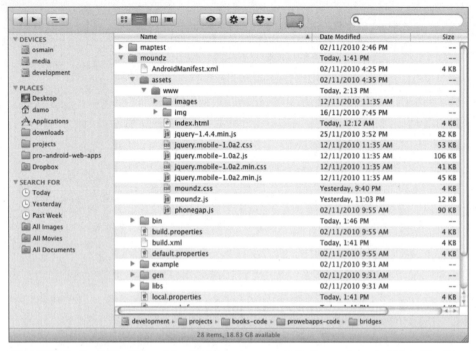

Figure 12–11. *Our HTML, CSS, and JavaScript assets are copied to the assets/www folder of the PhoneGap project.*

We now need to update references in the application to Moundz from their previous values. For detailed instructions on how to do this, revisit the Chapter 9 section "Tweaking the Sample PhoneGap Project."

After we have completed these steps and then installed the application to the emulator (remember `ant debug install` in the project folder), you should be able to open the emulator and see a Moundz application in the Android application launcher. Figure 12–12 shows an example of what you will likely see.

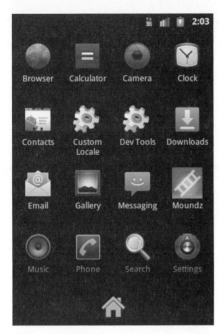

Figure 12–12. *We have successfully installed our application into the emulator, but it's time for a different icon.*

Supplying an Application Launcher Icon

One thing that we didn't cover in Chapter 9 was customizing parts of the PhoneGap application beyond just the name references. If we are going to deploy an application to the Android marketplace, it's probably a good idea to provide a custom icon for our application rather than simply use the PhoneGap default icon.

With regard to application icons, Google provide some excellent documentation that covers some of the dos and don'ts around icons in your application. This is definitely worth a read and can be found at the following URL: http://developer.android.com/guide/practices/ui_guidelines/icon_design.html.

Additionally, if you have Photoshop (http://adobe.com/photoshop) available, then Google also provide a useful template for building application icons, which can be found with the icon design guidelines that we referenced in the previous paragraph.

Now, we aren't going to go through the process of creating an application icon here, as this is more of a design-related task than a programming one, but you can use a variety of different tools to create the icon as long as a file named icon.png is generated at the end of the process. Additionally, as per the icon design guidelines provided by Google 3, different resolutions of the launcher icon should be supplied:

- A 72×72-pixel icon.png file for high-dpi (hdpi) devices

- A 48×48-pixel icon.png file for medium-dpi (mdpi) devices

- A 36×36-pixel icon.png file for low-dpi (ldpi) devices

Once you have your relevant icon files, these are simply copied to the relevant res/drawable-*?dpi* folder (where *?dpi* would be hdpi, mdpi, or ldpi, depending on the icon size). Figure 12–13 shows where each of the files have been placed in our working copy of the sample, and, while it's not visible in the screenshot, the 72-pixel image is in the drawable-hdpi folder, the 48-pixel image is in the drawable-mdpi folder, and the 36-pixel image is in the drawable-ldpi folder.

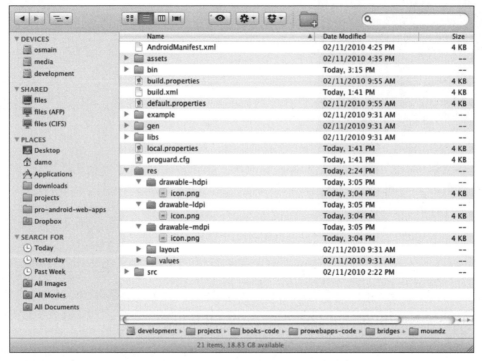

Figure 12–13. *Our updated icon.png file is placed in the res area of the project.*

With the icon in place, we are ready to rebuild and reinstall the application to the emulator. If everything has gone to plan, you should see an updated launcher icon, as shown in Figure 12–14.

Figure 12–14. *Our updated launcher icon now displays in the Android application launcher.*

With our application now looking the part, there is one more thing we have to do before it's ready to package up and ship to the Android marketplace.

Tweaking Application Permissions

If you have ever installed a native Android application, you are probably familiar with the screen that tells you what permissions the application is asking for before you complete the installation procedure. Figure 12–15 shows a screenshot of the permissions installation screen for the native Gowalla application, which gives you an idea of the kind of thing that applications request on installation.

Figure 12–15. *The Gowalla installation screen provides an example of the permissions that an application may request.*

Now, we really don't want to have an application that requests permissions for operations that it does not use. This is because users may have an objection to granting certain permissions, and in this case the more permissions our application requests, the more chance it has of being rejected by a user during installation. As such, it is best to keep the required permissions to a minimum.

As part of the default sample PhoneGap project, we have an AndroidManifest.xml file that requests a large number of permissions, and most of these aren't required for Moundz. For example, the following is an excerpt from the AndroidManifest.xml file showing the permission requests.

```
<uses-permission android:name="android.permission.CAMERA" />
<uses-permission android:name="android.permission.VIBRATE" />
<uses-permission android:name="android.permission.ACCESS_COARSE_LOCATION" />
<uses-permission android:name="android.permission.ACCESS_FINE_LOCATION" />
<uses-permission android:name="android.permission.ACCESS_LOCATION_EXTRA_COMMANDS" />
<uses-permission android:name="android.permission.READ_PHONE_STATE" />
<uses-permission android:name="android.permission.INTERNET" />
<uses-permission android:name="android.permission.RECEIVE_SMS" />
<uses-permission android:name="android.permission.RECORD_AUDIO" />
<uses-permission android:name="android.permission.MODIFY_AUDIO_SETTINGS" />
<uses-permission android:name="android.permission.READ_CONTACTS" />
<uses-permission android:name="android.permission.WRITE_CONTACTS" />
<uses-permission android:name="android.permission.WRITE_EXTERNAL_STORAGE" />
<uses-permission android:name="android.permission.ACCESS_NETWORK_STATE" />
```

While we won't go into the specifics of every permission here, details on what particular permissions provide can be found on the following page in the Android developer docs: http://developer.android.com/reference/android/Manifest.permission.html.

For the purposes of Moundz, it is pretty safe to remove the majority of these permissions and just reduce it to the permissions that provide our application web access and allow us to access location information. The reduced set of permissions would be something more like this:

```
<uses-permission android:name="android.permission.ACCESS_COARSE_LOCATION" />
<uses-permission android:name="android.permission.ACCESS_FINE_LOCATION" />
<uses-permission android:name="android.permission.ACCESS_LOCATION_EXTRA_COMMANDS" />
<uses-permission android:name="android.permission.INTERNET" />
```

Depending on the type of application you are building, additional permissions may or may not be required, which is probably why they are included in the default AndroidManifest.xml file.

PhoneGap, Authentication, and Intents

Before our application is ready for native deployment, we need to make some modifications to the way the authentication flow in the application behaves—or, rather, we need to properly equip our application to be able to respond to the authentication process that we put in place back in Chapter 10.

Our Previous Web Authentication Flow

Our final authentication process involved opening a new browser window, which is where we let Geominer and Twitter work through the authentication process before passing control back to our main Moundz web application. While this worked seamlessly in a browser environment, it doesn't work as effectively when we have our web application wrapped in a native application. Why? That's an excellent question— let's take a look.

In our web application, our authentication flow went something like this:

1. The user clicks the "Sign in with Twitter" button, a session ID is created within Moundz, and a new browser window is opened to the Geominer session initialization script.

2. Geominer handles the "OAuth dance" with Twitter, at which point the user may be asked to validate that they are OK with allowing Geominer to log them in.

3. Once the authentication process is completed, the new browser window is closed.

4.   At this point, the user is implicitly returned (when the browser window is closed, the last browser window is refocused) to our Moundz application window. Behind the scenes, Moundz has been communicating with the Geominer API in the background and has determined that we are authenticated. It then sends us to the application map.

Once Moundz is wrapped in a native application, the process fails at step 3 due to the way opening a new window is handled from within a PhoneGap application. Essentially, the WebView that is used in a PhoneGap application represents a single browser window, and, if any links are opened that require a new window, the native Android browser (not the application itself) handles this. This is understandable and the right way to handle such requests; however, it does have an impact when Geominer attempts to close the browser window in step 3. Essentially, it fails, and the user is left in the native browser on the Geominer authentication screen with no obvious way to get back—not exactly optimal usability.

The good news is that we are able to implement a workaround; however, we do have to work at a native level to do this. Don't worry, though—the process is quite simple and won't involve having to write any Java code.

An Overview of Android Intents

Android intents are structured mechanisms for passing messages between applications on the Android platform. Essentially, each application runs in its own sandbox and doesn't have access to another application's data—which is fair enough. To communicate with another application, an intent is sent to the Android OS itself, and, if one or more applications are configured to respond to that intent, then the OS provides them an opportunity to do so.

While intents are a native application concept, they make a lot of sense from a web developer's perspective, primarily because they respect the web URI scheme (http://en.wikipedia.org/wiki/URI_scheme) naming conventions. While we aren't interested in how to use intents from the perspective of native application development, using intents can provide us with an almost seamless way to transition from a web page back into our native application. In our particular case, we are providing a transition from the Twitter authentication process, back into the PhoneGap application wrapper for Moundz.

If you own and use an Android device, then you have probably experienced this already—for example, if you were browsing a web page, and then after clicking a link were taken to one of the native Android apps, as if by magic. Both the Android Market and YouTube use intents in this way.

So, let's see how complicated it is to have Moundz respond to some Android intents. The first thing we need to do is modify the `AndroidManifest.xml` file that resides in the root directory of our Moundz PhoneGap project. In this file, we will be adding an additional `intent-filter` to the `application` definition:

```
<application android:icon="@drawable/icon" android:label="@string/app_name"
```

```
        android:debuggable="true">
        <activity android:name=".Moundz"
                 android:label="@string/app_name"
android:configChanges="orientation|keyboardHidden">
        <intent-filter>
            <action android:name="android.intent.action.MAIN" />
            <category android:name="android.intent.category.LAUNCHER" />
        </intent-filter>
        <intent-filter>
            <action android:name="android.intent.action.VIEW"></action>
            <category android:name="android.intent.category.DEFAULT"></category>
            <category android:name="android.intent.category.BROWSABLE"></category>
            <data android:host="moundz" android:scheme="content"></data>
        </intent-filter>
    </activity>
</application>
```

Our new `intent-filter` definition is setting up Moundz to receive intents with the `VIEW` action, and we are marking our filter with the categories of `DEFAULT` and `BROWSABLE`. Both of these category definitions are required to have the intent filter work properly from the native web browser.

Finally, the `intent-filter` definition contains a data tag that provides information on how the URI scheme will look when placed in an HTML anchor. For instance, our definition specifies a host of `moundz` and a scheme of `content`, which means that links in web pages that start with `content://moundz` are going to match this filter, and the Moundz native application would be opened in response to these links being clicked.

> **NOTE:** The content URI scheme is an official registered URI scheme that maps to content providers for the Android platform. Note that it is also possible to use a custom scheme (e.g., we have URIs starting with `moundz://`); however, it is often discouraged, as URI schemes are meant to be unique, and this uniqueness is controlled through various Internet standards bodies.
>
> Additionally, it is also possible to register the filter using the HTTP (or HTTPS) scheme should you want to allow users to either complete the action using the Android browser or via a native application. If we had actually deployed to a public URL, then this might be an excellent way to go, but at this stage we are focusing on a deployment through PhoneGap, so the content scheme is probably the best fit.

To test our new filter, we simply need to create a very simply web page with a link that matches the rule specified in the `intent-filter`:

```
<!DOCTYPE html>
<html>
<head>
<title>Intent Test</title>
<meta name="viewport" content="initial-scale=1.0, user-scalable=no" />
</head>
<body>
<a href="content://moundz/test">Moundz Local Test</a>
```

```
</body>
</html>
```

All right, let's give it a go. Save the preceding code and then browse to it using the native Android browser. You should see a simple link and, when you activate the link, the native Moundz application should be launched. Figure 12–16 displays an example of what you should see.

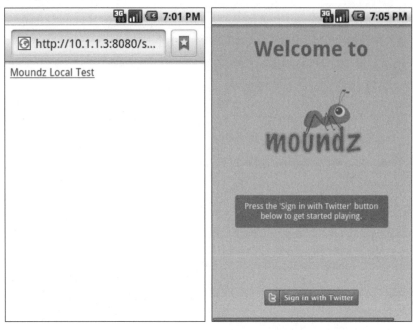

Figure 12–16. *Clicking the test link takes us directly into the Moundz application.*

Excellent, it worked. With that functionality, we should be able to make some tweaks to our Moundz application code and have it take appropriate action in response to the intents. We will, however, need a little help.

Using PhoneGap Plug-Ins to Handle Intents

We made a commitment earlier regarding not having to write Java code to work with the intents from within PhoneGap, and, despite intents being a native Android OS feature, we are going to be able to keep that promise. This is all thanks to the fact that someone has already done the hard work for us. In this section, we will be making use of a PhoneGap plug-in called WebIntent, which was created by Boris Smus. Boris has written a blog post on his motivations for writing WebIntent and it is well worth a read (see www.borismus.com/android-phonegap-plugins).

Essentially, Boris's plug-in provides the ability to invoke Android intents from your JavaScript, and also to respond to them if your application has intercepted and responded to an intent. Installation of the plug-in is very simple:

1. Download the `WebIntent.java` and `webintent.js` files from the following github repository: `https://github.com/borismus/phonegap-plugins/tree/master/Android/WebIntent`.

2. Tae the `webintent.js` file and place that in the `assets/www` folder of the Moundz PhoneGap project.

3. Take the `WebIntent.java` file and place that in a new `borismus` directory in the `src/com` folder of the PhoneGap project.

Figure 12–17 provides a screenshot of how the application folder should look after completing these steps.

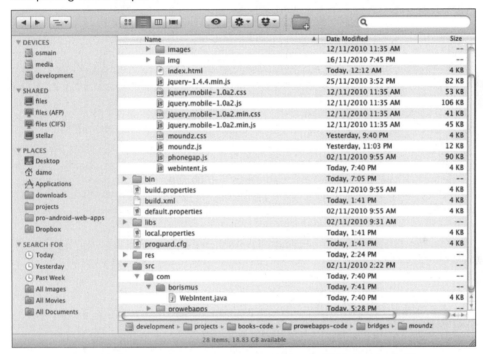

Figure 12–17. *Our Moundz PhoneGap project folder after adding the WebIntent plug-in files*

With the plug-in files in their correct place, it's time to wire everything up. The first step in this process is including the `phonegap.js` file in the project and also adding a script include for the `webintent.js` file. At the same time, we'll also move the script include for `moundz.js` to just before the closing body tag, as this is required for trapping particular events.

Additionally, while we are making modifications to the `index.html` file, we will remove the body `onload` event handler, as we now need to start making some PhoneGap-specific modifications to our code.

```
<!DOCTYPE html>
<html>
<head>
```

```
...
<script type="text/javascript" src="phonegap.js"></script>
<script type="text/javascript" src="webintent.js"></script>
...
<!--
<script type="text/javascript">
function initialize() {
    MOUNDZ.init();
} // initialize
</script>
-->
</head>
<body>
...
<script type="text/javascript" src="moundz.js"></script>
</body>
</html>
```

MAINTAINING A SINGLE CODEBASE

Until now we have maintained a single code base for an application version that could be deployed to both the web or a native application using PhoneGap. Now we are starting to make modifications that are specific to a PhoneGap version.

In our sample applications, we will simply be removing and adding code to suit our PhoneGap version, and having that code live in a location separate from our previous web-only version. If you are working on a real-world project, however, and find yourself in a similar situation, then look to alternative solutions that allow you to maintain a single code base while still allowing parts of the code to be customized for certain situations.

One way this could be achieved is through implementing a build process using previously mentioned tools like Ant or Rake. The build script selectively combines particular JavaScript files into a single JavaScript file designed for a particular platform distribution.

Another option is through using detection techniques within your JavaScript code. Given that we do not include phonegap.js in our pure web version of the application, we can make some runtime checks around the availability of PhoneGap within our moundz.js file. This allows us to maintain a single version of our core JavaScript files, and simply requires some small tweaks to the application HTML files (which are likely to differ somewhat anyway).

With the changes to our index.html file done, we now turn our attention to the moundz.js file. Here, we will make some modifications to attach to the custom PhoneGap deviceReady event rather than onload. This will ensure that PhoneGap-dependent code will only run once PhoneGap has been properly initialized. Additionally, we will wire in the WebIntent plug-in to monitor for details that will be passed through if the application is launched using a native intent.

```
MOUNDZ = (function() {
    ...

    /* private functions */
    ...
```

```
function parseUrlParams(url) {
    return {};
} // parseUrlParams

...

var module = {
    ...
};

// bind to the PhoneGap deviceReady event
document.addEventListener('deviceReady', function() {

    window.plugins.webintent.getDataString(null, function(dataString) {
        module.init(parseUrlParams(dataString));
    }, function() {
        module.init();
    });

}, false);

    return module;
})();
```

In the preceding code, we are making two changes to ensure that we properly handle the PhoneGap initialization:

1. Just before we return the module definition at the end of moundz.js, we add an event listener for the deviceReady event that is triggered by PhoneGap. Within this event handler, we ask the WebIntent plug-in to provide us details on any additional data that it has received.

   If the Moundz application has been started directly from the launcher, this call will simply pass a null value through; however, if the application has been called from a URL in the browser (such as our test page), this will be available to the native application.

2. Once we have successfully retrieved the value passed through, this value is passed through a new function called parseUrlParams before being passed on to our init method. For the moment, this function is just a placeholder and simply returns an empty object literal; however, we will add some meaningful code next.

The code we need to add to our parseUrlParams function will allow our application to translate URL query string parameters into a JavaScript object literal, which will then be interpreted in the MOUNDZ.init module function.

The following is the code required to have parseUrlParams perform that operation:

```
function parseUrlParams(url) {
    var matches = /^.*?\?(.*)$/.exec(url),
        keyPairs = matches ? matches[1].split('&') : [],
        params = {};

    // iterate through the key pairs we found
```

```
    for (var ii = 0; ii < keyPairs.length; ii++) {
        // split the pair on the = as we are only going to process these
        var pair = keyPairs[ii].split('=');

        // update the parameters
        params[pair[0]] = pair.length > 1 ? pair[1] : null;
    } // for

    return params;
} // parseUrlParams
```

This may not be the most readable code in the world, being littered with regular expressions and ternary operators, but its purpose is simple. As previously stated, parseUrlParams needs to extract that query string parameters from a URL and return them in a JavaScript object literal.

For instance, if we passed the following URL to the function: http://test.com/test.htm?param1=foo&param2=bar, then the parseUrlParams function would return an object literal of the following:

```
{
    param1: 'foo',
    param2: 'bar'
}
```

Once we have our query string parameters in that format, we can pass them to a modified version of our MOUNDZ.init function to be processed intelligently. Our modified init function follows:

```
MOUNDZ = (function() {
    ...

    var module = {
        ...

        init: function(args) {
            // initialize the parameters
            args = $.extend({
                zoomLevel: null
            }, params);

            // initialize the geominer bridge
            geominer = new GEOMINER.Bridge($.extend({
                app: 'moundz',
                login: '#login',
                returnUrl: 'content://moundz/'
            }, args));

            $(geominer).bind('authenticated', function(evt) {
                $('#splash').hide();
                $('.noauth').removeClass('noauth');

                // run the app
                run(args.zoomLevel);
            });
```

```
        // initialize the screen
        initScreen();
    },

    ...
};

...

return module;
})();
```

Let's quickly walk through the modifications we are making here; once we are done, Moundz will be ready to be packaged up for deployment.

1. We change the init function from taking a zoomLevel parameter to taking a more generic args parameter. This args parameter is then used to pass multiple values through (using an object literal) to the constructor of our GEOMINER.Bridge object. This is particularly useful when combined with our earlier code that converted the url parameters for the current web page into an object literal (as we will see in step 3).

2. Next, we update the initialization of GEOMINER.Bridge to include a returnUrl configuration parameter. This returnUrl parameter will be displayed on the page that Geominer presents as the final step in the Twitter authentication process. So now, rather than attempting to close the window, a link will be displayed that we can then click to return to the Moundz native application.

3. Additionally, we pass through the values specified in the args parameter through to the GEOMINER.Bridge using the $.extend function ($.extend is equivalent to jQuery.extend). This is a concise and effective way of passing parameters that have been sent to our application as part of the Android intent right through to our JavaScript module code.

4. Finally, we modify our call to the run function to remove the mock location that we have been using up until this point while developing the application.

That's it. The coding, tweaks, and refinements are all done. It's now time to package this application up for Android Market distribution.

Packaging Our Application for Release

We finally made it. Our coding is done, we have an application icon, and it's time to package the application for deployment. This involves a number of steps:

1. Building our application in release mode, and then signing our application for deployment.

2. Registering for the Android Market.

3.   Publishing our application to the market.

In this final section of this chapter, we will cover what is required to complete step 1 successfully, and then we will point you in the right direction so you can complete steps 2 and 3 with your own application once you reach that point. While there are some nuances to building the application for release (most of which are now handled during the build process), the registration and application-publishing processes are made very simple by Google. Additionally, they provide an excellent guide on the topic of publishing your application (see `http://developer.android.com/guide/publishing/publishing.html`).

The first step in building our application for release is using ant to build a binary of the application in release mode. This is achieved by running the following command from the Moundz PhoneGap project directory: `ant release`.

When run, this command should generate output similar to that shown in Figure 12–18.

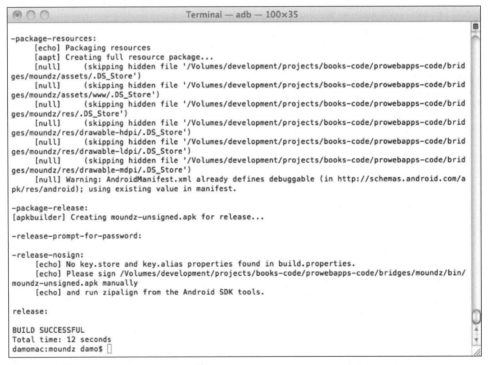

Figure 12–18. *Output from running the build in release mode—note the comments regarding signing.*

In this figure, you may notice some output generated by the Ant build referring to not having `key.store` or `key.alias` properties available with which to sign our application. This has prevented the build script from successfully signing our application, which is required if we wish to distribute our application.

To sign our application, the first thing we must do is generate a private key. This can be achieved by running the following command (however, you should change both the keystore and alias to something more appropriate for your own configuration):

```
keytool -genkey -v -keystore my-release-key.keystore -alias alias_name -keyalg RSA -
keysize 2048 -validity 10000
```

Running this command shows output similar to that displayed in Figure 12–19.

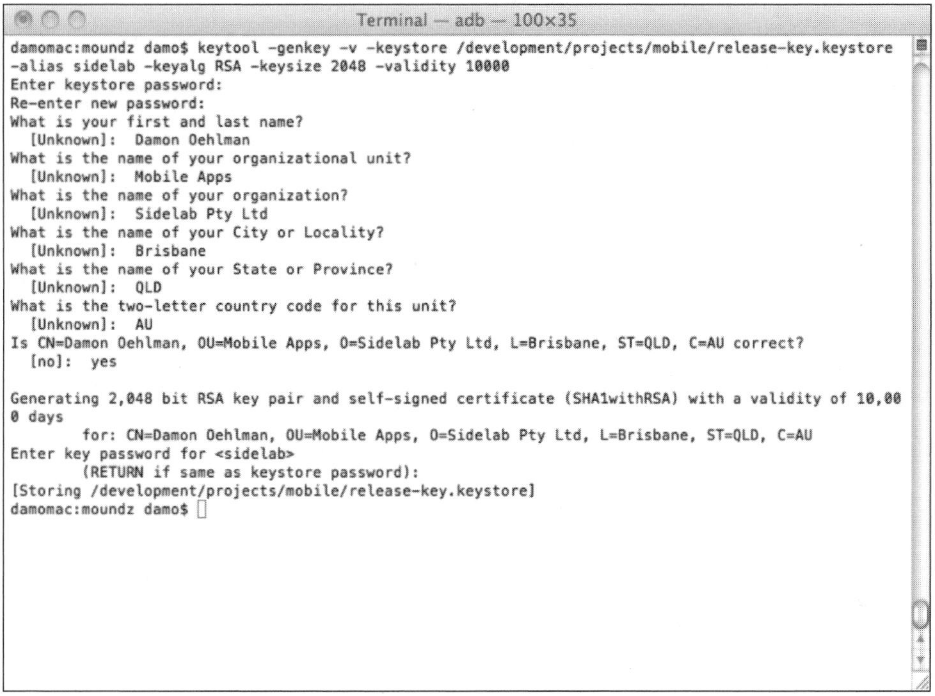

```
damomac:moundz damo$ keytool -genkey -v -keystore /development/projects/mobile/release-key.keystore
-alias sidelab -keyalg RSA -keysize 2048 -validity 10000
Enter keystore password:
Re-enter new password:
What is your first and last name?
  [Unknown]:  Damon Oehlman
What is the name of your organizational unit?
  [Unknown]:  Mobile Apps
What is the name of your organization?
  [Unknown]:  Sidelab Pty Ltd
What is the name of your City or Locality?
  [Unknown]:  Brisbane
What is the name of your State or Province?
  [Unknown]:  QLD
What is the two-letter country code for this unit?
  [Unknown]:  AU
Is CN=Damon Oehlman, OU=Mobile Apps, O=Sidelab Pty Ltd, L=Brisbane, ST=QLD, C=AU correct?
  [no]:  yes

Generating 2,048 bit RSA key pair and self-signed certificate (SHA1withRSA) with a validity of 10,00
0 days
        for: CN=Damon Oehlman, OU=Mobile Apps, O=Sidelab Pty Ltd, L=Brisbane, ST=QLD, C=AU
Enter key password for <sidelab>
        (RETURN if same as keystore password):
[Storing /development/projects/mobile/release-key.keystore]
damomac:moundz damo$ []
```

Figure 12–19. *If you don't already have one, you will need to generate a private key to sign your application.*

With our keystore created, we can now modify our `build.properties` file and specify its location so the build script can sign our application as part of the build process. With our application requirements, there are no additional settings required in this file, so, after the `key.store` and `key.alias` properties are added, our `build.properties` file should look something like the following:

```
key.store=/path/to/release-key.keystore
key.alias=your_alias
```

Now, with those settings in place, we are ready to attempt rebuilding our application in release mode. If everything has gone correctly, you should now be prompted for your keystore and alias password as part of the build process. Provide the password correctly, and your application will be signed and ready for release. Figure 12–20 shows an example of the output that will be generated in a successful build.

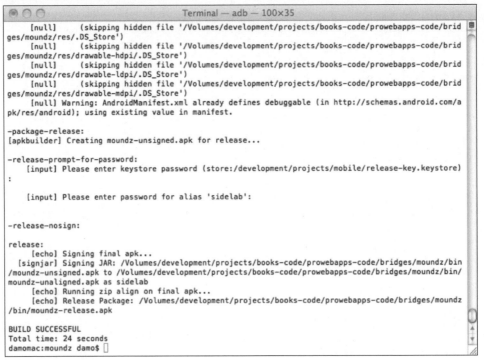

Figure 12–20. *After generating a private key and providing details to the build script, our build process successfully signs our application.*

If you have a look in the bin folder of your Moundz PhoneGap project folder, you should see a number of files. The most important one as far as a project release is concerned is moundz-release.apk. Figure 12–21 shows an example screenshot of what your bin folder might look like.

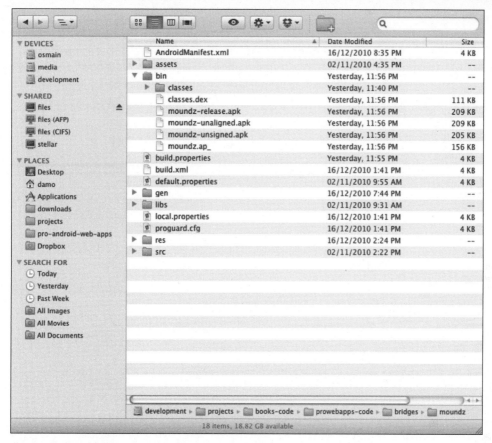

Figure 12–21. *The bin folder of the Moundz PhoneGap project folder should contain a moundz-release.apk file after our successful build.*

That's it. We now have the main application file, which will enable us to publish an application to the Android Market.

If you decide to go down this path with your own Android web apps, then from this point you should register with the Android Market (http://market.android.com/publish) and, as mentioned previously, familiarize yourself with Google's publishing guide that we referenced early in this section of the chapter.

In terms of the tasks that remain, you will need to gather a few screenshots, make some larger icons, and think of some text that describes your application well to potential users. If you are looking to sell applications through the market, then you should also investigate a Google Merchant account.

From here on, you enter the land of pictures, text, and promotion.

Summary

In this chapter, we covered a lot of material, ranging from some additional information on jQuery Mobile and visual tweaks to our application, to information on how to package an Android web app using PhoneGap for release to the Android Market.

In the next chapter, we will finish off the book by looking at some potential future trends in mobile computing. Hopefully, these will provide some food for thought, and perhaps even give you some ideas of things you might possibly like to explore in the world of mobile web application development.

Chapter **13**

The Future of Mobile Computing

Through the course of the book, we have looked at some code examples and exercises that will enable you to build web apps for Android and Chrome OS using the features available both on the phone and in the cloud. What's coming though? How are new technologies and trends going to change our development approach?

What is presented in this chapter is a developer's perspective on the potential future of mobile platforms and subsequently applications. Of course, the contents of this chapter represent only one possible view of the mobile future, and many possibilities exist. Given current trends in both desktop and mobile computing, though, we certainly believe that we will see components of this chapter implemented over the next few years.

The Era of Mobile Computing

The era of mobile computing is upon us. The adoption of web-connected mobile devices is one of the fastest-moving trends worldwide. Consumers have become accustomed to mobile technology, and for most of us that now includes mobile web access.

This in turn affects the way we will choose to consume and produce information. For instance, rather than making sure we are prepared before leaving the house or office for things such as appointments, we can now just get up and go. We can access the information that we need via our mobile device of choice when we need it, whether that is checking the exact time of the meeting or accessing driving directions on how to get there. We are definitely becoming accustomed to getting information "just in time"—assuming we have good connectivity.

A Worldwide Phenomenon

The take-up of mobile computing is not limited to established markets. In fact, for many emerging markets and nations, mobile broadband technologies are being rolled out in favor of traditional "landlines" due to the cost-effectiveness of the solution. Figure 13-1 helps demonstrate this point by showing a graph of monthly traffic for a mobile Twitter client, Tweete (`http://m.tweete.net`). In this particular graph, we can see that the majority of traffic for Tweete comes from Indonesia. The primary reason for this is due to mobile broadband being more prolific than fixed broadband in countries like Indonesia, and thus lightweight mobile clients can get very good traction over more heavyweight desktop (and nonoptimized mobile) clients.

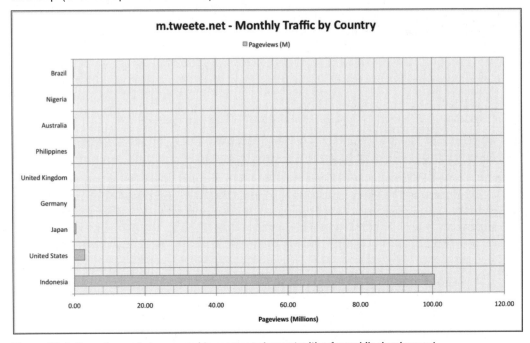

Figure 13-1. *Emerging markets can provide unexpected opportunities for mobile development.*

TIP: Many of you may look at the above graph and think—so what? We would like to challenge that thinking and recommend considering how you could build mobile applications for emerging markets (http://en.wikipedia.org/wiki/Emerging_market) as well as established markets. When doing this, though, you will also have to consider the fact that these nations will still have large numbers of simpler mobile devices in circulation. These devices often have web connectivity, but don't have the HTML5 support that we have been looking at using over the course of the book.

Effectively implement your web application or site with *progressive enhancement* (discussed in the section titled "Embracing Progressive Enhancement") and you may be able to start making inroads into those markets now, and still offer a rich experience with HTML5 features for more advanced devices.

Death of the Desktop?

Smartphones and tablets are really just the tip of the iceberg when it comes to mobile computing. The Mobile Internet Report (www.morganstanley.com/institutional/techresearch/mobile_internet_report122009.html) delivered by Mary Meeker (http://en.wikipedia.org/wiki/Mary_meeker) of financial services firm Morgan Stanley makes a number of predictions with regard to mobile device penetration and Internet usage of mobile platforms compared with desktop platforms.

Without going into the detail of the report, it suggests that mobile devices will likely be the platform of choice for Internet connectivity by about 2014. If this turns out to be an accurate estimate, then we need to start designing both sites and applications for the mobile web now.

Embracing Progressive Enhancement

Progressive enhancement (www.alistapart.com/articles/understandingprogressiveenhancement) is a web design strategy in which web designers and coders design web sites and application interfaces for the lowest common denominator (within reason) first and foremost. The application or site is then enhanced if the visitor's browser is able to support more advanced features. JavaScript libraries such as Modernizr (www.modernizr.com) are very useful here.

As to why this is important, take a look at Figure 13-2, which shows the breakdown of mobile-browser market share from August 2009 up until August 2010.

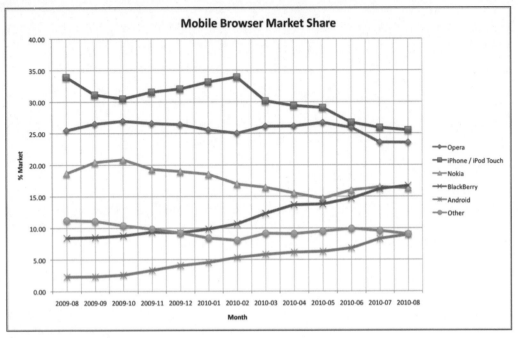

Figure 13-2. *Mobile browser market share from August 2009 to August 2010*

This data (sourced from StatCounter: `http://gs.statcounter.com`) shows a few things:

- Android device usage is on the rise, but is still a small part of the market.

- While the most popular *mobile* platform for browsing the web is iOS (iPhone, iPod Touch, iPad), there are still many browsers out there in active use that do not support HTML5 and CSS3 (e.g., Opera Mini: `www.opera.com/mobile`).

To assist in showing the current HTML5 vs. non-HTML5 device trending, Figure 13-3 has simplified the data into two categories: HTML5 supported and non-HTML5.

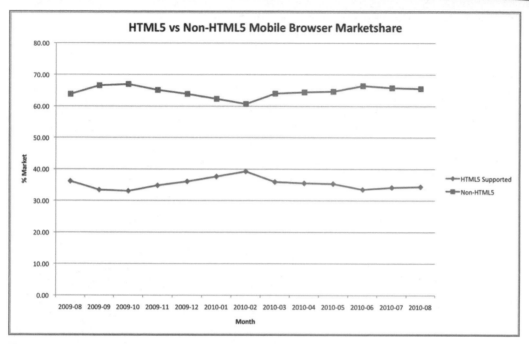

Figure 13-3. *HTML5 vs. Non-HTML5 mobile browser market share*

As shown in Figure 13-3, HTML5 devices have a smaller market share than non-HTML5 devices.

NOTE: These statistics aren't what we expected them to be. Over time, the graph actually shows less HTML5 compatible devices accessing the Web—and this is extremely suprising, at least at first. We think there are a number of potential explanations for why this is the case.

ONE such explanation could be the recent interest and promotion of the mobile Web. This in turn raises consumer awareness of the mobile services that are available online, and thus people with existing handsets are accessing mobile web services.

We would be lying if the statistics didn't make us second-guess our certainty of HTML5 adoption across a large number of mobile devices. However, this is not the only information we have about HTML5 adoption in mobile. Established vendors have provided HTML5 support in their new devices. For instance, RIM recently released the BlackBerry Torch and put an emphasis on HTML5 support and development options. We believe this is evidence validating the claim that HTML5 support in mobile browsers will trend up quickly over the next couple of years.

While it won't always be possible to build web applications and sites using progressive enhancement, it is worth spending some time at the start of a project evaluating the potential to support less advanced devices. If you can, you will broaden the reach of your application, and, while this book is focused on building Android web apps, minimizing the amount of work you have to do to cater for another platform is always a good thing.

Mobile Technology Predictions

The future is far from certain, but it is likely that mobile device development and architecture will play out in a similar way to desktop computing. This being the case, we can probably be brave and make a few predictions.

> **NOTE:** While there is an obsession with mobile development using native technology at present, we strongly believe that history will repeat itself in mobile the same way it did for desktop devices.
>
> This is definitely a risk-vs.-reward situation though, as many roadblocks stand in the way of web-oriented mobile development. We believe the community has sent device manufacturers a message, though, and that is that web development for mobile is important and something that needs to be prioritized. We also believe they have heard this message, and things are starting to change for the better.

Improvements in Tools and Libraries

The maturity and availability of both tools and libraries to streamline mobile web development is quite limited at the moment. This is changing, though, and we will certainly see a lot more options become available over the next year. One of the most promising libraries under development (at the time of writing) is the jQuery mobile framework (http://jquerymobile.com).

The research that has gone into this library and the focus on broad-spectrum mobile device support is very encouraging. From this research, the jQuery team has produced what is called the graded browser support (http://jquerymobile.com/gbs) chart, shown in Figure 13-4.

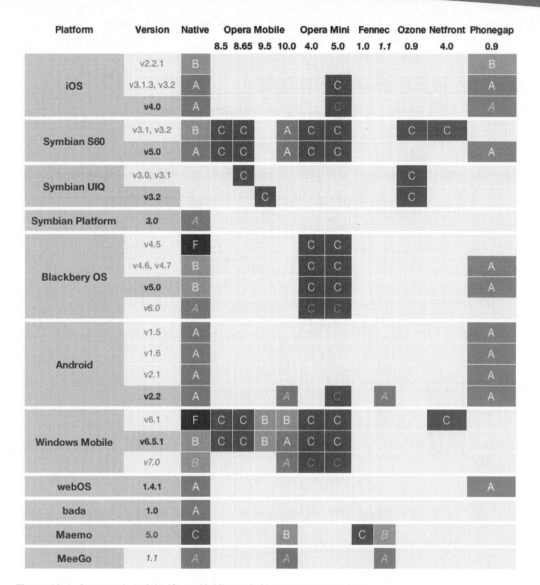

Platform	Version	Native	Opera Mobile 8.5	Opera Mobile 8.65	Opera Mobile 9.5	Opera Mobile 10.0	Opera Mini 4.0	Opera Mini 5.0	Fennec 1.0	Fennec 1.1	Ozone 0.9	Netfront 4.0	Phonegap 0.9
iOS	v2.2.1	B											B
iOS	v3.1.3, v3.2	A						C					A
iOS	v4.0	A						C					A
Symbian S60	v3.1, v3.2	B	C	C			A	C	C		C	C	
Symbian S60	v5.0	A	C	C			A	C	C				A
Symbian UIQ	v3.0, v3.1				C						C		
Symbian UIQ	v3.2					C					C		
Symbian Platform	3.0	A											
Blackbery OS	v4.5	F					C	C					
Blackbery OS	v4.6, v4.7	B					C	C					A
Blackbery OS	v5.0	B					C	C					A
Blackbery OS	v6.0	A					C	C					
Android	v1.5	A											A
Android	v1.6	A											A
Android	v2.1	A											A
Android	v2.2	A				A			C		A		A
Windows Mobile	v6.1	F	C	C	B	B	C	C				C	
Windows Mobile	v6.5.1	B	C	C	B		A	C	C				
Windows Mobile	v7.0	B					A	C	C				
webOS	1.4.1	A											A
bada	1.0	A											
Maemo	5.0	C				B			C	B			
MeeGo	1.1	A				A			A				

Figure 13-4. *A screenshot of the jQuery Mobile graded browser support chart*

Hopefully, this will finally provide a mobile web UI that can be used across devices, presenting a web UI in a device-neutral sense (rather than styling all UI elements with an iPhone look and feel).

Additionally, as developers, we can only hope for the maturity of mobile web development tools to improve. While integrated development environments (IDEs) tend to get in the way of web development in general, having suitable testing and debugging tools for mobile devices will be important for pushing mobile web development forward (in the same way that Firebug contributed to moving web development forward). There is a lot that can be done using desktop browsers such as Chrome, but there really is no substitute for device-targeted development tools.

Changes in Device Architecture

While Palm is not one of the dominant market players at the moment, there is a lot that can be learned from the way it architected its webOS (http://developer.palm.com) platform. From the ground up, webOS has been built with a strong web technology focus, providing developers a first-class way of building applications for the platform with HTML, CSS, and JavaScript.

Given this is an Android web apps development book, that might be considered to be a strange comment, but let's look at a couple of industry trends around both mobile and desktop computing:

- There is a lot of interest with regards to web operating systems as a replacement for current desktop operating systems. The implementation of a web operating system is generally achieved by using something like Linux to manage the interaction with the hardware, and then a web presentation layer providing the operating system "desktop" to the user. Two examples of web operating systems are Google's Chrome/Chromium OS (www.chromium.org/chromium-os) and Joyent's Jolicloud (www.jolicloud.com).

- Modern mobile operating systems are demonstrating continued innovation, and they could quite possibly move to implementing web operating systems (as Palm has demonstrated) before broader adoption on desktop platforms.

With those trends and the current Palm webOS architecture in mind, what will mobile device architectures look like in the future? Certainly one possibility is a device architecture that has a very strong web flavor to it, and this is shown in Figure 13-5.

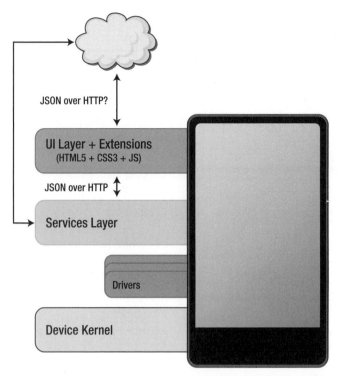

Figure 13-5. *More mobile devices may incorporate web-centric architectures in the future.*

In this architecture we see a services layer that is exposed to a web UI. This services layer would then expose functionality of the device, very similar to the way that existing web applications expose RESTful web services.

Using this technique for interacting with the device, combined with the fact that client-side web technologies are becoming more powerful, the need to build a mobile application interface with native languages should definitely become the exception rather than the rule.

This will probably first be evident in an increasing number of mobile applications being implemented using web technologies as opposed to native technologies. Once mobile web applications are predominant, removing some of the intermediate layers to more tightly couple the web UI to the underlying system layers will likely be the next step.

> **NOTE:** It is doubtful that this will occur on all mobile operating systems, as some will likely remain as primarily native development platforms. We would estimate, however, that by 2013 around 30 to 50 percent of mobile operating system vendors will either release or announce a mobile web operating system and complementary dashboard UI.
>
> Interestingly, some momentum is already building in this area, with the European Union announcing a project called Webinos (http://webinos.org), which appears to be designed to build exactly what is suggested above.

Coding for Future Architectures

If things do continue to progress in a web-oriented direction, then there will be very little that experienced mobile web developers will have to change. One exception to that may well be the way we interact with client-side storage. For instance, while HTML5 offers three very interesting APIs for working with local data, we discovered in Chapter 5 that synchronization with online services was not available out of the box.

Given that mobile devices currently have (and may always have) less reliable connections than their desktop cousins, it is expected that offline data synchronization will become a consumer requirement in the not-too-distant future. Therefore, either the HTML5 APIs will have to mature to support this requirement, or some alternative options will need to be investigated. A very interesting possibility is the use of an embedded CouchDB (http://couchdb.apache.org) instance within the mobile device, which would serve both the mobile app code and data, and keep that synchronized with the cloud automatically.

Imagine that—an embedded database capable of serving local web applications and supporting data, and keeping that in sync with the cloud so when you use the application from your desktop everything is synchronized.

The Internet of Things

As the number of web-connected mobile devices increases, not only does the number of potential consumers of information increase, but also the number of potential producers. As discussed back in Chapter 1, the modern smartphone already features a large number of hardware sensors, and this opens up some quite amazing possibilities.

The increasing number of web-connected devices that are present in our society (mobile phones and tablets are part of that larger group) has resulted in the creation of some interesting research projects and applications that could influence the way our society and we as individuals operate in the future.

The collection of these web-connected devices has been termed the *Internet of Things* (http://en.wikipedia.org/wiki/Internet_of_Things), and is well worth getting involved with if you are interested in building some really cool mobile apps.

Another term that is sometimes used to describe this connected network of devices is the *Web of Things* (http://en.wikipedia.org/wiki/Web_of_Things). The Web of Things and Internet of Things are very similar in that they both involve a massive number of interconnected devices feeding real-time information between each other and centralized services. The Web of Things model, however, specifies the use of existing web communication standards such as HTTP, REST (http://en.wikipedia.org/wiki/Representational_State_Transfer), and RSS to enable that communication.

> **NOTE:** From our observations, very few things that happen on the Internet are planned and executed in a way that people expect. We believe that the evolution of the Internet of Things will be no different, and that it will begin with mobile devices communicating information to web applications and sites. This in turn will probably mean that the Web of Things implementation will be the one that eventuates, rather than a new way of doing things. Whether that is a good thing or not is another conversation, but suffice to say there will be a significant increase in active web clients (desktop plus mobile plus embedded devices) in coming years. It will be interesting to see how the current way of doing things scales to that volume of information.

Hardware Sensor Networks

As stated previously, mobile devices can have many hardware sensors. Picture those sensors being able to (through appropriate privacy controls) share information with centralized systems. This could include data such as weather and traffic information at particular locations.

A couple of examples of existing mobile applications and companion web sites that have already created sensor networks are Waze (http://waze.com) and NoiseTube (www.noisetube.net). Waze is a mobile application that collects GPS readings as you drive around your local area. That information is fed back into Waze and used to generate mapping information that can be shared among all users. Figure 13-6 shows a screenshot of the Waze mobile interface, which is currently implemented as a native interface, but could easily be implemented as a mobile web application in the future.

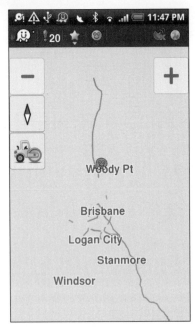

Figure 13-6. *The Waze mobile interface—not a web UI, but with HTML5 it could be.*

Waze is an excellent example of an application that makes use of sensors to collect information. A more generic example of a platform that supports sensor networks is a site/application network called Pachube (www.pachube.com). Figure 13-7 shows a screenshot of the front page of Pachube displaying the number of sensors contributing information back into the network. These sensors are typically small embedded devices, but could be mobile devices just as easily.

Figure 13-7. *Pachube is a site with API-supporting distributed sensor networks.*

The Human Sensor

In addition to the applications that focus on using device sensors to collect and communicate information, consider the phenomenon known as the *Human Sensor*. This is where individuals are reporting information about their surroundings back into a central system for processing.

An excellent example of this is a mobile application and supporting web site called Ushahidi (`www.ushahidi.com`). This application is designed to allow individuals to submit location-specific reports to a central Ushahidi server. Figure 13-8 shows some device shots from the current Ushahidi Android application, which like Waze is currently a native application.

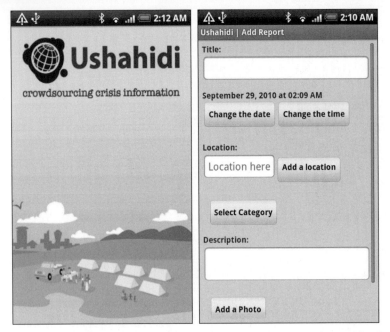

Figure 13-8. *Ushahidi is a crowdsourcing crisis information system with mobile clients.*

As can be seen in the device shots of Ushahidi, it markets itself as an application that does a particularly good job of collecting crisis information. In fact, the Ushahidi platform was used to assist with the relief efforts after the earthquakes in Haiti.

In addition to specialized applications like Ushahidi, things like geosocial networking (as covered in Chapter 10) are also good examples of sensor networks driven from human interaction.

Summary

In this chapter, we have had a look at some trends in mobile computing and how mobile web development fits into the picture. There are many opportunities opening up in the mobile space, both in established and emerging markets.

Additionally, with more and more devices coming online, there are some very interesting projects that can be explored both for mobile app development and in the cloud.

The best thing any developer can do right now is to get involved, and, while we would highly recommend working with mobile web technologies, the more important thing is to get started somewhere. Hopefully, over the course of the book you have been exposed to both the basics of mobile web development and some more advanced topics, plus some ideas about the kinds of applications you could build.

Now, get out there and build great mobile apps.

Debugging Android Web Apps

Debugging JavaScript applications and libraries is something that traditionally haunts web developers. You may have read forum comments or articles by people who have been less than enthusiastic about going down this mobile web application path. We will admit that it is more difficult than debugging an application that has a nice, shiny IDE; however, with the right tools and techniques, you can learn to track down and fix JavaScript errors with relative ease. Before you debug your scripts, though, you can use certain tools to scan and check your code and report any issues. This is a huge time-saver in the development process. In this appendix, we will see how we can increase our productivity and at the same time improve our code quality. This is an essential aspect of software engineering, especially when you start to work on bigger projects. A good starting point is the JSLint tool.

JSLint: Prevention Is Better Than Cure

JSLint (http://jslint.com) is a tool created by Douglas Crockford to assist developers in writing their JavaScript code consistently. JSLint is a code quality tool, and it can be run either online at the JSLint web page or from the command line. Depending on the text editor you are using, you may even be able to get a plug-in/extension that automatically runs JSLint over your code each time you save—which is very handy.

JSLint checks for common mistakes that can occur during coding, such as missing semicolons and portions of "dead code," which is code that will never be executed because it's unreachable. It will also warn you about code that runs without errors but is considered bad practice or violates a style convention, and it will produce a report for you that lists all the problems. In general, JSLint will help you fix code errors faster, as well as learn good JavaScript practices, especially if you are a novice.

In most cases, using the online JSLint tool is sufficient, and it's recommended when working through the sample code in this book. In the online JSLint tool, you paste your code into an input text area and then just press a button to generate the report. But, if you are working on a big project with a team, at a certain point you may want to provide some automation in your build and release process, instead of checking it manually each time by pasting it into the online tool. For this type of situation, there are some options available, including a plug-in for Hudson, a continuous-build server that automatically retrieves from source control servers, tests and distributes your code (see http://hudson-ci.org), and more basic bash scripts that can be integrated to crone jobs, for instance. Another option is to use Mozilla Rhino, which is a Java-based JavaScript interpreter (see www.mozilla.org/rhino). You can pass your script and the JSLint library to Rhino as arguments, and Rhino will run JSLint's check process. And because it's a Java program, Rhino is very easy to integrate with other Java-based frameworks, including the famous Ant build tool (discussed in more detail in Chapter 9; see http://ant.apache.org). Check this blog post to see how Ant and JSLint can be combined: www.ifisgeek.com/2009/05/05/running-jslint-in-automated-build-scripts.

However, even if you take all these precautions to produce well-written, robust code, you'll still have to confront the debug process at some point, especially if the complexity of your script is growing or if you're dealing with third-party libraries where the implementation is unknown by you. The following sections discuss some of your debugging options.

Debugging with the Google Chrome Developer Tools

The maturity of tools for working with JavaScript has improved dramatically over the last few years. The first notable mention goes to Firebug for enabling the debugging of so much brilliant code during the course of the Ajax movement (see http://getfirebug.com). Secondly, and more importantly for us working in the Android mobile space, Chrome and the Chromium project (http://chromium.org) are taking that tool maturity even further.

The main advantage to working with the Chrome developer tools (www.chromium.org/devtools) in Chrome or Chromium is that you'll be working once again with the WebKit rendering engine, which means that your JavaScript code will be interpreted the same way. This provides developers with some common ground between the desktop and mobile platforms for identifying and debugging problems.

We will have a look at some of the most useful tools now. The tools suite is integrated with the Chrome browser (www.google.com/chrome), so just be sure to have it installed before moving on.

Catching Messages and Errors in the Console

The developer tools console is probably the least advanced of the tools available in the suite, but almost certainly the most useful. Quite simply, the console is both a reporting interface and a manual code execution tool. Figure A-1 shows an example of how the developer tools console appears after running the following snippet of code:

```html
<html>
<body>
<script type="text/javascript">
// write some console messages
console.debug("debug message");
console.info("info message");
console.warn("warning message");
console.error("error message");

// throw an exception
throw new Error("This is a test exception");
</script>
</body>
</html>
```

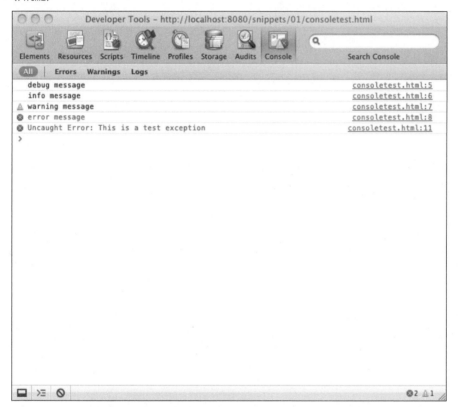

Figure A-1. *The Chrome developer tools console after running our console test snippet*

The console displays messages that you placed in JavaScript code using console debugging. Additionally, it shows the location of any uncaught exceptions that have been raised while executing a script.

To see an error in the context of the code that it was running against, simply click one of the underlined files displayed on the right of the screen. You will then be taken to the Resources section, which shows where the warnings/errors were generated from.

Debug and info messages aren't displayed. Figure A-2 shows an example of the Resources screen.

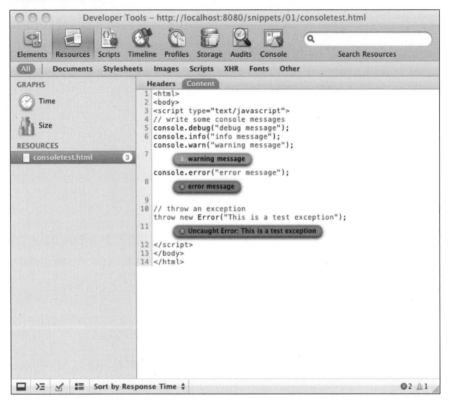

Figure A-2. *The Resources section of the developer tools shows warnings, errors, and exceptions in context.*

For the most part, the functionality provided by the console and Resources view is adequate for catching the small and frustrating errors that can occur when working with JavaScript. For example, try to insert your console statements at strategic places and using the right log type ("warning," "info," "error" or "debug"). Your catch closure should always log the reason why it was caught. Good log output is always very instructive and helpful before using heavier tools such as the debugger, which will be explained now.

Script Debugging

Every now and again, you may hit a problem that is either difficult or inefficient to solve using logging to the console in isolation. For a long time, the console method was the best that JavaScript developers could hope for, but more recently both Firebug and the Chrome developer tools have provided interactive debugging features. This enables the creation of breakpoints, watches, and other goodies that are usually reserved for IDEs and compiled code. Figure A-3 shows the script debugger, and, while we won't go into an in-depth tutorial on its use here, we will just explain the basic concept of a breakpoint.

A *breakpoint* functions just like the Pause button on your DVD player. It stops the code from running at whatever point you set it. You can set a breakpoint anywhere you want—just click the line number label, and the code will pause when it reaches the line. Why is it useful to pause code execution? Well, at the moment you enter a breakpoint, you get an instant picture of the state of your script, including all the variables' states. This is very useful, for example, to see whether a variable has been set yet or is still null. You can even change the value of a variable at runtime. You can also check the *call stack*, which shows the hierarchy of function calls; this can be very handy when you're working with complicated flows and you want to know exactly who is calling whom. For example, if you set a breakpoint inside the function retrieveTaskDetails() which was called by the function getNewestTask(),you will be able to see this arborescence in the debug tool.

After inspecting your script, you have different options: *step over*, *step in*, and *stop*. Stepping over is just like hitting the Play button on your DVD player after a video has been paused—your script will continue to run until it reaches the end or another breakpoint. Stepping in can be used if your breakpoint is on a code line that calls another function. You can step into this function, and the script will freeze at the first statement of this function. Of course, you can stop running the script at any time by clicking the Stop button.

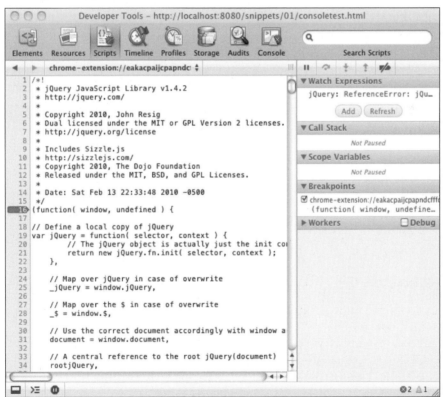

Figure A-3. *The script debugger provides breakpoints and variable watches for more trying times.*

NOTE: You'll often hear the statement "Smart developers don't use the debugger." The idea behind this is that, if you put your console log statements in the right places and trace the right info, it won't be necessary to use the debugger, and you'll be spared a lot of time (checking your console output is quicker than stepping into your code). The fact is, however, that you won't always be testing your own code, and you'll sometimes have to test code that you wrote a long time ago and don't remember the details of—in these cases, the debugger offers some flexibility for seeing exactly what's happening.

Inspecting the DOM with the Elements Tab

It is pretty easy to end up with typos in HTML, and sometimes strange things can happen in terms of your layout—especially when you are modifying the DOM (Document Object Model) at runtime. To see what the current state of your HTML is, the Elements tab in the developer tools is invaluable. Figure A-4 shows an example of the Elements tab.

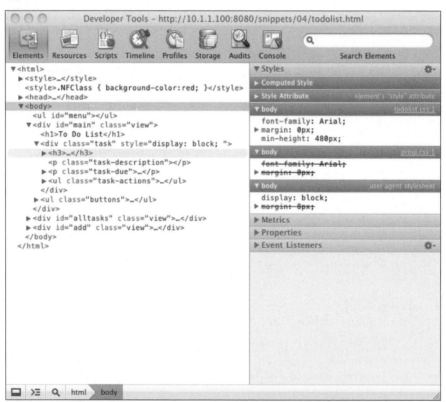

Figure A-4. *The Elements tab shows the current state of the mobile app's HTML.*

When an element is selected in the HTML pane on the left, details of the element (including applied styles, bound event listeners, etc.) are displayed on the right. Additionally, you can use the DOM inspector (http://en.wikipedia.org/wiki/DOM_Inspector) to dynamically apply styles and change properties at runtime to experiment with what impact a change to a stylesheet would actually have before implementing it. If you change a property at runtime, be aware that it will only be temporary; when your page is reloaded, this property will return to its original value, so don't forget to update and save your source file if you find a suitable property for an element.

Debugging with the Android Debug Bridge

While Chrome is invaluable for testing your web apps, spending time in the Android emulator is crucial to seeing how the application will actually behave once deployed to a device.

> **NOTE:** In addition to running tests in the emulator, it is also important to test your application on an actual device before deploying either to a publicly accessible web site or the Android marketplace (if you are using a bridging framework). Information on how to configure USB debugging to gain similar debugging features as described below can be found at the following web page: http://developer.android.com/guide/developing/device.html.

Once you start working with the browser in the emulator or on an actual device, and you attempt to debug your application, it will start to feel like you are back working in the early versions of Internet Explorer. JavaScript errors occur silently, and the Android browser doesn't even have a console similar to mobile Safari on the iPhone.

That's certainly how it appears on the surface, but it's not as bad as it seems. By using the *adb* tool that comes packaged with the Android SDK, you can actually see JavaScript errors that occur within the browser on the emulator.

Running adb logcat will generate output similar to that displayed in Figure A-5. In this particular example, the events pertaining to JavaScript console events have been sent from the WebCore application. It can be useful to see what other events are going on in the emulator, though—such as when garbage collection and other system-level events are occurring.

```
●○○                    Terminal — adb — 80×24
lling back to default line: 744 source: http://train.tripplanner.racq.com.au/mob
ile/scripts/tile5.js
D/dalvikvm( 176): GC freed 4295 objects / 663112 bytes in 180ms
D/WebCore ( 176): Console: populating grid, x shift = 0, y shift = 0 line: 744
source: http://train.tripplanner.racq.com.au/mobile/scripts/tile5.js
D/dalvikvm( 176): GC freed 3470 objects / 368264 bytes in 118ms
D/dalvikvm( 176): GC freed 5853 objects / 818136 bytes in 119ms
D/dalvikvm( 176): GC freed 5495 objects / 312720 bytes in 99ms
D/WebCore ( 176): Console: Not able to tap element. line: 290 source: http://tr
ain.tripplanner.racq.com.au/mobile/jqtouch/jqtouch.js
D/WebCore ( 176): Console: populating grid, x shift = 0, y shift = 0 line: 744
source: http://train.tripplanner.racq.com.au/mobile/scripts/tile5.js
D/dalvikvm( 176): GC freed 2628 objects / 224864 bytes in 108ms
W/KeyCharacterMap( 176): No keyboard for id 0
W/KeyCharacterMap( 176): Using default keymap: /system/usr/keychars/qwerty.kcm.
bin
W/IInputConnectionWrapper(  52): showStatusIcon on inactive InputConnection
D/dalvikvm(  93): GC freed 7461 objects / 406792 bytes in 316ms
D/WebCore ( 176): Console: Not able to tap element. line: 290 source: http://tr
ain.tripplanner.racq.com.au/mobile/jqtouch/jqtouch.js
D/WebCore ( 176): Console: populating grid, x shift = 0, y shift = 0 line: 744
source: http://train.tripplanner.racq.com.au/mobile/scripts/tile5.js
D/dalvikvm( 176): GC freed 10128 objects / 894896 bytes in 148ms
```

Figure A-5. *Output from adb logcat is extremely useful when debugging JavaScript in the emulator.*

If you find this log a bit too noisy, there is a tip to extract only the lines from the
WebCore process:

```
adb logcat WebCore: * *:S
```

Index

D

H

I